AMERICA'S FUTURE

OPPOSING VIEWPOINTS®

Other Books of Related Interest in the Opposing Viewpoints Series:

American Foreign Policy
American Government
American Values
Economics in America
Japan
Social Justice
The Superpowers: A New Detente

Additional Books in the Opposing Viewpoints Series:

Abortion
AIDS
America's Elections
America's Prisons
Animal Rights
Biomedical Ethics
Censorship
Central America
Chemical Dependency
China
Civil Liberties
Constructing a Life Philosophy
Crime and Criminals
Criminal Justice
Death and Dying
The Death Penalty
Drug Abuse
The Elderly
The Environmental Crisis
Euthanasia
Genetic Engineering
The Health Crisis
The Homeless
Israel
Latin America and U.S. Foreign Policy
Male/Female Roles
The Mass Media
The Middle East
Nuclear War
The Political Spectrum
Poverty
Problems of Africa
Religion in America
Science & Religion
Sexual Values
The Soviet Union
Teenage Sexuality
Terrorism
The Third World
The Vietnam War
Violence in America
War and Human Nature

AMERICA'S FUTURE

OPPOSING VIEWPOINTS®

David L. Bender & Bruno Leone, *Series Editors*

William Dudley & Bonnie Szumski, *Book Editors*

OPPOSING VIEWPOINTS SERIES ®

Greenhaven Press, Inc. PO Box 289009 San Diego, CA 92128-9009

Library of Congress Cataloging-in-Publication Data

America's future.

(Opposing viewpoints series)
Includes bibliographical references.
1. United States—Forecasting. I. Dudley, William, 1964- . II. Szumski, Bonnie, 1958- .
III. Series.
E839.4.A85 1990 303.4973 89-25885
ISBN 0-89908-448-6 (lib. bdg.)
ISBN 0-89908-423-0 (pbk.)

"Congress shall make no law . . . abridging the freedom of speech, or of the press."

First Amendment to the U.S. Constitution

The basic foundation of our democracy is the first amendment guarantee of freedom of expression. The *Opposing Viewpoints Series* is dedicated to the concept of this basic freedom and the idea that it is more important to practice it than to enshrine it.

Contents

Why Consider Opposing Viewpoints?

"It is better to debate a question without settling it than to settle a question without debating it."

Joseph Joubert (1754-1824)

The Importance of Examining Opposing Viewpoints

The purpose of the Opposing Viewpoints Series, and this book in particular, is to present balanced, and often difficult to find, opposing points of view on complex and sensitive issues.

Probably the best way to become informed is to analyze the positions of those who are regarded as experts and well studied on issues. It is important to consider every variety of opinion in an attempt to determine the truth. Opinions from the mainstream of society should be examined. But also important are opinions that are considered radical, reactionary, or minority as well as those stigmatized by some other uncomplimentary label. An important lesson of history is the eventual acceptance of many unpopular and even despised opinions. The ideas of Socrates, Jesus, and Galileo are good examples of this.

Readers will approach this book with their own opinions on the issues debated within it. However, to have a good grasp of one's own viewpoint, it is necessary to understand the arguments of those with whom one disagrees. It can be said that those who do not completely understand their adversary's point of view do not fully understand their own.

A persuasive case for considering opposing viewpoints has been presented by John Stuart Mill in his work *On Liberty*. When examining controversial issues it may be helpful to reflect on this suggestion:

> The only way in which a human being can make some approach to knowing the whole of a subject, is by hearing what can be said about it by persons of every variety of opinion, and studying all modes in which it can be looked at by every character of mind. No wise man ever acquired his wisdom in any mode but this.

Analyzing Sources of Information

The Opposing Viewpoints Series includes diverse materials taken from magazines, journals, books, and newspapers, as well as statements and position papers from a wide range of individuals, organizations and governments. This broad spectrum of sources helps to develop patterns of thinking which are open to the consideration of a variety of opinions.

Pitfalls to Avoid

A pitfall to avoid in considering opposing points of view is that of regarding one's own opinion as being common sense and the most rational stance and the point of view of others as being only opinion and naturally wrong. It may be that another's opinion is correct and one's own is in error.

Another pitfall to avoid is that of closing one's mind to the opinions of those with whom one disagrees. The best way to approach a dialogue is to make one's primary purpose that of understanding the mind and arguments of the other person and not that of enlightening him or her with one's own solutions. More can be learned by listening than speaking.

It is my hope that after reading this book the reader will have a deeper understanding of the issues debated and will appreciate the complexity of even seemingly simple issues on which good and honest people disagree. This awareness is particularly important in a democratic society such as ours where people enter into public debate to determine the common good. Those with whom one disagrees should not necessarily be regarded as enemies, but perhaps simply as people who suggest different paths to a common goal.

Developing Basic Reading and Thinking Skills

In this book, carefully edited opposing viewpoints are purposely placed back to back to create a running debate; each viewpoint is preceded by a short quotation that best expresses the author's main argument. This format instantly plunges the reader into the midst of a controversial issue and greatly aids that reader in mastering the basic skill of recognizing an author's point of view.

A number of basic skills for critical thinking are practiced in the activities that appear throughout the books in the series. Some of the skills are:

Evaluating Sources of Information The ability to choose from among alternative sources the most reliable and accurate source in relation to a given subject.

Separating Fact from Opinion The ability to make the basic distinction between factual statements (those that can be demonstrated or verified empirically) and statements of opinion (those that are beliefs or attitudes that cannot be proved).

Identifying Stereotypes The ability to identify oversimplified, exaggerated descriptions (favorable or unfavorable) about people and insulting statements about racial, religious or national groups, based upon misinformation or lack of information.

Recognizing Ethnocentrism The ability to recognize attitudes or opinions that express the view that one's own race, culture, or group is inherently superior, or those attitudes that judge another culture or group in terms of one's own.

It is important to consider opposing viewpoints and equally important to be able to critically analyze those viewpoints. The activities in this book are designed to help the reader master these thinking skills. Statements are taken from the book's viewpoints and the reader is asked to analyze them. This technique aids the reader in developing skills that not only can be applied to the viewpoints in this book, but also to situations where opinionated spokespersons comment on controversial issues. Although the activities are helpful to the solitary reader, they are most useful when the reader can benefit from the interaction of group discussion.

Using this book and others in the series should help readers develop basic reading and thinking skills. These skills should improve the reader's ability to understand what they read. Readers should be better able to separate fact from opinion, substance from rhetoric and become better consumers of information in our media-centered culture.

This volume of the Opposing Viewpoints Series does not advocate a particular point of view. Quite the contrary! The very nature of the book leaves it to the reader to formulate the opinions he or she finds most suitable. My purpose as publisher is to see that this is made possible by offering a wide range of viewpoints which are fairly presented.

David L. Bender
Publisher

Introduction

"The American system of ours . . . gives each and every one of us a great opportunity if we only seize it with both hands and make the most of it."

Al Capone

In the United States, the emphasis on individual rights, achievements, and goals has always been an important and appealing part of our nation's identity. Ironically, it is this same emphasis on the individual that many blame for the economic and social problems facing the U.S. today—it is a country of individuals, they say, who care little about the common fate of the nation. As Eugene O'Neill once declared, "We talk about the American Dream, and want to tell the world about the American Dream, but what is that dream, in most cases, but the dream of material things? I sometimes think that the United States, for this reason, is the greatest failure the world has ever seen."

Yet others believe that it is the entrepreneurs, immigrants, and other individualists that promise to continue to revitalize and remake this country. As Woodrow Wilson summed up, "This is the only country in the world which experiences . . . constant and repeated rebirth." These opposing views pose a scintillating question: Can Americans work together to stem the economic and social crises that plague the nation, or will the U.S. become a second-rate power, torn asunder by individuals pursuing their own short-term material goals?

There are many who would argue that America's future is secure. This optimism is based on the idea that Americans are as unpredictable in conquering problems as they are ethnically diverse. James Fallows, author of *More Like Us*, claims that the current economic and social conflicts that plague the U.S. may be the incentive America needs to pull together in the years ahead. He likens America's current hardships to the bombing of Pearl Harbor. Just as Pearl Harbor was necessary to jar the American public into involvement in World War II, the budget deficit, rampant drug abuse, and other crises may jar Americans out of complacency toward these problems. Others, like Marvin Cetron and Owen Davies, authors of *American Renaissance*, are even more optimistic: "We believe firmly that anyone who looks clearly at the facts, unbiased by any partisan political agenda, must feel an unfashionable optimism about the future of our country." They believe that Americans' innate ingenuity will allow them to overcome the problems the U.S. faces in the next century.

Others see this eternal optimism as the epitome of American naivete and lack of realism. These critics argue that America is running out of options—the economy is a shambles, and social problems like drug abuse and AIDS threaten to overwhelm the nation. These pessimists believe Americans are too caught up in accruing individual wealth at the expense of the country as a whole. Daniel Burstein, author of *YEN!* believes the U.S. is especially blind when it comes to the threat from Japan. He cites the Japanese buyout of U.S. real estate as an example of short-term profits made at the expense of the nation. As America's first poet laureate Robert Penn Warren expressed in an interview shortly before his death, American optimism has "led us, bit by bit, to believe that solutions would be almost automatic: pass a law, take a poll, draw up a budget, take a body count, hire an expert or PR man, believe only optimistic reports. There is no use in rehearsing the long list of consequences of this attitude, but we may name a few: sick cities, blighted landscapes, an irrational economy, a farcical educational system, and a galloping inflation."

Will America's supposed strength—its belief in the individual—be its ultimate downfall? This question permeates every issue in *America's Future: Opposing Viewpoints.* The following topics are debated: Is America in Decline? What Is America's Economic Future? Is America Falling Behind in Technology? How Can American Education Be Improved? What Lies Ahead for America? As the United States faces the next century, which view of Americans will ultimately prevail?

CHAPTER 1

Is America in Decline?

AMERICA'S FUTURE

Chapter Preface

The United States became a global superpower after World War II. With its major economic and military competitors ravaged by the war, the U.S. was able to profit from its unique position. Consequently, it dominated the world economic scene for the next thirty years. In the 1980s, however, external factors, such as the economic rise of Japan and the prospect of a united European market coupled with internal factors, such as budget and trade deficits and huge military outlays affected the U.S. position. It has now become popular to forecast the decline of the U.S. and to argue that it must cede its place in the world to a number of rising powers.

Is this decline, if actual, a negative state of affairs? Some commentators argue that America's economic dominance was inevitably temporary. Some, like James Griffin, president of Aetna Insurance Company, assert that the U.S. has always aimed to spread its prosperous example throughout the world. The success of nations such as Japan is testimony to the achievement of America's goal, Griffin maintains.

Whether the U.S. is truly experiencing a decline in economic and world status is the subject of this chapter.

VIEWPOINT 1

"There is no blinking the fact that the United States has lost its relative *place in the sun."*

The U.S. Is in Decline

Paul Kennedy, interviewed by Robert Heilbroner

Paul Kennedy became a well-known and controversial figure when his book, *The Rise and Fall of the Great Powers* became a national bestseller. In this book and in the following viewpoint, Kennedy argues that the U.S. is declining in power in the same way that Britain declined in power. He believes that Americans must recognize the danger of their country's decline or the U.S. will fall behind countries like Japan. Kennedy is a professor of history at Yale University in New Haven, Connecticut. He was interviewed by Robert Heilbroner, a professor of economics at the New School for Social Research in New York City.

As you read, consider the following questions:

1. Why does Kennedy argue that Americans' perception of defeat is more important than the defeat itself?
2. Why does Kennedy doubt that America will be able to reverse its decline?
3. What changes does the author suggest the United States make?

You perceive some kind of grand design in the rise and fall of the great powers—a theme that repeats itself in the stories of imperial Spain and Austria and Napoleonic France and nineteenth-century Britain and twentieth-century Germany. . . .

To the extent that there is a grand design, one element of it is surely a nation's institutional adaptability to changing circumstances—or perhaps, more precisely, its institutional capacity to encourage innovation and creativity.

Once a nation rises to dominance the dynamics change. The dominant country's interests expand. It develops far-flung commitments. Fleets and armies are needed to protect its newly won territory. Its national power is not only much larger but much more expensive. The problem becomes one of expanding its economic base to keep pace with the expansion of its political and military role. . . .

An Invasion of Foreign Products

Do you think the loss of our markets is a sign that America is losing its status as a great power?

There is no blinking the fact that the United States has lost its *relative* place in the sun. After World War II this country was the steelmaker to the world, the breadbasket of the world, the auto manufacturer for the world. America's predominance in manufacturing and in agriculture—a mighty combination, you must admit—was without peer. Not surprisingly, the American dollar was also the strongest currency in the world. All these elements of economic superiority have been eroded. The United States is still the single largest economic entity on the planet, but it is not any longer the entity whose performance puts it in a class by itself, hopelessly beyond the reach of any would-be competitor.

On the contrary, we have seen the most astonishing "invasion" of this economy by foreign products. What is perhaps even more significant is the rapidity with which the American sense of its economic superiority has given way to a feeling of its having lost its bearings—of not knowing how to compete or where to compete.

Why do you say "even more significant"?

Perhaps because the present mood of soul-searching in the United States reminds me so strongly of a very similar kind of self-questioning in Edwardian times, when many thoughtful people in England felt that greatness was slipping through their fingers and didn't know what to do about it.

No Single Power Can Dominate

How do your investigations and historical perspective help us see our situation more clearly?

The thing that strikes me the most strongly is that the general world situation has become much more complicated over the last few years. That is probably what sets the stage for the American frame of mind. And I'm not just thinking of the advent of nuclear weapons. I am thinking about the end of a world in which any single power can exercise global hegemony of the kind we had at the height of the British Empire and again in the heyday of American power in the decades following World War II.

A Downward Slope?

The question can be asked: is America, like many other great nations before it, on a downward slope into becoming a second-tier nation, as has already happened in this century to Britain and France? This slide is neither inevitable nor irreversible, but present trends may continue at an accelerating pace if the United States does not fundamentally change its present policy priorities. The country must make concerted efforts to regain its balance, its sense of proportion between domestic and foreign demands, and to reallocate its resources in ways that rebuild its economic foundations.

Ray C. Rist, *Society*, October 1989.

The main reason, I think, lies in the growing fluidity of economic power. There are no more impregnable geographic bastions of manufacturing strength, as once there were. There are no dominant centers of financial power comparable to the London-based finance of the late nineteenth century or the New York-based finance of the 1950s. West Germany and Japan are major players in the manufacturing and financial worlds, and will continue to be. Other economies, like the Korean, are on the rise. Still other countries, such as perhaps Brazil, are waiting in the wings. India may soon be heard from. What of China? Of course, America is today and will be tomorrow a great military and economic power. But not the *only* power.

What are the consequences of this more complex map of world power?

One consequence, I feel, should be the rise in the importance of diplomacy. A bipolar world leads inevitably to military trials of strength—an arms race. A multipolar world leads much more naturally to diplomacy. We are entering a world that is much more open and indeterminate than the one we've left. Such a world could be more promising—or more unstable.

The Stability of Rome

Why unstable?

Because one-power hegemony has an obvious stability—think of the Roman Empire!—and even a two-power world has a certain stability, so long as it does not lead to runaway rivalries. Multipolar worlds, such as Europe in the early nineteenth century, do not possess these natural equilibriums. They require a sensitive adjustment and adaptation to a map of power that is constantly being redrawn, not a dogged pursuit of policies designed for a map that never changes. However, we must not think that today's new instability poses problems only for the United States. Aren't the Soviets also challenged by the new state of affairs, with the rise of new military and economic centers in the East? One cannot any longer meaningfully describe the overall historical situation simply in terms of a free world against an unfree world, or of the capitalist system against planned systems, or even of East against West. At the end of David Calleo's *Beyond American Hegemony*, he tantalizingly suggests that, as two "older" powers, Washington and Moscow may find they have many common interests in the emerging unstable world. One can only speculate about that. What I think is quite clear is that diplomacy must play a far more important role in the coming decades.

How well equipped do you think this country is to carry on such a world diplomacy? Don't I pick up from your book a deep ambivalence about the way you assess the United States—at once admiring its vitality but deploring its tendency to see everything in oversimplified terms?

Of course I have my uncertainties about America's diplomatic capabilities. I suppose I would about anyone's. I often think that a country's particular weaknesses are the obverse side of its strengths. The American strength has been its wonderful optimism, its "can do" attitude. That has given the United States great energy. But it also brought the belief that sheer optimism and resolve would by themselves always carry the day. This is a view that can prevent its holders from taking a critical stance with respect to their own situation. Historical self-confidence carries a price at those times when reexamination and fresh stock taking may be the order of the day.

To me this lesson seems to apply especially in the economic sphere. The United States rose to power in a period when all-out entrepreneurship, combined with a generally negative view of government, carried everything before it. I'm thinking of the time when you built your vast railways and your unparalleled steel industry, then your electric utility industry, your consumer appliance industry, your automotive industry, and later your computer industry. Under that general outlook the United States had a triumphant economic career for a century.

Americans and Japanese

Therefore, it is very difficult psychologically to accept the possibility that today other ways of mobilizing and organizing the economy may be more effective—for instance, the ways in which the Japanese openly use the state as a kind of partner, often the senior partner, of private enterprise. Americans find it hard to imagine that ministries and bureaucrats can work successfully with entrepreneurs and captains of industry. Mind you, I am not saying that Japanese methods are intrinsically better than the American or that they could be imported, as we import their cars. But the very possibility of doing things in another way does not come easily to you.

The same is true, of course, of other countries. What has been called the British Disease used to refer to the inability of my own countrymen to change English ways of running a business to American ones. Perhaps today it refers to their difficulty in running them in an Italian or a Swedish fashion. Maybe one day in the future that challenge will come full circle, and the Japanese will be worrying about why they can't match the new American—maybe by then even the new English—way of organizing their national economic effort.

For the moment, though, the gauntlet is at the feet of the United States. This is the country whose established ways of thinking and doing are being challenged. That brings us back to what we talked about earlier, the problem of adaptation and flexibility. That has

been the great secret of success and failure, of rise and fall. I suspect it will be the same today and tomorrow.

I take it you have some doubts about America's capacity to adapt.

I don't regard the American future as anything like foreclosed. But I'm concerned lest there be barriers in the American outlook that will make it hard to respond to challenge, especially on the economic front. To my way of thinking, in the face of so much uncertainty the best chance of remaining flexible and adaptive—competitive—is to raise the share of resources going into infrastructure. I don't just mean roads and water mains. I mean first-class educational systems, basic scientific research, the production of scientists, engineers, skilled workers of all kinds. That is not, right now, a generally shared urgent priority for most Americans.

Warning Signs

What course should we pursue?

I see the answer in a group of coordinated responses, not in any single effort. Let me begin with the military/diplomatic sphere. The United States is carrying an immense military burden, which it imposes upon itself because it still perceives itself as the world leader it was forty and thirty or perhaps even twenty years ago. It is that no longer.

Soviet military strength quite aside, both the American experience in Vietnam and the inability of the United States to control the Persian Gulf situation are clear warning signals that the days of unchallengeable American military might are in the past. Do not forget that there was a time when the United States could (and did) unseat an Iranian premier whose policies were regarded as unfriendly and oust or install whatever regimes it wanted in Central America with a few Marines. That period is past. So I sense that America's military commitment—perhaps I should say its conception of its role—is unrealistic.

That is, I am sorry to say, an old story that we can trace back to the Hapsburg monarchy in the sixteenth century, and no doubt much earlier: too many fronts to defend; too many "enemies," too large a military burden to be borne by the economy. In America's case it means devoting too large a proportion of its best scientific and skilled manpower to ends that do not add to the growth of the economy. If history teaches us anything, it is that an emphasis on military power over economic vitality leads to a deterioration of both.

And what about the nuclear question?

In a sense we have to put the nuclear issue to the side. There is simply no precedent for the possibility that using a weapons system might destroy not only the enemy but also oneself. But non-nuclear military force is still extremely important. So I think the President should seize the opportunity presented to us by

Russian *perestroika* to say to Gorbachev: "Look, we both have to modernize and improve aspects of our societies. We have our own *perestroika* to attend to—different from yours but also needing our full attention. So let us seek to de-escalate together, realizing that we are very different kinds of societies that nonetheless have some common problems ahead of us."

Then I would like to see this country mount a new diplomatic effort to persuade its allies to share the burden of European and Pacific defenses more equitably. That does not mean that America should pull out its troops from West Germany or South Korea with a shrug of its shoulders. It does mean that the United States is today well placed *because of its economic problems* to persuade the rising nations of the West and of the Pacific that it is in their long-term interest to share more proportionately the expenses of an adequate military defense.

Massive Deficits

I am also worried about the massive American domestic deficit and the unprecedented foreign deficit. The loss of this country's accustomed competitive edge in manufacturing and the loss of its traditional place at the apex of world finance is a dangerous combination. The answer here is not to resort to defensive measures, such as old-fashioned protectionism, but once again to encourage the innovation, flexibility, and adaptation that seem to me the keys to success. This will certainly involve such changes as new management structures and attitudes in business; one already sees these appearing. Sooner or later I believe it will have to lead to new ways of coordinating public and private activities. These are matters about which economists and political scientists will argue. Speaking as a historian, however, I am certain that adaptability will necessitate a shift away from national consumption—the credit-card way of life as well as unproductive government spending—into formation of human and physical capital. That last may be a painful process.

Perhaps not so very painful if we consider that a great deal of that shift should result in an improvement of the quality of our lives—that is, in our inventories of skills and knowledge.

Painful even then. I recently heard of a state legislature that was considering lengthening the school year to match that of the Japanese—about 240 days instead of 185. What a furor that started! The tourist industry protested. The kids protested. Some of their parents protested. The teachers wanted more compensation. So the trade-offs for redistributing resources into the capacity for future growth and flexibility are not painless. Politicians running for office may use slogans like "Hard choices," but they don't spell out those choices. None of them are willing to talk about raising taxes in order to increase the growth potential of the nation. None of them are even willing to mention raising taxes to the levels that were around before Mr. Reagan gave people a lot of pocket money. What I call the "thinking classes" are already wrestling with these notions. But the American electorate in general is not, and neither party wants to be the first to mention it. What is fascinating to me is that Gorbachev faces something of the same kind of problem—indeed, a much more difficult one.

Can the United States manage such a remarkable transition? Can it undertake the difficult process of pulling back its military commitments and of undertaking those changes needed to help us find a productive and contributive place in the world economy? History doesn't give us answers to questions like that. I see my task as pointing to the lessons of the past, so that this nation—I should say all nations, not just this one—will not have to learn those lessons over again. . . .

A Sober Picture

You present a very sobering picture. But isn't it likely that the very growing awareness of our problems will lead us to overcome them? Isn't it the challenge that generates the response?

Of course, there is such a possibility. But I wouldn't want to count on it. To turn around the vast inertial system of a country like the United States *quickly* is no easy matter. I remember a newspaperman asking a British minister in the midst of some crisis in the 1970s, "Are we at the edge of a precipice?" and the minister answering, "No, but I wish we were."

I get the point.

The danger, you see, is that of sliding *gradually* downhill, simply because no single dramatic event will come along to awaken Americans to the need for change and keep them awake for a decade. I am very far from composing a dirge for the United States. But it strikes me as the height of foolishness not to recognize its vulnerability—I do not mean to military attack but to a further worsening of its relative economic position in the world. That is not in itself a bad thing. It is good for Europe and the Pacific to catch up. The hope, as I see it, is for the United States to take its place among the concert of nations fortified with the knowledge that it is, and with intelligence can remain, a great power, yet no longer perceiving itself as, or even desirous of being, *the* great power.

2 VIEWPOINT

"Although there are current weaknesses in the American Empire, they are not irreparable."

The U.S. Is Not in Decline

Susan Strange

So many prominent writers have been predicting America's decline that a new term, "the school of decline" has been dubbed for the theory. In the following viewpoint, Susan Strange takes issue with these doomsayers. Strange believes that predictions of America's decline are based on false assumptions. Strange is professor of international relations at the European University Institute in Florence, Italy. Her recent books include *Casino Capitalism* and *States and Markets*.

As you read, consider the following questions:

1. Why does Strange believe that U.S.-controlled businesses outside the U.S. are more important than industries in the U.S.?
2. Why is the comparison with Britain faulty, according to the author?
3. What does America have to do in the coming decade, according to Strange?

Susan Strange, "The Future of the American Empire," *Journal of International Affairs*, Fall 1988. Published by permission of the *Journal of International Affairs* and the Trustees of Columbia University in the City of New York.

Make no mistake. Questions about American decline—true or untrue, avoidable or inevitable—which have been much in the public eye, are not just the subject of an academic debate, a kind of intellectual jousting match of absorbing interest to the protagonists but of only passing interest to the spectators. In my opinion, it is much more than that. This is one of the comparatively rare occasions on which the perceived outcome of an academic debate actually has some significance and impact outside the classroom and beyond the pages of professional journals. At the end of the day the apparent victor in the argument, and the broad conclusions that the spectators draw, will crucially affect decisions in the real world. It cannot help but affect the policy choices made in the future by people in business, banking and government, in the United States and in other countries around the world. . . .

It looks as though the "school of decline" as it has been called has thus far got the best of the intellectual joust. Although a few voices of dissent have been heard in America, and though opinion outside the United States is still far from convinced that American power is declining, the challenges that have been made to the major propositions of this school have not registered much of a dent. But the tournament is far from over and the verdict of the present and coming generation of students in the social sciences, and especially in international relations, has still to be given.

Three Propositions

To that end, it may help first to disentangle the three major propositions of the school of decline. These are:

• American power, once predominant, is now less than it was, and, that it is (or soon will be) matched or exceeded by that of others.

• Such declines of great powers are normal and explicable and are to be anticipated, especially when such states are committed to heavy military spending.

• When such states do decline in power, one likely consequence is political instability and economic disorder in the international system. . . .

By laying out the main grounds on which I think each of the three propositions can be legitimately questioned, a different conclusion becomes possible. It is based on the analysis of structural power in international political economy which I have developed at greater length elsewhere. It leads to the conclusion that although there are current weaknesses in the American Empire, they are not irreparable and they are much less important than its continuing structural power. However, a necessary condition for the needed reforms is the development of a political will to change. And that will not come until it is more widely recognized that the school of decline has grossly overdone its Cassandra act. . . .

Where I think we are all in agreement is on the critical nature of the present end-of-century decade. We share a common perception that mankind—and more particularly the governments it acknowledges as possessing the authority to make decisions—is standing at a fork in the road, at the end of a long stretch of comparative order and stability, and facing momentous choices in the way ahead. That is why there is shared concern to understand where we are now and how we got there and to seek in the lessons of history some guidance for future action. . . .

My contention (which should surely be sustained by the champions of American service industries) is that it is the information-rich occupations, whether associated with manufacturing or not, that confer power, much more now than the physical capacity to roll goods off an assembly line. Secondly, I contend that the location of productive capacity is far less important than the location of the people who make the key decisions on what is to be produced, where and how, and who design, direct and manage to sell succesfully on a world market. Is it more desirable that Americans should wear blue collars and mind the machines or that they should wear white collars and design, direct and finance the whole operation?

An Arrogance to the Decline Theory

The gap between American living standards and those of Europe and Japan has shrunk dramatically over the postwar period. If the shrinkage of that gap is the national decline about which some now fret, how would they address it? Should we have frozen time in the 1950s, keeping other nations poor and weak? . . .

There is an arrogance to those who see America sliding. They suggest that a melting pot world economy is less good than one we dominate, that our institutions and way of life are so highly evolved they can only be degraded by foreign influence. That is not true to our history as a nation of immigrants, nor to our economic ideology that the best will prove out in open competition.

James Griffin, *Fortune*, August 29, 1988.

That is why all the figures so commonly trotted out about the U.S. share of world manufacturing capacity, or the declining U.S. share of world exports of manufactures are so misleading—*because they are territorially based.* Worse, they are irrelevant. What matters is the share of world output—of primary products, minerals and food and manufactured goods and services—that is under the direction of the executives of U.S. companies. That share can be U.S.-directed even if the enterprise directly responsible is only half owned by an American parent, and even, in some cases of technological dependence, where it is not owned at all but where the license to produce is granted or refused by people in the United States. The largest stock of foreign direct investments is still held by U.S. corporations—even though the figures are neither precise, complete nor comprehensive. The fact that the current outflow from Japan is greater than that from the United States merely means that the gap is narrowing. But the Japanese still have a long way to go to rival the extent of U.S. corporate operations in Europe, Latin America, Australasia, the Middle East and Africa, the assets of which are often valued at their historical prices not at their current values.

U.S. in Other Countries

U.S.-controlled enterprise outside the territorial United States is still growing very fast in new fields of technology like software services, biotechnology, medical products, data retrieval, environmental management or new basic materials. IBM is still unrivaled in its field and has stayed so by strategic agility in overcoming its rivals and imitators. Genentech is still the world's biggest biotechnology corporation and Cray Research is the largest producer of supercomputers. What these leading American companies have in common is that more of their output is produced outside the territorial United States than is produced inside it. For example, an estimate of middle-sized U.S. companies associated within the American Business Conference found that 80 percent of their revenues in 1986 came from production overseas, only 20 percent from exporting from the United States. Two conclusions were drawn from their success. One was that Jean-Jacques Servan Schreiber had been quite wrong in seeing the "American Challenge" to the rest of the world as coming from the giant corporations like ITT or General Electric. Today, the challenge is more likely to come from relatively new and smaller American enterprises. The other conclusion was that trade figures are not the best measure of competitiveness and that it would be better to judge by corporate world market shares.

In these terms, Japanese companies just now beginning to shift production to America, Europe and mainland Asia are only following the American lead—and the trade figures so eagerly (and wrongly) watched for indications of competitiveness will soon begin to show it.

At this point some people will object that when production moves away from the territory of the United States, the authority of the U.S. government is diminished. At the same time, the same people sometimes complain against the "invasion" of the United States by Japanese companies, as if "selling off the farm" is diminishing the authority of the United States government. Clearly, both cannot be right. Rather, both perceptions seem to me to be wrong. What is happening is that the American Empire is spilling out beyond the frontier and that the very insubstantial nature of frontiers where production is concerned just shows the consolidation of an entirely new kind of nonterritorial empire.

America's Decline Is Overrated

The rhetoric of decline is wrong because it portrays a past that wasn't, a present that isn't, and a future that probably won't be.

Charles Wolf, *The Wall Street Journal*, May 12, 1988.

It is that nonterritorial empire that is really the "flourishing economic base" of U.S. power, not the goods and services produced within the United States. One obvious indication of this fact is that foreign central banks in 1987 spent roughly $140 billion supporting the exchange value of the dollar. Another is that Japanese and other foreign investors financed the lion's share of the U.S. government's budget deficit by buying U.S. government securities and investing in the United States. An empire that can command such resources hardly seems to be losing power. The fact that the United States is still the largest and richest (and most open) market for goods and services under one political authority means that all successful foreign companies will want to produce and sell there and will deem it prudent also to produce there, not simply to avoid protectionist barriers but in order to be close to the customers. And the worldwide reach of U.S.-controlled enterprises also means that the capacity of the United States to exercise extraterritorial influence and authority is also greater than that of any other government. If only for security reasons, the ability of Washington to tell U.S. companies in Japan what to do or not to do is immeasurably greater than the ability of Tokyo to tell Japanese companies in the United States what to do.

This points to another major fallacy in the decline school's logic—its inattention to matters of security. The U.S. lead in the ability to make and deliver the means of nuclear destruction is the complement to its lead in influencing, through past investments overseas, the nature, modes and purposes of modern industrial production. Here, too, the gap may be narrowing as South Africa, Israel, India and others claim nuclear capability. Yet there is still no comparison between the military power of the United States to confer, deny or threaten the security of others with that of minor non-Communist states. That military power is now based far less on the capacity to manufacture nuclear weapons than on the capacity to recruit scientists, American or foreign, to keep ahead in design and invention, both offensive and defensive.

The decline school so far has succeeded in promoting the idea that history teaches that it is "normal" for great states and empires to decline, especially when they become militarily overextended; or else when they become socially and politically sclerotic, risk-averse and resistant to change or when they overindulge in foreign investment; and for any or all of these reasons when they lose preeminence in agricultural and industrial production, or in trade and military capability. In almost all this American literature on the rise and fall of empires, great attention and weight is characteristically (and for reasons of language and culture, perhaps understandably) given to the British experience. But the trouble with history, as the first great realist writer on international relations, E.H. Carr, rightly observed, is that it is necessarily selective—and that the historian selects facts as a fish shop selects fish, choosing some and discarding or overlooking others. In this debate, the historical analogy between Britain and America is particularly weak; and the other examples selected for consideration show a strong tendency to concentrate on the empires whose decline after the peaking of their power was more or less steady and never reversed.

First, it is not too difficult to show that what Britain and America have had in common—such as a tendency to invest heavily overseas—is much less important than all the differences that mark their experience. Britain's economic decline, beginning around the 1880s, was the result of a neglect of the then advanced technologies—notably in chemicals and engineering. This neglect reflected the weakness and low status of manufacturing industry in British politics and society—a social disdain such as American industry has never had to contend with. Even more important was the effect of two long debilitating wars on the British economy, by comparison with which the American experience of Vietnam was a flea bite. It is arguable that the British economy, dependent as it was on financial power, would not have suffered so great a setback if the whole international financial system on which it lived and prospered had not been twice destroyed—first in the Great War and then in the Second World War. The interwar period was too short—and policies were also ill-chosen—to allow a reversal of this British decline.

A Tiny Offshore Island

Finally, there is the great difference between a small offshore island running a large territorial empire and a great continental power managing (or sometimes mismanaging) a large nonterritorial empire. The island state made the fatal mistake after the Second World War of relying on sheltered colonial and sterling area markets—with disastrous effects on the competitiveness of its export industries and even some of its old, established multina-

Table 1
Is U.S. Power Declining?
(Public Opinion Poll)

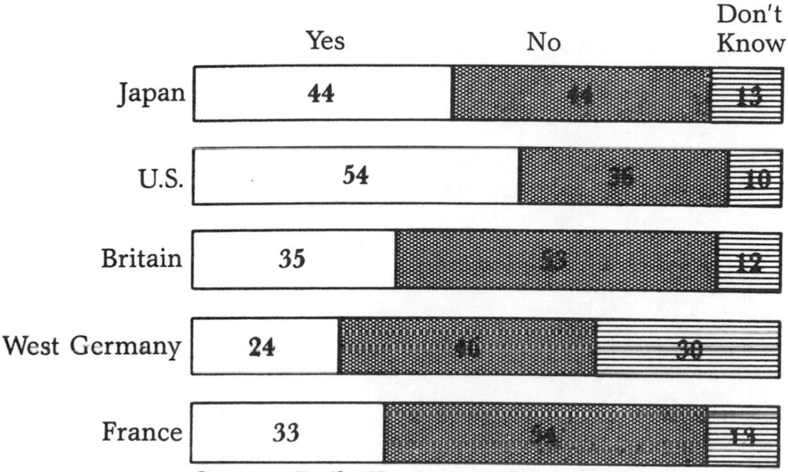

Source: *Daily Yomiuri,* 18 June 1987.

tionals. The continental power's confidence in its ability to dominate an open world economy, plus the strong commitment to antitrust policies at home, has created no such weakening crutches for its major transnational corporations.

Secondly, any historical study of empires of the past fails to reveal any standard or uniform pattern of rise and fall. They are like trees. Some grow fast and fall suddenly without warning. Others grow slowly and decay very gradually, even making astonishing recoveries from shock or injury. One author, Michael Doyle, who has shared less in the media attention perhaps because his work lent itself less readily to deterministic interpretations, drew an important conclusion from an analytical survey of empires that included those of the ancient world as well as the later European ones. It is worth quoting:

> The historical alternatives had divided between persistence, which necessitated imperial development in both the metropole and the periphery, and decline and fall. Persistence in an extensive empire required that the metropole cross the Augustan threshold to imperial bureaucracy, and perhaps became in effect an equal political partner with the metropole.

In plainer language, what I interpret this to mean is that the empires that lasted longest were those that managed to build a political system suited to the administration of the empire out of one suited to managing the core. In addition, those empires that survived managed to blur the distinction between the ruling groups of the core and the participating allies and associates of the periphery. . . .

A Corporation Empire

I would argue that America's "legions," in the integrated financial and production economy of today's world, are not military but economic. They are the corporate enterprises on which the military depends—as President Dwight Eisenhower foresaw in talking about the military-industrial complex. The American Empire in sociological terms therefore could be described as a "corporation empire" in which the culture and interests of the corporations are sustained by an imperial bureaucracy. But this bureaucracy, largely set up after the Second World War, was not simply a national American one based in Washington, D.C. A large and important part of it was and is multinational and works through the major international economic organizations such as the International Monetary Fund (IMF), the World Bank, the Organization for Economic Cooperation and Development (OECD) in Paris and the General Agreement on Tariffs and Trade (GATT) in Geneva.

The other feature of the Roman Empire that I believe is relevant to the current debate is that citizenship was not a matter of domicile, and that there were gradations of civil and political rights and responsibilities, ranging from slaves to senators, which did not depend on what we, today, understand by "nationality," indicated by possession or nonpossession of a passport. If we can once escape the corset-like intellectual constraints of the conventional study of international relations and liberate our minds to ask new questions we begin to see new things about America's nonterritorial empire. Here, too, citizenship is becoming much more complex and graded than it used to be. The managers of U.S. corporations, in Brazil, for example, may hold Brazilian and not U.S. passports. But they are free to come and go with indefinite visas into the United States and they often exercise considerable delegated power in the running of U.S.-directed enterprises vital to the Brazilian economy. Participation in the cultural empire depends not on passports but on competence in the American language and in many cases participation in U.S.-based professional organizations—like the International Studies Association for example. Similarly, participation in America's financial empire depends on the possession and use of U.S. dollars and dollar-denominated assets and the ability to compete with U.S. banks and in U.S. financial markets.

Rather like a chrysalis in the metamorphosis from caterpillar to butterfly, the American Empire today combines features of a national-exclusive past with features of a transnational-extensive future. In military matters, it is still narrowly exclusive—though where advanced technology is concerned, even that is changing. Certainly, in financial and cultural matters, the distinction between first-class, passport-holding citizens and second-class, non-passport-holding participants is increasingly blurred. The peripheral allies have been unconsciously recruited into the American Empire. . . .

One obvious feature of the American Empire, like that of Venice, has been that despite the political rhetoric on the subject of liberty, democracy and free trade, its governments have been remarkably unfussy on all three counts in their choice of allies and associates. . . .

America Is Structurally Superior

I find that a structural analysis of the basic issues in any political economy, when applied to the world system, strongly suggests that on balance American structural power may actually have increased in recent decades. It has done so through four interlocking structures. These structures concern the power conferred by the ability to offer, withhold or threaten security (the security structure); the ability to offer, withhold or demand credit (the financial structure); the ability to determine the locus, mode and content of wealth-creating activity (the production structure); and, not least, the ability to influence ideas and beliefs and therefore the kind of knowledge socially prized and sought after, and to control (and, through language, to influence) access to and communication of that knowledge (the knowledge structure).

Such a structural analysis suggests the existence under predominant American power and influence of an empire the likes of which the world has never seen before, a nonterritorial empire, whose only borders are the frontiers of the socialist great powers and their allies. It is not, in fact, such an eccentric idea. Two former U.S. secretaries of state wrote:

> Far into the future, the United States will have the world's largest and most innovative economy, and will remain a nuclear superpower, a cultural and intellectual leader, a model democracy and a society that provides exceptionally well for its citizens.

3 VIEWPOINT

"A Japanese empire is being born that will pose a fundamental challenge to American power in every sphere."

The U.S. Is Losing Its World Status to Japan

Daniel Burstein

Daniel Burstein is a New York-based journalist who has covered East Asia and trade issues for more than a decade. His articles have appeared in *The New York Times, Los Angeles Times*, and other major periodicals. In the following viewpoint, excerpted from his controversial book, *Yen!: Japan's New Financial Empire and Its Threat to America*, Burstein argues that Japan's growing economic and international status may allow it to displace America as a world leader.

As you read, consider the following questions:

1. What does Burstein say are the dangers of ignoring the Japanese threat?
2. In what areas has Japan gained world prominence, according to the author?
3. Why does the author believe it is important to recognize Japan as a threat?

Today's global prosperity hinges as never before on a delicate set of balances, interdependencies, and confidences. And the U.S.-Japan relationship lies at the very nucleus of that belief system.

With just 7 percent of the world's population, the two economies produce 30 percent of the world's goods and control a similarly disproportionate percentage of global trade. Together the two countries account for nearly three-quarters of world stock and bond market value and half of all bank lending. They issue 80 percent of the money used by other nations as reserve currencies.

The instruments of debt and equity that flow instantly across borders these days are so sophisticated that it is easy to forget how conditional their value is on the unspoken assumption that the rules of the global economic game will be the same tomorrow as they are today. But if the U.S.-Japan relationship is severed and the two sides are thrust into conflict, many of those rules will be thrown open for question. Therein lies a recipe not only for panic, but for global economic meltdown.

At the moment, U.S.-Japan economic activity remains symbiotic, if grudgingly so. A few skirmishes have been fought, giving world markets a faint hint of the dangers inherent in any sort of full-dress showdown. But to date no credible political or economic faction in either country actually advocates or desires a rupture.

That is the good news. The bad news is that forces of national interest are likely to prove more powerful determinants of the future than the wishes or intentions of today's decision makers. The argument is not that such a confrontation is inevitable. Rather, it is only inevitable if we ignore it as a possibility and fail to take preventive action, or if the preventive action we choose to take is of the knee-jerk, protectionist type that could serve to bring the clash on sooner and more destructively. And here lies the great American quandary: we are being pushed and pulled between two political and economic trends of thought, both of which are dangerous and neither of which is addressing the fundamental problem.

Ignoring the Threat

The leading trend in the 1980s has been to ignore the depth of the threat. According to this line of reasoning, America is still number one and always will be; a globalized economy benefits Americans who have the intellectual and technological powers to dominate it; the flow of foreign capital is a testament to American strength, stability, openness, and the general superiority of our system. Therefore we should maintain the status quo domestically. Our "competitiveness" problems should be solved principally by persuading foreigners to be more like us in their home markets.

The reality is that this rosy view has already been responsible

for a rapid decline of American economic vigor and a similarly rapid rise of Japanese power. To continue to pursue such policies invites the prospect not of *interdependence*, but of a one-sided and highly destabilizing U.S. *dependence* on foreigners whose agenda is different from our own. . . .

Having reached decade's end, the Hollywood-style fantasies that concealed the underlying crisis in the U.S. economy earlier in the 1980s are finally being challenged publicly in some influential quarters. "Wake Up, America!" say the editors of *Business Week*. "We have spent too much, borrowed too much, and imported too much. We have lived beyond our means, relying on foreigners to finance our massive budget and trade deficits. The bill is now coming due."

When America does awaken, we are told by former commerce secretary and investment banker Peter Peterson, it will be "the morning after." We will face a country that has "let its infrastructure crumble, its foreign markets decline, its productivity dwindle, its savings evaporate, and its budget and borrowing burgeon." The "day of reckoning" will be at hand.

We hear this talk, and even recognize a ring of truth to it, yet we still don't want to believe it. We cling to illusions about "rebuilding American greatness," but we fail to define what that means in light of today's changed global environment. As Nobel economics laureate Paul Samuelson suggests, the United States, responsible for around 20 percent of the world's output today, simply cannot expect to exercise the same kind of dominant role in the world that it did after World War II when it accounted for 40 percent.

We continue to maintain an extensive military capability in far corners of the world, but Paul Kennedy, the historian who has made an academic career of studying rising and falling empires, hypothesizes that in so doing, we are falling victim to the classic syndrome of "imperial overstretch" that has doomed great powers throughout history. By spending so much on armies and weapons systems, we are draining the economy of resources necessary to compete successfully with Japan and other less encumbered powers.

Hidden behind the glittery facade of the "Roaring Eighties" in American business lies the reality that the United States has lost control over the central features of its own economy, thereby foreclosing many of the potential solutions to current dilemmas. Interest rates, the value of the dollar, the financing of U.S. government operations, the flow of imports and exports—none of these areas of fundamental importance to national well-being can be fully controlled any longer by American policymakers, even in those rare moments when they can agree on policy.

It would be an overstatement to say that Japan now controls these strategic areas instead. Some of the power relinquished has gone to our other old adversary, Germany; some has been claimed by a diverse lot of other foreigners. Much of the economic architecture we once relied upon has simply broken down in the wake of volatility in the global marketplace. But having said that, it is still imperative to recognize that Japan has gained a measure of control over our economy unwise to cede to any foreign country, even the friendliest, best-intentioned ally.

Americans' Willingness to Lose

No evil cabal in Tokyo planned things this way. Rather, it is a case of Americans willingly, if not always knowingly, surrendering our own destiny. It is an epic tale with a theme worthy of the

Bible: the American Esau—a strong, prideful hunter—has sold his birthright to the Japanese Jacob—a quiet, clever strategist—in return for a mess of consumption and debt. Nothing in the Bible suggests that Jacob is to blame for taking advantage of Esau in this way.

In the case of Japan, moreover, it is not just any foreign country to whom we've sold our birthright. Japan is our mirror image and our fiercest competitor. Japan is strong precisely where we are weak; its economy reverberates with the equal and opposite reactions to our American actions. Thus, while the United States has become the world's leading debtor, Japan has become its leading creditor. While we consume more than we produce, Japan produces more than it consumes. While our dollar weakens, Japan's yen strengthens. While we lust for imports, Japan's passion is for exports. While we deregulate and fragment our society, Japan maintains a strong central plan and national cohesion. While we find ourselves unable to rebuild our industrial and social infrastructure, Japan embarks on what will likely be the world's greatest domestic expansion of the nineties. And while we withdraw from global obligations, Japan begins to assume them.

Blinded by wartime victory and our long-standing role as senior partner in the U.S.-Japan relationship, we ignore the obvious: Japan is becoming a global superpower in its own right. We casually acknowledge Japan as a great manufacturing and trading nation that has surpassed us in certain product areas. We even accept the idea that "Made in Japan" means higher quality than "Made in USA." But we still shrink from recognizing the essential reality. A Japanese empire is being born that will pose a fundamental challenge to American power in every sphere.

Power at Stake

The central issue here is not which country can produce better-quality automobiles or pack more circuits on a computer chip, important though such talents are to a national economy. Instead, what is at stake is the power that allowed Britain to dominate the nineteenth century and the United States to dominate the twentieth, and will, in all probability, allow Japan to dominate the twenty-first. It is the power that, when possessed by a nation, propels it beyond all others in its wealth, standard of living, technological development, productive capacity, and even its art, culture, and intellectual life. And conversely, the kind of power that, when lost by a nation accustomed to thriving on it, triggers economic chaos, stagnates growth, deepens the cleavage between rich and poor, and induces a profound crisis of identity and national spirit.

Japan is not only our mirror image and our fiercest competitor, it is also the only country that has ever bombed United States territory. It is not necessary to believe in the cliché of a Japanese conspiracy seeking to win back what was lost in 1945 to recognize that Japan's great wealth is regenerating a new nationalism, an ugly arrogance, and a certain imperial swagger. It is possible that the Japanese will resist the temptations of this trend in favor of a course that could influence world history in a much more humanitarian way. The fusion of Japan's rich cultural legacy with its new financial power could create a socioeconomic model that would inspire the rest of the world in the next century. Japan could be the engine that pulls the Third World out of its misery and teaches the superpowers that the arms race and economic development are incompatible. But although such ideas are sometimes voiced in Japan today, current events are not moving in their direction. The logic of contemporary Japanese policy, coupled with the leadership's need to defend itself from the illogic of American policy, creates fertile ground for crystallizing the almost inevitable consensus that Japan must convert the economic empire it has obtained into a political and military one as well.

Japanese Expansion/American Decline

Today's financial world is the razor's edge in this explosive process of Japanese expansion and American decline. The U.S.-Japan trade war is fast becoming an issue of the past, won for all intents and purposes by Japan. Now, the financial war is brewing. By following the trail of dollars and yen, we can see the accelerating pace at which the new Japanese empire is gaining momentum and the American empire is losing ground.

Japan's new role as the leader of world finance isn't taken terribly seriously by Americans. . . . Its bankers and brokers don't have "the right stuff" to go up against the freewheeling, risk-taking American bulls.

It is shocking how much this reasoning sounds like Detroit's auto executives speaking about the threat of Japanese competition in the 1960s. What is even more shocking is how much greater the stakes are now. Not surprisingly, the new dimension of the U.S.-Japan rivalry is better understood on the other side of the Pacific. Tokyo's chief trade negotiator acknowledges that he is preparing for U.S.-Japan "financial friction" to be worse than the acrimonious trade war of the 1980s.

An executive with Daiwa, Japan's second biggest securities house, frames the issue bluntly: "It is one thing to compete for a share of the automobile market, but it is quite another to compete on the financial battleground. Money is the blood that runs through every economy, carrying food to the nation's brain and heart. There are those who will see competition in the field of finance as competition for control of the body's bloodstream."

I am one of those people.

4 VIEWPOINT

"The 20th century was the American century. . . . And the 21st century will be the American century."

The U.S. Is Not Losing Its World Status

Karen Elliott House

An economically stronger Europe and the emergence of Japan have led many to believe the U.S. will inevitably lose its status to these and other nations. Karen Elliott House argues in the following viewpoint that the U.S. really has no rivals. House examines the potential of other countries, and finds that the U.S. is far more powerful in more areas than Japan is. House is a staff reporter for *The Wall Street Journal*.

As you read, consider the following questions:

1. What makes a nation powerful, according to House?
2. How does House rank the U.S. as a military power?
3. Why will America remain a world leader, according to the author?

Karen Elliott House, "The '90s and Beyond," *The Wall Street Journal*, January 29, 1989.

Everywhere these days, there is head-shaking and hand-wringing over the decline of America. Doomsayers are busily handicapping entrants in the race to replace America as world leader.

"Kiss No. 1 Goodbye, Folks," blares a headline in the *Washington Post*.

"America, Europe Is Coming," warns another in the *International Herald Tribune*.

"Emergence of Superrich Japan as Major Superpower" is the title of yet another gloom-and-doom article, in *Time*.

And Yale historian Paul Kennedy's book *The Rise and Fall of Great Powers*, the bible of American doomsayers, topped the best-seller list in the U.S. for 24 weeks.

Topsy-Turvy

Clearly, pessimism about America is in vogue. The sudden emergence of America as the world's largest debtor, Japan as the globe's richest creditor and the Soviet Union as its most ardent preacher of pacifism seems to many Americans to have turned the world upside down, raising doubts about whether America any longer can or should lead.

But as with many fashionable ideas, this one doesn't bear up well on closer scrutiny. In an effort to draw a reliable picture of the world that will develop in the next century, *The Wall Street Journal* undertook an exhaustive survey: talks with several hundred leaders and laymen in America, Japan, Europe, China and the Soviet Union, involving 100,000 miles of travel. The picture that emerges is clear, if surprising: whether America relishes the role or not, it is the pre-eminent power in the world today and will remain so for at least the next generation—and probably longer.

This will not be the America of the immediate postwar era, the lone Western power dictating a global agenda, but rather the America of this generation, a team captain cajoling and corralling others in the interests of global peace and prosperity.

Can Do

"America is the most vital nation in the West and will remain so," says Helmut Schmidt, the former West German chancellor. "It is a nation of vitality and optimism, and that helps a lot even if it sometimes blinds wisdom."

Most of those interviewed expect the world to be both politically and economically a far better place—with reduced chances of superpower war and increased prospects for prosperity—than anyone dreamed possible even a decade ago. The coming era, most predict, will be one of competition, not confrontation. To the extent that is so, it is largely because America has matched the Soviets militarily, bested them ideologically and buried them economically, forcing Moscow to focus on internal overhaul if it is even to remain in the great-power race.

But negativism about America's chances dies hard. Many of the same post-Vietnam pessimists who a decade ago doubted America's ability to compete with the Soviets politically and militarily now have decided that the real global contest is simply economic, and that in this arena Americans can't compete with the Japanese—even though America's economy in 1988 was nearly twice the size of Japan's.

Paradoxically, many foreigners, like Mr. Schmidt or former French President Valery Giscard d'Estaing, are more upbeat about America's prospects than are many members of America's own financial and foreign-policy establishment. Here in America, a fair generalization would be that politicians are more pessimistic than financiers, the money men are more gloomy than businessmen, and businessmen more downbeat than men on the street.

Notably, America's most enthusiastic cheerleaders are the emerging nations of the Pacific, often cited as the new center of global gravity and sometimes simplistically seen as Japan's economic vassals. There, America remains the preferred leader and Japan the distrusted and often detested neighbor.

"If Japan doesn't play an international role equal to its economic power, it's a problem," says Lee Hun Jo, president of South Korea's Lucky Gold Star. "If it does play a big role, that's a problem too, because they will dominate us."

No Withering Empire

The U.S. is not declining. It is not a withering empire, militarily overcommitted, spending too much on defense, or incapable of competing with Japan and other economic giants. It is a vibrant nation, which has all the ingredients for world leadership well into the next century: it has a flexible and growing economy. It has military power on a global scale. But more important, it stands for something more than getting rich or acquiring more military power.

Kim R. Holmes, speech before the Alabama Retail Association, July 24, 1989.

In the contest for global power and influence, each of the contenders for power has some ardent boosters. Many cite Japan's huge trade surpluses and its increasing technological prowess as proof Japan will lead in the 21st century. Others look at Europe's effort to create by the end of 1992 a unified market—one that would exceed in size even that of the U.S.—and predict Europe's rapid emergence. Still others hail Mikhail Gorbachev's public-relations coups and Moscow's continuing military clout as evidence of an eventual Soviet resurgence. And a few predict the unstoppable triumph of the unleashed entrepreneurial instincts of one billion Chinese.

But there are fundamental flaws in all these forecasts. Power is not simply money, market size, might or masses. Power—the elements that enable a nation to influence events in a fashion favorable to its own interests—derives from a combination of military, political, economic and cultural clout, including the intangibles that make a nation admired and respected.

A close look at America's mix of strengths compared with those of other pretenders to power indicates why America should have little competition for pre-eminence in the 1990s and beyond. "We have a winning hand," says former Secretary of State George Shultz. "We just have to play it."

Arms and Economics

Militarily, the U.S. is certainly a leader. Few Western experts any longer talk of Soviet superiority, even though Moscow boasts greater numbers of troops, tanks and missiles. This isn't just because of Ronald Reagan's military buildup; it is basically because as military might becomes more reliant on modern technology, the natural advantage tips toward America's technological society. Also, for all the talk about budget pressures in the U.S., America remains infinitely richer and more capable than the Soviets of funding defense.

Economically, America remains the world's largest producer, and no one interviewed for this series, even the pessimists, believes it won't still have the largest economy 20 years hence. Indeed, a recent study by American wise men projected that America's share of total global output will rise by 2010 to nearly 30% and then, as now, be twice Japan's share.

Some skeptics insist America's economy is shrinking relative to others in the world. And it is true that for a time in the 1950s America accounted for nearly half of the world's gross national product, a far larger proportion than now. But that period was a historical aberration when Japan and Europe were still devastated by World War II. By the mid-1960s, with the world fully recovered, America's share of global GNP stood at 25%, and it has held steady at around that level ever since. In short, nothing in these numbers supports any hand-wringing over American decline.

Others say Japan is growing much faster than the U.S. But again, recent trends show otherwise. During the 1960s Japan's economy grew at a blistering 11% a year, compared with America's average growth rate of 3% a year. Through much of the '80s, however, the Japanese and American economies have both grown in the range of 3% to 4% a year.

But there is much more to its strength than size. America is the world's free-enterprise model. And the free-enterprise system, with its incentives to grow and prosper, is demonstrably far more robust than statist systems, whether socialist or merely bureaucratic. Free enterprise is catching on world-wide among the booming nations of East Asia, in the rapidly deregulating economies of Western Europe, in the recent experiments of Eastern Europe and most notably in the bastions of socialism, China and the Soviet Union.

No American Decline

How can Americans consider themselves in decline? Consider: The US is a continental power with enormous natural resources—even more so if a free-trade zone with Canada and Mexico develops. Also, in many areas of high technology, including software, the originality and creativity of American technology dominates. . . .

I do not think the US is in decline. Europe and Japan are optimistic about America because leadership in the United States, both political and economic, is very strong.

Jiro Tokuyama, *New Perspectives Quarterly*, Summer 1988.

Paradoxically, some American pessimists, such as economist Lester Thurow, see the need for America to "manage" its economy to become more globally competitive. Yet it is precisely the open, free-wheeling nature of American free enterprise that its practitioners consider its greatest source of strength. "I have a flexibility a Japanese or German company can only dream of," says John Welch, chairman of General Electric Co., a company that earns 25% of its $40 billion in annual revenues from exports and overseas production. "I can make a deal to put a plant in Spain without asking my government, my banker or even my shareholders. A Japanese company must consult its government. A German company consults its bank. I act." To try to mimic German or Japanese "economic management" is to "play to our weaknesses not our strengths," Mr. Welch adds.

In fact, Japanese companies increasingly are trying to emulate America's emphasis on individual initiative and creativity rather than simply marching in state-orchestrated step. "The easy path of following America's lead is over," says Jiro Tokuyama, head of Mitsui's research center. "Now Japan must find its own way. We can produce capable technocrats but not yet creative visionaries because we emphasize lifetime security, not individual leadership here."

Economic strength, of course, ultimately rests on human resources. Here, too, America has the advantage. While Japan, despite a rapidly aging population, works hard to maintain its racial purity by closing its doors to outsiders, America's human resources continually are replenished by waves of immigrants. Some 600,000 legal immigrants arrive each year, far more than go anywhere else in the world. And many more arrive illegally.

These people restore national energy and enthusiasm and bring new talents. They live and thus keep alive the American dream. In this sense, America isn't doing immigrants a favor by letting them in; it is the immigrants who strengthen and thus favor America by coming. Moreover, while Japan largely excludes women from its work force, America has led the industrial world in recognizing and using the talents of its women.

It is certainly true that America has its economic problems. Chief among them is that its people consume more than they produce and save very little of what they earn. As a result, America in 1988 recorded a $130 billion trade deficit and a $150 billion budget deficit. These deficits are cause for concern but hardly for despair.

"It's a little like having a kid who has a tough flu," says John Reed, the chairman of Citicorp. "You worry about the kid; you are solicitous. But probably in this day and age, you don't view it as life-threatening. America has a tough flu, that's all."

The budget deficit is twice as large as it ever was in the Ford or Carter years. Yet the U.S. economy has grown so much that as a percentage of GNP, the deficit now is roughly equivalent to the 2.8% in Mr. Carter's last year, and it is half the 1983 peak. A nation, like an individual, can afford more debt if its wealth is growing.

Solutions at Hand

More important, the deficit could be slashed rather quickly if Americans were, for example, ready to pay for gasoline even what they paid at its 1981 price peak. Then, with crude oil at about twice its current price, gasoline cost roughly $1.35 a gallon, compared with around 95 cents now. If the U.S. chose to pay that difference in a gasoline tax, the federal Treasury—collecting about $1 billion for each penny of tax—would reap some $40 billion a year, and the budget deficit could be slashed by nearly one-third. That is more than even the most pessimistic economists say is necessary to restore investor confidence.

While politicians call a higher gasoline tax regressive and unrealistic—and while any deficit-closing move carries economic risks—the point is that if politicians can convince Americans that the deficit is truly a problem, solutions are available. "It's hard to take seriously that a nation has deep problems if they can be fixed with a 50-cent-a-gallon gasoline tax," says former French Foreign Minister Jean Francois-Poncet.

The trade deficit, the other bugaboo in America's future, appears to be on the way to fixing itself. With the dollar weak against other currencies, American goods are cheaper and thus easier to sell

How Fast the Superpowers Are Growing

Average annual growth rate of real gross national product, in percent

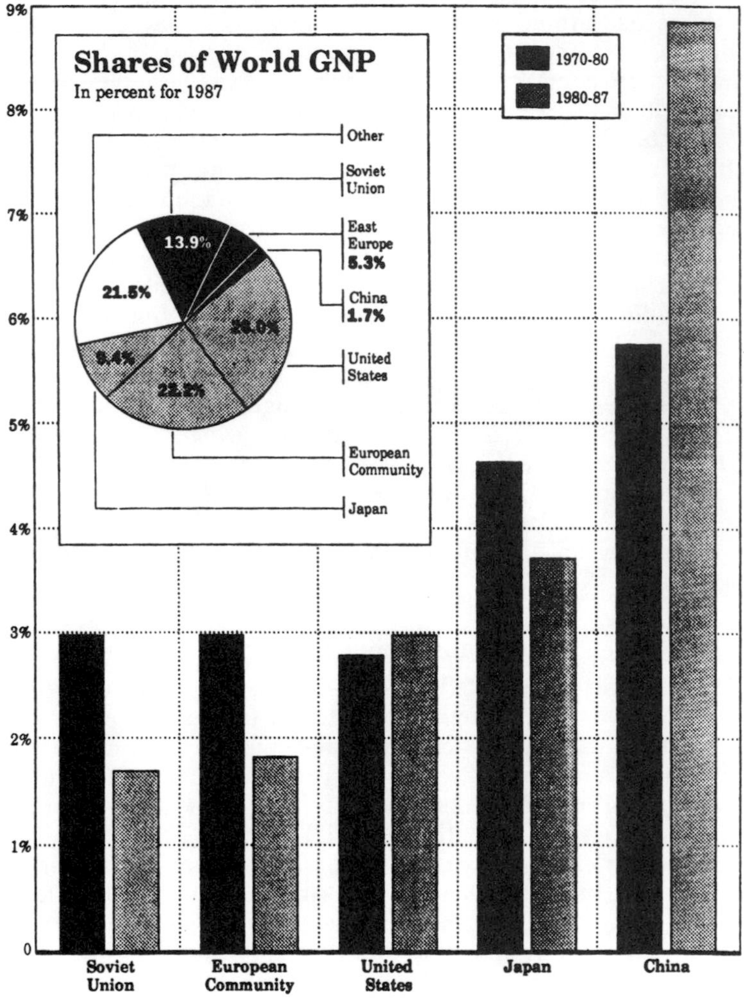

Note: Growth rates are based on data translated into U.S. purchasing power equivalents.
Source: CIA Handbook of Economic Statistics

abroad, and the trade gap is gradually shrinking. "The U.S. already has become competitive again," says Alain Chevalier, former chairman of LVHM Moet Hennessy Louis Vuitton of Paris. "America's isn't a problem of productivity but of consumption."

Nevertheless, economists such as Fred Bergsten of the International Institute of Economics in Washington and Mr. Thurow, dean of the Sloan School of Management at MIT in Cambridge, Mass., decry America's dependence on foreign money to finance its deficits. The U.S., they warn, is borrowing some $15 billion a month, largely from Japanese and West German investors. Much of this, of course, finances imports from those countries.

Pressure to Lend

While this borrowing does make America vulnerable to the decisions of Germans and Japanese, those countries and their investors know that if the lending stops, America stops consuming their goods. Because America is such a major market for the entire world, a halt in purchases here would mean that not just America, but along with it the world, would plunge into recession. Citicorp's Mr. Reed recalls that in the late 1970s the global economy was booming and some abroad were beginning to believe they could continue to do so irrespective of America. But Paul Volcker, then chairman of the Federal Reserve, imposed his anti-inflation measures, throwing the U.S. into an economic slump.

"We put on the brakes, and the result was a global recession," says Mr. Reed. "Global trade didn't return to 1980 levels for another six years."

So Japan and West Germany seem unlikely to stop financing U.S. deficits. In short, economic interdependence is a two-way street, and America is still living in the biggest house.

America's major strength, however, isn't its military or even its economic might, but rather its democratic ideal. To countless millions around the world, America really is, in the phrase Ronald Reagan so often has used, "a shining city on a hill." The big question for America isn't whether others want her to lead—most still do—or whether she has the ability to lead. The question is does America have the will to lead.

"If you decide the U.S. is the natural world leader, and act like it, you would be, of course," says Alfred Herrhausen, the chairman of Deutsche Bank, in a comment paraphrased by businessmen and politicians from Bonn to Beijing.

National will is no small issue. Yet the other contenders for global leadership—Europe, Japan, China and the Soviet Union—by and large face greater liabilities and have fewer innate advantages.

Japan is, at best, a major commercial and economic power. It is a physically small country all but devoid of natural resources. It has an aging population of modest size (120 million) that it chooses not to invigorate with immigrant infusions. Above all, it is an insular nation, in Asia but not part of Asia, superficially westernized but not Western. For all of its international economic clout, it remains a cultural and political island.

While America isn't always loved as a leader, at least since the end of the Vietnam War, it rarely has been hated. While some Americans and Europeans talk nervously of an Asian trading bloc with Japan as its leader, Asians do not. To them, the idea is something between a myth and a nightmare.

First of all, Japan still is widely resented in Asia for its World War II brutalities in Korea, China, the Philippines and elsewhere. No Asian neighbor looks forward to another era with Japan the region's pre-eminent power.

Secondly, the differences among Asian economies are so great that a trading bloc similar to the one European nations envision after 1992 is simply impossible, Asians say. Japan and China are the East's largest economies, but Japan's per capita income is over $13,000 while China's is $280. The conditions for trade among equals simply don't exist.

So, while Asia is a major market for Japan, it isn't likely to be a self-sufficient trading zone. . . . Japan is eager to import its neighbors' natural resources, but it shows no interest in becoming the market of last resort for the manufactured goods of all the developing economies of the area.

Those countries thus continue to rely on the American market, a dependence that gives Uncle Sam both economic and political leverage in Asia. "Economically, Asians want the U.S. in North Asia to counterbalance Japan, and politically Japan and all Asia want the U.S. presence to counterbalance the Soviet Union and China," says Park Ungsuh, a South Korean economist.

Japan's Lack of Military Might

Besides its other handicaps, Japan lacks military might. While it spends more on arms than all but the two superpowers, its military is defensive in nature. And all the world, especially its Asian neighbors, hopes fervently to keep it that way.

Finally, to the rest of the world, Japan stands for no political ideal beyond its own economic self-interest. It can export Mazdas, microchips and even management techniques, but none of this amounts to leadership. "The Japanese haven't shown any inclination to lead," says Mr. Volcker. . . .

In terms of America's status, all this is basically favorable news. It means that the U.S. now faces a future with the Soviet threat—both military and ideological—sharply reduced, though still potentially destabilizing. It is a world in which a growing number of nations are seeking to experiment with democracy and free enterprise in direct emulation of America. And America, of course, can take a good deal of credit even for the success of its competitors, having helped reconstruct postwar Japan and Western Europe as dynamic forces in a global economy.

It might seem all this should be cause for self-congratulation, not self-flagellation. Most of the world doesn't see America declining. One German strategist, Josef Joffe, opened a speech to an American conference on the topic of decline by mockingly saying, "Oh Lord, if I have to live in a declining country, please let it be America."

Self-Doubt

But America's establishment often tends toward self-doubt, even as Americans are fond of proving the experts wrong. When the Soviets launched Sputnik in the late 1950s many of the leading minds of America deplored its decline and hailed the inevitable pre-eminence of the Soviets. . . . It was said then of the Soviets, as it is now said of the Japanese, that they were producing tens of thousands of scientists while U.S. education was producing football players.

In the late 1960s, Richard Nixon and Henry Kissinger began to prepare Americans for a multipolar world in which American decline was inevitable. The superpowers' military might would take a back seat to the economic power of Europe and Japan. Since then, Mr. Kissinger and others have successively written off Europe as plagued by Eurosclerosis, only to proclaim it now an Olympic sprinter.

By the mid-1970s, it was the Arabs who were seen as invincible. Saudi Arabia was a super "petropower." Its hard-currency reserves of at least $200 billion in 1980 dwarfed those Japan has now. Yet few talk today of Saudi power, or even influence.

In the late 1970s, the establishment moved on to worrying about American political and military decline. The Soviets had invaded Afghanistan. Iran had grabbed 52 American hostages. Jimmy Carter proclaimed malaise. A humiliated nation tossed him out to bring in Ronald Reagan, with his simple promise to restore American power and prestige.

Now, with the U.S. having spent $1.8 trillion on defense, having stood down the Soviets in Afghanistan, the micromarxists in Grenada, Col. Gadhafi in Libya and the Iranians in the Strait of Hormuz, many of these same American officials and experts have decided military power is virtually useless, that money is what matters and America doesn't have enough of it.

The syndrome amuses many America-watchers. "I do not believe at all in American decline," says Hubert Vedrine, national security adviser to French President Francois Mitterand. "Americans adore frightening themselves."

Seizaburo Sato, a Japanese political scientist and adviser to former Prime Minister Nakasone, is even more emphatic. "The 20th century was the American century," he argues. "And the 21st century will be the American century."

VIEWPOINT 5

"We must continue to assume the burden of leadership not just for the sake of others but also for our own sake."

The U.S. Should Continue to Act as a World Leader

Richard Nixon

The U.S. has one of the largest military complexes in the world. It maintains a military presence in dozens of countries, and its only rival in nuclear weapons is the Soviet Union. Richard Nixon, in the following viewpoint, argues that the U.S. must continue to support this vast military network. He believes that the only impediment to the U.S. remaining the world's most prominent superpower is a lack of will to do so. Nixon was U.S. president during the height of the Vietnam war from 1969 to 1974, and became the only president to resign from office—after the Watergate scandal. He is author of seven books, including *1999*, from which this viewpoint is excerpted.

As you read, consider the following questions:

1. What are the beliefs of the "new negativists" and why are they wrong, according to Nixon?
2. Why must the U.S. continue to maintain its influence throughout the world, according to the author?
3. How does Nixon view the Soviet/American relationship?

With the beginning of the twenty-first century, there will be added appeal to call for a new America. A growing sense will develop that we need to gear up for new times, to prepare America for leadership in the next century. What we choose to do will profoundly affect what will become of the world. How we choose to lead and who is chosen to lead us are vitally important questions. What is at stake is nothing less than the future of civilization. Our actions will determine in large part whether the next century will be the best or the last one for mankind.

We have to ask ourselves what role the United States should play in the twenty-first century. Will the baton of world leadership pass to another nation after 1999? Is the United States—the oldest democracy in history—over the hill after two hundred years? To paraphrase Churchill, are we witnessing the beginning of the end or the end of the beginning of the great American experiment? All individuals go through the same experiences—birth, life, and death. Most individuals die when they no longer have a reason to live. Nations also experience birth and life. But for a nation, death is inevitable only when it ceases to have a reason to live. America has powerful reasons to live—for the sake of our posterity and for the sake of others. . . .

America in the Past

To understand America's role in the future, we must first understand what America has meant to the world in the past. We have not been just another country on the world scene. We have been at the center of the revolutionary progress in man's material condition and have often been a decisive influence in the great political and military struggles of recent times. But we have been more than that. We have also been an ideological beacon—the physical embodiment of a unique philosophy of the relationship between the individual, society, and the state.

At the beginning of the twentieth century, America was not a world power. Economically, we were behind Britain and Germany in relative terms. Militarily, we were not even in the picture. While the great fleets of the imperial powers ruled the seas, we had only recently succeeded in sending a small flotilla around the world—and our land forces were even weaker than our navy. Politically, we were following a policy of deliberately avoiding involvement in the snits and quarrels of the Old World.

At the same time, the ideals that animated the American system carried a profound effect. They gave us boundless optimism about the promise we held out to the world. From the time of our national independence, Americans have believed that we represent ideals that are bigger than ourselves. Thomas Jefferson said, "We act not just for ourselves but for all mankind." Abraham Lincoln spoke of America as the "last, best hope of earth." Albert Beveridge spoke lyrically of America's "manifest destiny." Woodrow Wilson said, "A patriotic American is never so proud of his flag as when it comes to mean to others as to himself a symbol of liberty."

All these statements were made *before* the United States became an authentic world power. We believed deeply in the principles for which we stood. Our influence stemmed not from our military or economic power but from the enormous appeal that our ideals and their success had in the rest of the world. We were the only great power in history to make its entrance on the world stage not by the force of arms but by the force of its ideas.

The Power of America's Message

In the end the greatness of America depends not so much on its force of arms, or even the opulence of its economy, but upon the power of its message to the world. Lacking a sense of mission, the nation will likely continue to flounder, unsure even of its true identity. Only by rediscovering our revolutionary charter, and applying it to the realities of the post-European world, can the United States in its third century enjoy a renaissance equal to the great vision of its founders and the uniqueness of its people.

Joel Kotkin, *Current*, December 1988.

In the course of this century, we have stayed true to our ideals. We have been a force for good in the world. We sought to temper the vindictive peace of the Treaty of Versailles. We were a decisive factor in preventing Hitler from making good on his promise of a thousand-year Reich. We have tried to hold the line on Soviet expansionism in Europe and Asia. We have certainly made mistakes in trying to uphold our ideals. But American idealism—sometimes naive, sometimes misguided, sometimes overzealous—has always been at the center of our foreign policy. One of our greatest strengths and greatest weaknesses as a world power has been the fact that we have never learned to act with the cold cynicism of Old World *Realpolitik*. . . .

As great as these changes have been, they will seem insignificant by comparison to those coming in the twenty-first century. It is therefore imperative that we decide today what role America should play in the future.

Our potential seems unlimited. We are the strongest and the richest country in the world. We can project our military power around the world, and we can influence all the great political issues of our time. Our culture, our ideas, and our economic and political systems have greater international appeal than ever before. It is no exaggeration to state that if allowed, hundreds of millions of people from around the world would emigrate to the United States.

But ironically, a new negativism afflicts America today. A growing chorus of pundits, professors, and politicians speak of the decline of American economic power and political leadership. They say that we have seen the end of the American century. They argue that American civilization has peaked and now faces an irreversible decline. They point out all around us the symptoms of decline—the problem of drug addiction among our young people, the crisis in education, the call for protectionism, and the appeal of isolationism. Brazil even beat us in basketball!

Are the new negativists correct? Does all this prove America's greatest days are behind us? Those who propound the new negativism will prove correct only if we permit their pessimism to become a self-fulfilling prophecy. Unlike the Marxists, we do not subscribe to a determinist view of history. We know we have a choice to make. We have the resources, the power, and the capacity to continue to act as a world leader. We can be a force for good in the twenty-first century. But there is still one unanswered question: Do we have the national will to play that role?

The American People Are Not Negative

The new negativists argue that American national will power has collapsed. After his famous seance with his advisers at Camp David, President Carter declared that the United States was suffering from a deep-seated malaise. He was right in identifying a problem. But he was wrong in arguing that the malaise afflicted the American people. In fact it was a deadly virus which had infected the American leadership class. The same is true of the new negativism. The American people are not defeatist. They will respond to strong, responsible leadership. The problem has been that our leader class has failed to provide it.

If Moscow ever wins the U.S.-Soviet rivalry, the reason will be the failure of the American leadership class. As Robert Nisbet wrote, "We appear to be living in yet another age in which 'failure of nerve' is conspicuous; not in the minds of America's majority but in the minds of those who are gatekeepers for ideas and intellectuals." In the last forty years, the upper crust of America in terms of education, money, and power has lost its sense of direction in the world. It has become enamored of every intellectual fad that has caught its attention. Disarmament and pacifism are today's rage, and that could have a disastrous impact on the fate of the West. If our society's decision-makers and those who influence them lose the will to lead, there is a great danger that America's majority might not be able to reverse the slide to defeat. . . .

Yet there are those both on the right and on the left who ask why the United States should play a role on the world stage when we have so many urgent problems at home. Many were disillusioned by our failure in Vietnam. Others have despaired at the sight of corrupt leaders in developing countries wasting billions of dollars in American aid on graft and government boondoggles. And they have been outraged to hear those same leaders berate us at the United Nations. Critics on the right think the United States is too good to sully itself with the grimy politics of the world; critics on the left think the United States is not good enough to be able to contribute anything to the world. These old and new isolationists seek to shift to the Europeans and the Japanese, whose economies have long since recovered from the devastation of World War II, the primary burden of world leadership.

In addressing the future world role of the United States, we need historical perspective. At the beginning of this century, it did not matter whether America played a world role or not. Others who shared our values could do so. As we approach the beginning of the next century, that is no longer true. It is absolutely vital for America to play a major role. If the United States withdraws into a new isolationism, there is no other power that shares our values and possesses the resources and the will to take our place. At the same time, we can be sure that another power hostile to our values and interests, the Soviet Union, will do so.

Soviet Union Still a Threat

This is not to say that the power structures in the Soviet Union have been radically changed. They have not. The KGB is still there. The military remain in power. They might revert to a harsher control over the population, continue to extract large resources for the military from the rest of Soviet society, and return to a more aggressive foreign policy.

It is unlikely that the Soviet Union can recover its ideological strength. But it can become an expansionary military power again. If the Soviets succeed in expanding, their prestige might increase again as well.

Fred C. Iklé, *Policy Review*, Summer 1989.

If we pull back, we will turn over to Moscow the role of undisputed leadership; we will have made the world safe for Soviet domination and expansionism; we will see the rapid demise of peace and freedom, and the dawn of the twenty-first century will open a new age of barbarism on a global scale. If we pull back, we will eventually find that we have become an island in a red sea. We will have peace. But it will be the peace of retreat and defeat.

We must therefore reject the new isolationist agenda of

withdrawing from Europe, curtailing our nuclear guarantee to our allies, erecting a wall of protectionist tariffs, cutting off support to freedom fighters, and retreating from the battle of ideas. In the superpower rivalry, to the extent that the United States prevails, the world will be safe for free nations. To the extent that the Soviet Union prevails, the world will be unsafe for free nations. Soviet-style tyranny survives by expanding. Liberty will expand by surviving. But to expand, it must first survive.

The Burden of Leadership

We must continue to assume the burden of leadership not just for the sake of others but also for our own sake. De Gaulle wrote, "France is never her true self except when she is engaged in a great enterprise." This is true for all nations. It is true for individuals. But it is particularly true for America. Only if we commit ourselves to be an active force for good in the world can America keep faith with its founding principles. Only if we commit ourselves to take part in the great enterprise of shaping the future of human civilization can we be true to ourselves. . . .

Our task is to formulate an agenda to exploit those twenty years for the cause of freedom and real peace. We must first of all reject the counsel of the new negativists in our great universities, in the news media, in big business, and in politics. One of the most disturbing aspects of their approach is the new isolationism. Unlike the old isolationists, those afflicted with the new strain of this deadly virus oppose not only American involvement abroad but also defense programs at home. They are obsessed with the twin fears of another Vietnam and of nuclear war and are incapable of facing up to the threat posed by the Soviet Union. Whenever Western interests are at risk, they can only tell you how not to do it. Their knee-jerk response to a crisis is to turn it over to the United Nations—which means, in effect, to do nothing.

If we have only twenty years before a reinvigorated Soviet Union turns its sights to renewed expansion, we have no time to lose. We must think boldly and act boldly. We must seek to shape the world; but we should not seek to remake the world in our image. We must recognize that a system which works for us may not work for others with different backgrounds. We must reject the fashionable but intellectually sterile doctrine of moral relativism. We deeply believe in our values. But one of the fundamental tenets of those values is that we will not try to impose them on others. Only by example and never by force will our values be extended to others.

We must restore the credibility of the U.S. strategic deterrent by reducing its vulnerability to a Soviet first strike. We must bolster our conventional forces for key theaters—like Europe, Korea, and the Persian Gulf—so that Soviet leaders will never believe they could win a war with conventional forces alone.

We must take advantage of Moscow's flagging economic strength to improve our competitive position around the world, fortifying our friends and improving ties with those we wish to be our friends. We must continue to build our cooperative relations with the other major power centers in the world: Western Europe, Japan, and China. We should help those who are fighting to prevent a communist victory and those who are trying to overturn a communist victory. We should also work to improve living conditions in other countries in order to undercut the political appeal of communist slogans. We should make it clear that even if there were no communist threat we would devote our efforts to reducing the poverty, misery, disease, and injustice that plague most of the people in the world. By investing in progress abroad, we are ensuring progress at home.

We should use our negotiations with Moscow to demonstrate our resolve in areas of irreconcilable conflict, to work toward mutually beneficial accords in areas of possible agreement, to increase contact between Soviet society and the West, and to structure as constructive a relationship with the Soviets as their international behavior permits.

A Supreme Irony

It is time to acknowledge the irony of the situation: The Soviet Union has produced a bold, visionary leader who is appropriating American ideas to capture that most elusive and valuable of political commodities, popular imagination. Meanwhile, the United States has been willfully ignoring its major problems, enmeshing itself in small-minded, partisan bickering at home, and in international forums emulating the grudging, reactive recalcitrance long associated with the Soviet bureaucracy. . . .

In failing to contend with fundamental changes in the economy and in security conditions, we are forfeiting our claim to leadership and our chief rival is filling the void. It is time, as once was said, to get the country moving again, but don't look to the government to move first. And don't complain about our fate until we all have made a more reflective effort than has been our recent habit.

John D. Steinbruner, *Los Angeles Times*, December 17, 1988.

Most of all, we must not fall into the trap of thinking that a reduction in U.S.-Soviet tensions means the end of the conflict. If Gorbachev stresses the need to solve his internal problems, we should not be conned into thinking that the system has changed or that the threat to the West has ended. Those in the West who believe he has abandoned the Soviet goal of a communist world should note the conclusion of his speech on the seventieth anniversary of the Bolshevik revolution: "In October 1917, we parted with the old world, rejecting it once and for all. We are moving toward a new world, the world of communism. We shall never turn off that road." Even as he pushes forward with reforms, Gorbachev will still press for Soviet interests and challenge ours—and he will be back in full force in twenty years. If we take the needed actions in the years before 1999, we will be ready for him.

We must avoid the danger of complacency. As Paul Johnson wrote, "One of the lessons of history is that no civilization can be taken for granted. Its permanency can never be assured; there is always a dark age waiting for you around the corner, if you play your cards badly and you make sufficient mistakes." We cannot allow Western civilization to meet with that fate. We have the needed physical and moral reserves, but we still have to demonstrate that we have the skill and the will to prevail. . . .

The Future in Our Hands

Are we witnessing the twilight of the American revolution? Are we seeing the first stages of the retreat of Western civilization into a new dark age of Soviet totalitarianism? Or will a new America lead the way to a new dawn for all those who cherish freedom in the world?

In his Iron Curtain speech at Westminster College in 1946, Winston Churchill said, "The United States stands at this time at the pinnacle of world power. It is a solemn moment for the American democracy. For with primacy in power is also joined an awe-inspiring accountability for the future." Those words are as true today as when he spoke them forty-two years ago. We hold the future in our hands.

6 VIEWPOINT

"We ought to adjust our burdens and privileges to our (relatively shrinking) power, and encourage others to play the roles and carry the responsibilities."

The U.S. Must Reduce Its World Obligations

Stanley Hoffmann

Major world trends have led many commentators to conclude that the U.S. carries too much of the world's economic and military burdens. These critics argue, as does Stanley Hoffmann in the following viewpoint, that the U.S. must scale back its burdens and allow itself to let other countries share in the leadership of the world. Hoffmann is the chairman of the Center for European Studies and the C. Douglas Dillon Professor of the Civilization of France at Harvard University in Cambridge, Massachusetts. He is the author of many books including *The Mitterand Experiment.*

As you read, consider the following questions:

1. How does the author view the state of America's economy? What solution does he recommend?
2. How does the author view the Soviet/American relationship? How does it differ from that of Richard Nixon, the author of the previous viewpoint?
3. What is Hoffmann's vision of America's future?

Stanley Hoffmann, "What Should We Do in the World?" *The Atlantic Monthly,* October 1989. Reprinted with permission.

There are periods of history when profound changes occur all of a sudden, and the acceleration of events is such that much of what experts write is obsolete before it gets into print. We are now in one of those periods, which obliges the United States to rethink its role in the world, just as it was forced to do by the cataclysmic changes that followed the end of the Second World War.

For more than forty years American foreign policy has been dominated by the contest with the Soviet Union. The strategy of containment, defined by George F. Kennan in 1946-1947 and applied by all American administrations since, often in a manner that displeased Kennan, may not have been an adequate compass at all times. The Soviet Union found ways of leaping across the barriers that the United States tried to erect, with military alliances and bases, all around the Soviet empire. Moreover, the imperative of containment failed to provide clear guidance for dealing with a host of regional and internal conflicts, especially in developing areas. Nevertheless, containment proved to be an extraordinarily sturdy concept. It was flexible enough to serve such diverse policies as the original strategy of alliance-building and confrontation, the détente of the early 1970s (aimed at providing Moscow with incentives for self-containment), and occasional attempts at "rollback," including the Reagan doctrine. . . .

Momentous changes have done more than any other trends or events since 1947 to deprive U.S. foreign policy of this overriding rationale. The détente of the early 1970s was a limited rapprochement between superpowers that were continuing to arm even while seeking to control jointly some parts of the arms race. It was a shaky convergence of contradictory calculations, in which the United States was trying to impose its version of stability and its own predominance on the Soviets, while the Soviets were hoping for condominium. Despite the defection of China, Moscow was still the center of a powerful empire. Today this empire is in serious trouble, China appears the more repressive and cruel of the two Communist giants, and Mikhail Gorbachev has gone far toward fulfilling the prophecy of Gyorgy Arbatov, the head of Moscow's Institute of USA and Canadian Affairs, who said that the new Soviet Union would deprive the United States of its main enemy.

Orphans of Containment

As if stupefied by the pace of events, many members of the American foreign-policy establishment behave like the orphans of containment—clinging to the remains of an obsolete strategy and incapable of defining a new one. And yet this is the moment coolly to re-evaluate American interests in the world. For many years our perceptions (often mistaken) of the Soviet threat drove our policy and defined, or distorted, our interests. Any great power has fundamental concerns, such as survival, physical security, and access to essential sources of energy, raw materials, and markets. In addition it has what specialists in international relations call milieu goals: promoting its values abroad, or at least preserving chances for the flowering of those values, and shaping international agreements and institutions in such a way that the nation's fundamental objectives and values are served. . . .

Managing U.S.-Soviet Relations

> We need to manage our relations with the Soviets in a way that reflects the increasing insufficiency of the notion of superpower domination. . . .
>
> Soviet military power has grown in the postwar period. But in our fixation with that fact, we have missed a major development—one that, in the long run, is more important. Other nations have grown in power relative to both superpowers to the point where the notion of a superpower has diminishing weight outside of the nuclear context. The rise of nationalism and the diffusion of power now mean that many secondary powers can frustrate the designs of a superpower; many regional powers are independent of both superpowers; and, ominously, several new forces are threatening to both the Soviet Union and the United States.
>
> Gary Hart, *New Perspectives Quarterly*, Spring 1987.

Some changes have taken place only in recent years. On the strategic and diplomatic front the most interesting trend has been the beginning of the end of the Cold War. Some of the reasons for this trend are external, or international, the main one being the extensive limitations on the effectiveness of force to which I have already alluded. In addition to the nuclear restraint, we must consider the increasing capacity for resistance among the victims of external force, especially if those victims get support from the outside, as usually happens, or if, like the Palestinians in the occupied territories, they fight at a level that makes successful repression difficult. Here recent experiences are telling. We have witnessed remarkably parallel American experiences in Vietnam and Soviet experiences in Afghanistan; the Israelis have been thwarted in Lebanon (which also gives Syria much trouble); the Vietnamese are calling it quits in Cambodia; and so on. Plainly there exists a wide inability to use force abroad for the control of a foreign people. These frustrations lead one to a conclusion once expressed by a former French Foreign Minister (a very shrewd man who liked to talk in apparent banalities): if you can't win a war, you might as well make peace. Thus the bizarre epidemic of peace in 1988. There is another external reason for the beginning of the end of the Cold War. Over time, inevitably, there had to be some loosening of the two blocs that have confronted each other; the compression of all the internal divergences and conflicts within them could not last forever. It was largely artificial: they were compressed as long as there was a cold-war condition, a kind of mimicked state of war; once it became clear that war was being postponed indefinitely, there was no reason for the blocs to remain as rigid as they once had been.

Ending the Cold War

Of course the dominant reasons for the ending of the Cold War are internal. In the United States, apart from economic factors to which we will come, there is what is quite improperly called the Vietnam syndrome, which is simply the marked reluctance of the American public to become engaged in protracted, uncertain wars for unclear purposes in secondary parts of the world. After all, Ronald Reagan, a rather popular President, did not succeed in getting the U.S. public to support the contra war against Nicaragua, nor did the American public support the presence of the United States Marines in Lebanon, once the awful cost became visible. In the Soviet Union the internal situation is far more serious, and there is a rather desperate need for retrenchment because of the economic predicament.

In the realm of economic interdependence, the evolution of recent years has two main characteristics. One is that despite the considerable difficulties of the past two decades, the economic relations among the advanced countries have developed successfully. To be sure, there has been a creeping erosion of the international principles of free trade established after the Second World War. Nevertheless, a relatively open and growing international economy has been preserved despite the economic shocks of the 1970s—no mean achievement, especially if one compares this with the situation that prevailed between the wars. The second trend, which is much more disturbing, has occurred in North-South relations; there we have not been so successful. An increasing differentiation has taken place between the developing countries that have been able to join the industrial world, and whose economic take-off has been spectacular, and the many other countries that have failed, and have fallen more and more deeply into debt. Between the latter countries and the rest of the world the gap has grown ever wider. . . .

In the arena of interdependence an increasing role is being played by a tightening European Community, by Japan, in some areas by Saudi Arabia. The aspect of this diffusion of power that is most significant for us here is the relative decline of the United States, to use the obligatory cliché (after all, a cliché is simply a truth that too many people have uttered and that many resist). Many public officials and academics have wrapped themselves in the American flag in the long debate on decline. They keep saying, quite rightly, that—if one compares the United States in the world today with the United States in the world of 1945-1950—a major part of this decline is not only normal but has been planned by the United States. Since 1945, when, after all, the world situation was completely abnormal, the United States has done its best to help the economies of Western Europe, Japan, South Korea, and Taiwan; as a result the American share of world GNP [gross national product] was bound to decrease.

A Global Partnership

For America to enjoy the peace and assurance that armaments afforded in a bygone era, our country now will have to direct its formidable economic, intellectual, and spiritual resources toward the building of a world order based on reason, nonviolence, democracy, and interdependence. This is exactly what our founders envisioned as the destiny of America, which is why they inscribed the Latin motto *Novus Ordo Seclorum* (a new order of the ages) on the reverse side of the Great Seal. America's world role today is to enter a global partnership with other nations—accepting our diversity—to help bring it to maturity before time runs out on us all.

Thomas J. Osborne, *USA Today*, July 1989.

However, there is more to it than that. The United States has become a debtor nation that depends on the willingness of others to provide the funds necessary to finance its budget deficit; we are going to be burdened for a long time by that debt. The United States has also seen its competitiveness decline for reasons that are largely internal and that cannot simply be dismissed by referring to the inevitable growth of other countries. The phenomena of overconsumption and underinvestment; insufficient industrial productivity; rigidity, waste, and shortsightedness in industry; and the problems in American education, particularly technical education, which have been much discussed though not much has been done about them, are the main culprits here. As a result the United States is simply no longer the leader in a number of key sectors in the world economy. Granted, this is less significant than it would have been in past international systems, where declining in key sectors meant a dangerous advantage for a major new military challenger. In the current system the United States faces no military challenger that is in better shape than it is. Nevertheless, this decline means that the American capacity to mold the international system of the future is not what it used to be, insofar as technological predominance often leads to wide influence abroad, and technological decline reduces the dependence of others on American civilian and military goods.

Given these features and trends of the world of the late 1980s, what ought American foreign policy to be? The point of departure must be the recognition of a paradox. The United States remains the only "complete" great power, the possessor of the largest military arsenal and of the most powerful economy in the world. On the other hand, both the diffusion of power in recent years and the partial impotence of military and economic power because of the restraints on its uses make it much more difficult for the United States to impose its will on others and to shape outcomes according to its preferences. We can still lead, toward goals that have a reasonable chance of being deemed by others compatible with their own interests. But we can no longer rule. Games of skill must replace tests of will. Our waning power to command and control needs to be supplemented by the new kind of power that the international system requires: the power to convince and to deal. In order to be effective, we have to define our national interest in a way that has a chance both of preserving a national capacity for steering toward world order (not because we are wiser than other nations but because there is no other candidate for the job) and of persuading others that their long-term concerns and ours mesh.

We cannot replace a fading vision—that of containment—with mere short-term management and avoidance of trouble, because the present offers opportunities for a decisive change in direction, and because there are simply too many dangers ahead to allow us to stumble from issue to issue in a "pragmatic" way. Nor can we follow the advice of neo-isolationists who believe that the United States ought not only to reduce its commitments and its military presence abroad, now that the Cold War is ending, but also to transfer to other powers the responsibility for dealing with the world's perils. That a great deal of what some call "devolution" needs to take place is not in doubt, but there is a gap between devolution and abdication. The truth is that only our continuing involvement is likely to draw other powers into an effort for world order, precisely because our past predominance has led others to rely on our initiatives and has led us to hug political control even as we rhetorically deplore the costs and burdens that come with it.

Toward Cooperation

We have to define first our goals, then our strategy. [One of our goals] ought to be the rearrangement of our relationship with the Soviet Union, away from both the old Cold War and the rather misleading exchange of misunderstandings that was the détente of the 1970s. This new relationship will inevitably be partly competitive, because our two nations will continue to have conflicting interests in many parts of the world, but it ought to be competitive without excessive militarization, and partly cooperative on issues in which there will be or already are converging interests. . . .

Thus it would be foolish for the United States to contribute to Gorbachev's fall, even if the contribution took the form of merely responding too grudgingly to some of his initiatives, and especially if it took the form of setting intemperate or untimely preconditions about internal changes or external retrenchment which could only embarrass and help derail him. Moreover, if Gorbachev should succeed, the result would not be a Soviet Union so much more efficient that it was more dangerous than the one we have known; in fact it would be less dangerous. *Glasnost* and *perestroika* are likely to produce a more open society, with a better informed and less manipulable public, with a greater role in the arena of interdependence and a smaller role in the military arena—precisely what we have always said we really wanted. Moreover, should Gorbachev fall after the United States had tried to cooperate with him, we would still have the means to return to our second nature—the Cold War—especially if we preserve our alliances while pursuing a new policy. . . .

Finally, we and the Soviets have a remarkably convergent interest in reducing the burden of arms that are very difficult to use and whose main purpose is to deter the other side from doing something that it has no particular desire to do. First, in arms control, the time has come to close the famous grand deal on strategic nuclear reductions that we might have obtained toward the end of the Reagan Administration, and that a large number of players in that administration wanted. . . .

For a More Balanced Order

Under [the] heading, "for a more balanced order," come the steps we must take in the 1990s to resolve numerous problems resulting from changes in the global distribution of power over the past fifteen or twenty years. We ought to adjust our burdens and privileges to our (relatively shrinking) power, and encourage others to play the roles and carry the responsibilities their power now requires. We should encourage the Western Europeans to develop and strengthen their identity. Whether or not they succeed in establishing a unified market is a detail; it is not the timetable that matters but the process itself. It may take a little longer, because the issues of pooling sovereignty over money, taxation, and fiscal policy, for instance, are very complicated, and because Margaret Thatcher exists, but even without Thatcher the issues would be difficult, and what counts is that things are again in motion. Fears that a "Fortress Europe" will exclude American goods are not justified; many powerful forces in Europe, including Great Britain and West Germany, and many multinational businesses operating in Europe, will not allow this to happen. It is in the American interest, in the long run, to encourage the European Community to play a larger role in diplomatic and security affairs, an arena where progress among the twelve members has so far been very limited. If we succeed in lowering the level of armaments in Europe, in agreement with the Soviets, the moment will come when we will indeed be able to withdraw a part of our forces. The NATO [North Atlantic Treaty Organization] alliance will then become more of an even partnership between the United States and its European associates. They are more likely to cooperate with one another on defense if the level of defense is lower overall than the present one. The situation that President Dwight D. Eisenhower, many years ago, thought would come very quickly will finally arrive: we will be able to disengage somewhat, and our allies will engage more. Western Europe has an extremely important diplomatic role to play in the eastern half of the continent. There the American and European objective ought to be to encourage as much Finlandization as possible. Each country in Eastern Europe is different, and it is much easier for the Western Europeans to pursue a discriminating policy—helping with economic ties and cultural agreements those countries that liberalize most convincingly—than it has ever been for the United States.

We should encourage Japan to be more active in international organizations, particularly in world institutions of assistance, development, and finance. Greater Japanese efforts at helping the developing countries would allow a partial reorientation of Japanese trade away from the developed world, where resistance to the volume of Japanese exports has been growing. Japanese consumers are likely to demand that their nation's economy also shift from the conquest of new external markets to the satisfaction of long-repressed domestic needs. . . .

We Can Do Nothing

In conclusion, in the world we have entered there will be many things that the United States can do nothing about. We should accept this state of affairs and, incidentally, perhaps even be grateful for it. It is a world in which war is no longer the principal and often inevitable mode of change; change comes more often now from domestic revolutions, about which we can and should do very little, because usually we do not understand the political cultures and trends of other countries and often we make mistakes. Change also, now that the pressures exerted by the Cold War are easing, comes from the rebirth of nationalisms. Many of the new forces of nationalism may lead to explosions and revolutions, about which, again, there will be very little that we or anybody else in the West can do. The task therefore is not to eliminate trouble everywhere in the world. Instead, we must devise what could be described as a new containment: not of the Soviet Union (although this will be part of it, insofar as conflicts of interest with the Soviets will continue) but of the various forms of violence and chaos that a world no longer dominated by the Cold War will entail. It is a complicated agenda, but it is at least different from the agenda we have had for so long.

A New Internationalism

If, as I have indicated, statesmen and citizens now operate not in a single international system but in two different fields, with different logics, actors, and hierarchies and tools of power, the question remains whether this duality can persist. An imperative for the United States is to prevent it from ending in the wrong way, as in the 1930s, when economic power was widely used for either self-protection or aggression. This is why we need to strive for the devaluation of hostile forms and uses of power in the strategic and diplomatic arena, and against a major recession in the field of economic interdependence. Our new strategy must aim at spreading the sense of common interests in the former and at strengthening it in the latter. It will require more "internationalism" than before, and the novel experience of cooperating widely with associates who are no longer satellites or dependents—as well as with the enemy of the past forty years.

a critical thinking activity

Distinguishing Between Fact and Opinion

This activity is designed to help develop the basic reading and thinking skill of distinguishing between fact and opinion. Consider the following statement: "By September 1989, the budget deficit was $160 billion." This is a fact which can be verified by many published sources. But consider this statement: "The budget deficit provides evidence that the U.S. is no longer the world's economic leader." This statement expresses an opinion about the deficit's impact on America's world status. Many people may have different assessments of the U.S. economy.

When investigating controversial issues it is important that one be able to distinguish between statements of fact and statements of opinion. It is also important to recognize that not all statements of fact are true. They may appear to be true, but some are based on inaccurate or false information. For this activity, however, we are concerned with understanding the difference between those statements which appear to be factual and those which appear to be based primarily on opinion.

Many of the following statements are taken from sentences in this chapter. Consider each statement carefully. *Mark O for any statement you believe is an opinion or interpretation of facts. Mark F for any statement you consider a fact. Mark U if you are uncertain.*

If you are doing this activity as a member of a class or group, compare your answers to those of other class or group members. Be able to defend your answers. You may discover that others come to different conclusions than you. Listening to the reasons others present for their answers may give you valuable insights in distinguishing between fact and opinion.

O = *opinion*
F = *fact*
U = *uncertain*

1. The U.S. and Japan together issue 80 percent of the money used by other countries as reserve currencies.
2. After World War II, U.S. currency was the strongest in the world.
3. America is today and will continue to be a great power.
4. The U.S. spends an enormous amount of money on its military.
5. The U.S. holds the largest amount of foreign direct investments in the world.
6. Foreign banks spent $140 billion supporting the exchange value of the dollar in 1987.
7. The United States' arsenal of nuclear weapons guarantees that it will continue to be a superpower.
8. Together the United States and Japan produce 30 percent of the world's goods.
9. The U.S. economy is becoming increasingly dependent on foreigners which could cause problems in the future.
10. Japan has taken control of the world market away from the United States.
11. Congresspeople, bankers, and financial experts in the U.S. have responded inappropriately to Japan's rise to economic power and remain unconcerned.
12. The idea that American world power is declining is ridiculous.
13. By the end of the 1980s, the budget deficit was double in size from the 1970s.
14. American culture, ideas, and economic and political systems have greater international appeal than ever before.
15. The United States must continue its role as world leader.
16. George Kennan defined the policy of containment in 1946 and 1947.
17. The American public is reluctant to see the U.S. involved in protracted wars in the Third World.
18. Now that the Cold War has ended, the U.S. must find a new ideology to guide its foreign policy.
19. In the 1980s, the value of the American dollar fell.

Periodical Bibliography

The following articles have been selected to supplement the diverse views presented in this chapter.

Georgi Arbatov	"Is America No Longer Exceptional?" *New Perspectives Quarterly*, Summer 1988.
Francis M. Bator	"Must We Retrench?" *Foreign Affairs*, Spring 1989.
Lawrence S. Eagleburger	"Uncharted Waters Ahead: U.S. Needs New Compass," *Los Angeles Times*, September 24, 1989.
Jeffrey E. Garten	"Is American Decline Inevitable?" *World Policy Journal*, Winter 1987/1988.
Paul Kennedy	"Does America Need Perestroika?" *New Perspectives Quarterly*, Spring 1988.
Paul Kennedy	"The (Relative) Decline of America," *The Atlantic Monthly*, August 1987.
Irving Kristol	"U.S. Foreign Policy Has Outlived Its Time," *The Wall Street Journal*, January 21, 1988.
Walter McDougall	"The Sick Eagle and the Politics of Despair," *The World & I*, May 1988.
Lance Morrow	"Welcome to the Global Village," *Time*, May 29, 1989.
Daniel Patrick Moynihan	"Debunking the Myth of Decline," *The New York Times Magazine*, June 19, 1988.
Karen Pennar	"Economic Prospects for the Year 2000," *Business Week*, September 25, 1989.
Peter G. Peterson	"The Morning After," *The Atlantic Monthly*, October 1987.
George W. Rathjens	"Global Security: Approaching the Year 2000," *Current History*, January 1989.
Jerry W. Sanders	"America in the Pacific Century," *World Policy Journal*, Winter 1988/1989.
Abu K. Selimuddin	"Will America Become Number 2?" *USA Today*, September 1989.
Marvin E. Wolfgang	"Whither the American Empire: Expansion or Contraction?" *The Annals*, November 1988.

CHAPTER 2

What Is America's Economic Future?

AMERICA'S FUTURE

Chapter Preface

America's preeminent world position following World War II was based not only on its military power, but also on its position as the "colossus of the world economy," in the words of economists Barry P. Bosworth and Robert Z. Lawrence. In 1950, the United States, with 6 percent of the world's population, had 48 percent of the world's wealth and accounted for 50 percent of the world's consumption of resources. In the 1950s and 1960s the U.S. dominated world manufacturing, became the biggest creditor and exporter of capital, and provided its citizens with the world's highest standard of living.

Although America's economy is still the world's largest measured in terms of gross national product, it is no longer as dominant as it once was. This is due in part to deliberate U.S. policies. The countries the United States defeated and then helped rebuild after World War II—Germany and Japan—are now powerful economic competitors. While U.S. consumers have benefited from foreign imports, U.S. companies have lost business and workers have lost jobs to foreign competition. Partly because of government budget deficits, the U.S. has also gone from being the world's largest creditor to being the world's largest debtor, owing more than four hundred billion dollars to foreign creditors at the end of 1987. Business professor and writer Abu K. Selimudden predicts, "If the U.S. does not meet the challenge of new competition, it surely will . . . slip to number two in the world economy by the end of this century."

Other observers, such as Paul Craig Roberts, economist and advisor to former president Ronald Reagan, strongly dispute the notion that the U.S. is in danger of losing its number-one status. They argue that America can only benefit from increased trade and foreign investment, and that fears about its economic future are unfounded. The viewpoints in this chapter debate the U.S. economy's future in an increasingly competitive global marketplace.

1 VIEWPOINT

"The world and the United States, instead of teetering on the edge of disaster, are really on the threshold of an almost unprecedented long-run economic boom."

America's Economic Future Is Bright

Charles R. Morris

Charles R. Morris is a business consultant, *Los Angeles Times* columnist, and author of several books. In the following viewpoint, he asserts that the United States is on the verge of an economic boom. Morris argues that the 1981-1982 recession and overseas competition have forced American industry to become more efficient and productive, and that the maturing of the "baby boom" generation will improve labor productivity and the U.S. savings rate. These and other trends, according to Morris, point to a strong U.S. economy. Morris argues that the U.S. will not dominate the world as it did following World War II, nor should it wish to, but will instead be an important part of a flourishing world economy.

As you read, consider the following questions:

1. What three general trends does Morris believe point to a future economic boom?
2. Why does Morris argue that it is becoming harder to distinguish between U.S. and foreign companies?
3. What will be the most challenging problems of the future, according to the author?

Charles R. Morris, "The Coming Global Boom," *The Atlantic Monthly*, October 1989. Reprinted by permission of Russell & Volkening as agents for the author.

The prevailing economic opinion in the United States, it sometimes seems, is one of unrelieved Spenglerian gloom. The world creaks beneath hopeless burdens of debt and deficit. Japan is destroying the international trading economy with its single-minded drive toward mercantilist conquest. America is besotted by the bright torrent of electronic gewgaws from Asia. Europe is retreating into its "Fortress 1992." . . .

But there is another view. A small but growing group of economists makes a strong case that the world and the United States, instead of teetering on the edge of disaster, are really on the threshold of an almost unprecedented long-run economic boom.

The Case for Optimism

The intellectual icon of the new optimists is Joseph Schumpeter, an Austrian economist who did much of his work in the United States. Schumpeter, who died in 1950, was one of the first to develop the theory of business cycles. He believed that economies progress in fitful starts and stops, interspersing long periods of economic dislocation with stretches of sustained growth and development. The driving forces behind Schumpeter's cycles of boom and bust are the pace of industrial innovation and the diffusion of new technology. In Schumpeter's terms, the optimists see the long run of economic turmoil that began in the early 1970s as a period of dislocation that is the prelude to a new industrial golden age.

Although there is some overlap between the new optimists and the supply-side publicists—the people, that is, who predicted we could have tax cuts without budget deficits—their case is not just blind Panglossism. It rests on sophisticated arguments, derived from economic and demographic developments around the world and in the United States. The gap between the optimists' view and that of most economists, according to Edward Yardeni, the chief economist at Prudential-Bache Securities, who is one of the most vocal of the optimists, is that mainstream economics focuses too much on formal macroeconomic models. "Most economists don't look much at the real economy," Yardeni says. "It's messy and doesn't translate well to models. But when you stop and look, the case for a long-run boom is almost overwhelming."

Three Arguments

The optimists' arguments reduce essentially to three. The first is the integration of the global goods markets. Everyone knows about global *financial* markets. Stocks, bonds, and bank deposits surge around the world in nanoseconds, riding the twinkling green blips on trading-room computer screens. Integration of the manufacturing economy is an even newer development. High productivity manufacturing technology, much of it pioneered in

Japan, is spreading rapidly throughout the world, at the same time that big companies, and even many medium-sized companies, are operating more and more on a global scale. The result is relentless global competition on price and quality, a steady, even startling, worldwide increase in manufacturing productivity, and solid increases in real world output.

The second argument is a demographic one. The population profile of the United States has been wildly misshapen over the past twenty years. Tens of millions of young adults born during the Baby Boom years of 1946-1964, unskilled, semischooled, and very unsettled, streamed into the job queues, playing havoc with the unemployment rate, personal savings, and the quality of American work output. The populations of Japan and Germany, in contrast, have been much more heavily weighted toward mature adults in their forties and early fifties. Starting just about now the center of gravity of the American population is shifting radically once again. For most of the next two decades the age mix in America will be very much like those in present-day Japan and Germany. The labor force will grow very slowly, if at all; the demographic pressures making for unemployment will decline; output, income, and savings per worker should go up steadily.

America's Economic Success

An analysis by the Organization for Economic Cooperation and Development (OECD) shows that "living standards in the U.S. continue to soar well above those of other Western countries." Using what they call "purchasing power parities" (PPP), OECD found that not only is U.S. real per capita GNP 10 percent ahead of its nearest competitor (Canada), it is 41 percent ahead of Japan, 33 percent ahead of West Germany, and 51 percent ahead of Great Britain, a clear proof that we remain competitive, with real U.S. PPP income rising another 4.3 percent in 1986 over 1985.

All in all, when you consider that the U.S. has created nearly 90 percent of all the new jobs in the Western world since 1980, this upward income performance in an era of exploding competition has been nothing short of incredible—and another testament to the fact that the U.S. economy, despite all its creaks and groans, continues to be a miraculous (if awfully quiet) success.

Warren Brookes, *The American Spectator*, August 1988.

Finally, the optimists foresee a steady decline in interest rates. Big-country governments, as a group—including the United States—have halved their budget deficits, measured as a percent of national income, over the past few years; some are already buying back their bonds. Over time reduced borrowing should mean lower rates. Meanwhile, global competition is already keeping a tight lid on inflationary wage and price increases. About half the long-term interest rate is a hedge against higher future inflation. As investors slowly come to believe that inflation isn't about to run out of control, the size of that hedge will drop. What's more, for a variety of complicated reasons, the demand for housing is expected to drop sharply. Real estate has absorbed an absurdly high proportion of American wealth over the past twenty years. Over the next ten much of that capital will become available for productive business investment, helping to keep interest rates low. . . .

The Third Industrial Revolution

For sheer compressed, earth-scorching savagery, it is difficult to match the violent recession that struck American manufacturing industries in 1981-1982. Whole sectors of the economy were brought to the brink of destruction. Just a few statistics convey the speed and extent of the humiliation. In 1975 America's machine-tool manufacturers dominated the world markets; by 1985 machine-tool exports were virtually nonexistent and German and Japanese machine tools were standard throughout American industry. In just a few years America's share of world semiconductor fabrication dropped from 60 percent to 40 percent. For all practical purposes, American companies simply exited the consumer electronics industry. *No* home radios, phonographs, black-and-white televisions, or cassette players are made in the United States any longer; American companies' share of the color-television market is minuscule. No American company makes VCRs or CD players. Industry after industry told the same story. "We were oxyacetylened," one Rust Bowl executive says—it was like being taken out with a blowtorch.

In retrospect, the storm warnings had been flying for years. American companies, feeling secure in their big home market, were complacent and lazy, running smug big-union and big-management cartels, turning out shoddy products that cost too much. And in industry after industry there are the same frantic struggle for global position and scrambling for strategic alliances that are reshaping the automobile industry. Texas Instruments and the Japanese computer-maker Hitachi are partners in developing the next-generation computer memory chip, the 16-megabit DRAM. The Japanese earthmoving-equipment-maker Komatsu is partnering with Dresser Industries in manufacturing and marketing throughout North and South America. . . .

The drive for global market share is forcing what Stanley Feldman, of Data Resources, calls the Third Industrial Revolution. A wholesale reordering of production technology is under way—computerized factory schedules and inventory controls to cut costs, intelligent production machinery that can shift processes in the middle of an assembly line. The object is to produce local products adapted to local markets, but reap world economies of scale in research and development, raw-materials sourcing, and production balancing.

IBM makes almost all its products in its local markets, but no other company can match its worldwide research-and-development base; and it enjoys the luxury of global sourcing of selected products from highly specialized factories. Sony has been steadily moving the design and production of its televisions to Europe and America, but a common worldwide chassis gives a cost advantage no local competitor can match. Engineers at General Electric-FANUC design factory controllers around the clock—at the end of each day the Americans download their work to a satellite link to Japan and then pick up the next morning where the Japanese left off. A global competitive standard squeezes out the small inefficiencies that build up in protected national markets—traditional labor practices, fustian management. "If you let your costs or your quality get out of line almost anywhere, someone is moving in to take advantage," says Steven Nagourney, the chief international strategist for Shearson Lehman Hutton.

Escalating Prosperity

The Free World is on the verge of an unprecedented epoch of escalating prosperity through expanded international trade and investment. An integrated global marketplace coupled with America's vast productive capacity and technological excellence will enrich every working man and woman in America and around the globe.

To realize the bountiful vision of a strong, productive and free America, we must lead the world into the economy of the future, not hide from it.

Phil Gramm, *The Washington Times*, June 30, 1987.

Support for the optimists' claims comes from the striking rise in global manufacturing productivity during the 1980s. Manufacturing productivity in the United States has grown at an annual rate of 4.3 percent since 1982, one of the fastest sustained run-ups on record. (American steel is now actually cheaper than Japanese steel.) After slipping badly, Japan has surged back to the head of the productivity-league tables, with a 5.9 percent growth rate over the same period. And right behind Japan is Great Britain, for twenty years the living symbol of "Eurosclerosis." Europe's second fastest rate of output growth was in Italy—yes, *Italy*—just a hair faster than the rate in the United States. France, Germany, and Sweden are clustered behind the United States, with quite respectable rates of improvement. . . .

Even accepting the optimists' claim that the world is on the brink of an industrial boom, the question remains whether the United States will get much benefit from it. National economic behavior for the past two decades has not been impressive. The problem seems almost to be a moral and intellectual flabbiness—an inability to make spending choices, a low savings rate, a culture of self-centered consumerism and restless mobility, a lack of commitment and loyalty on the part of careless workers and job-hopping executives. The optimists' answer is that the past twenty years have been a most unusual period in American economic history.

The world sings the praises of the "Great American Job Machine." Over the past twenty years the United States has created jobs for 38 million new workers . . . when employment was virtually flat in almost every other industrial country. But in the same breath economists lament the slowdown in American productivity; manufacturing excepted, the output of American workers has been stagnant since the early 1970s.

A Changing Work Force

The strong performance in job creation and the weak performance in productivity are, of course, two sides of the same coin. New workers swelled the American labor force by about 50 percent in the past twenty years, shifting the average age and experience of workers sharply downward. Not surprisingly, with lots of cheap new workers mobbing the doorway, businessmen increased hiring instead of investing in labor-saving machinery—a fancy industrial robot costs about as much as a year's wages for a hundred entry-level workers. Real wages and productivity were stagnant, and the business success stories were companies, like McDonald's, that learned how to pan for gold in that low-wage pool.

The transformation of the work force in the 1990s will be just as dramatic. People born at the Baby Boom's peak are in their thirties. About five years from now two-thirds of the Baby Boomers will be over thirty-four. Walking shoes are already pushing high-priced running shoes off the sports-store counters. Another sign of the times is that McDonald's is beginning to invest in labor-saving machinery—two-sided grills, for instance. As the size of the work force begins to stabilize, and the average age and experience of workers move rapidly upward, business will start substituting equipment for low-wage workers. Capital spending, in fact, has been strong throughout the 1980s expansion, and with time productivity should soar. "Couch potatoes" are not exciting people. The soul does not thrill at the sight of forty-year-old workaholics, raising kids and paying their mortgages, but as the economy's centerweight, they have it all over the long-haired pot-smokers of a couple of decades ago. . . .

The last thread in the bright economic tapestry the optimists are weaving is the forecast of steadily falling interest rates. Falling rates would ease debt pressures and spur industrial investment. The array of forces lining up to push rates down is, in fact, an impressive one. In the first place, interest rates are partly an anticipation of inflation. There is a good argument that global competitive pressures clamp a firm ceiling on prices. Coopers & Lybrand, the international accounting and consulting firm, says flatly that only the "fierce worldwide competition in price and quality" can explain the tame behavior of prices during the prolonged American economic expansion. Alan Greenspan, the chairman of the Federal Reserve, says that "integration of the world's production facilities" heads off inflation by unstopping production bottlenecks.

U.S. Remains Important

Although the United States no longer dominates all areas of the global economy, its ability to raise the living standards of its citizens is not thereby diminished. There may be less scope for the United States to exercise its will at the expense of others, but economic growth abroad brings with it important benefits to the United States, including a productivity boost from the technological innovations of others, access to larger markets as a producer, and greater variety as a consumer. In the near future, moreover, no other country is likely to approach the importance of the United States to the world economy. The United States remains the pivot of the global trading system; its trade flows with both Europe and Asia far exceed those between Asia and Europe.

Barry P. Bosworth and Robert Z. Lawrence, *The Brookings Review*, Winter 1988/1989.

At the same time, government borrowing is declining in virtually all the industrial countries, which should press rates down further. Roland Leuschel, the chief investment strategist at Banque Bruxelles Lambert, has even raised an unfashionable alarm over "a looming shortage of government bonds." On average, government borrowing as a percent of national income fell by about half from 1984 to 1988—in the United States from five percent of GNP [gross national product] in 1985 to about three percent (or two percent if state and local surpluses are counted, as they should be). Britain is already in surplus, retiring perhaps $23 billion of debt in 1989. Australia and Denmark are running surpluses, as will Japan and Germany within a year or two. America's cash deficit will disappear sometime after 1995, as collections for the next century's Social Security overhang begin to accumulate. Scarcer bonds mean higher bond prices—another way of saying lower interest rates. . . .

Yardeni has pulled together all the roses blooming in the economic garden into a bouquet he calls New Wave Economics. "After the stock market crashed in 1987," he says, "and everyone was filled with gloom, I decided to look at what might go right. Frankly, I was amazed at how positive all the fundamentals were. The work force is getting older, more skilled, and more productive. Savings should rise just as government borrowing and the demand for housing slow down. Global competition and a resurgence in manufacturing are a lid on inflation. We're looking at low interest rates, a long-term shift from housing to business investment, and a big increase in productivity and real incomes. It's a cycle that could go on for a long time."

U.S. Success in the Global Economy

There is still the pervasive worry that American industry has been weakened to the point where we are slipping to second-class economic status. It is a serious issue, and there *is* genuine cause for concern in specific industries.

But the question of America's future success in a global economy is too often confused with the issue of our regaining our postwar position as economic dictator to the world. That role is gone forever, and no one should wish it otherwise. The income of urban adults in the major industrialized countries is now practically uniform. That was the explicit objective of American statesmanship at the end of the war, the crowning adornment of our postwar foreign policy, a grand aim expressly adopted, pointedly pursued, and unambiguously attained. To seize upon that success as an index of relative "decline" is to miss the point.

The shock of the economic turmoil of the 1970s, the recessionary gales of the early 1980s, and the sudden onslaught of the Japanese have tended to exaggerate the perception of decline. There are real problems in many American industries, but they need to be kept in perspective.

Some statistics:

• According to a detailed study completed by the British Treasury, real output per American worker, abstracted from currency fluctuations, is still the highest in the world, and perhaps half again higher than output per worker in Japan.

• Over the past twenty years American companies have increased their share of world exports. But American companies have spread their operations around the globe, and their sales overseas do not show up in American trade data.

• The U.S. share of world output actually increased slightly during the 1980s. Asian and Japanese shares of world output also increased, but at the expense of Europe, not of America.

• The United States never "de-industrialized." Manufacturing's share of GNP, at about 23 percent, has been virtually unchanged since 1947. . . .

The importance of agriculture, mining, and logging in America is sometimes viewed as a measure of backwardness. But as practiced in the United States, these are becoming high-tech industries. The price of coal has dropped by about a fifth in recent years, primarily because of improvements in mining machinery. The continuing flaps over bovine somatotropin, the hormone that boosts cows' milk production, and over the use of recombinant gene products as pesticides or crop enhancers demonstrate the impact of technology on the modern farm.

America's Technology

And the American high-technology position is still very strong. In the booming market for mini-supercomputers—miniaturized powerhouses that can chew through scientific problems that would tie up even the largest business computers for years—the only manufacturers are still American. In the computerized-workstation market—very high-powered personal computers—Sony is still chasing the medium-sized California firm Sun Microsystems in Japan. America has no peer in medical technology, fiber optics, genetic engineering, or computer-aided design. . . .

America is too big, too rich, and too resourceful to be shut out of the global boom. Even the pessimist Gary Shilling sees America as regaining much of its competitiveness longer-term: "Japan may actually have a tougher time than the United States," he says, "because of demographics and excess capacity."

As global companies continue the relentless push into local markets, America will become a haven for high-productivity manufacturing. American companies will be clear winners in some global industries, and American companies that have taken to heart the lessons of the past ten years will be winners in every industry. To be sure, a large number won't make the grade and will be swallowed up by stronger Asian or European competitors, but it will be increasingly difficult for consumers or workers to tell the difference. . . .

Success will bring momentous problems of its own. But if the optimists are right, and the world really is on the brink of a Schumpeterian golden age, there should be energy and resources enough to solve them.

2 VIEWPOINT

"The nation is not keeping pace with changes in the world economy and has a serious competitiveness problem."

America's Economic Future Is Bleak

The Cuomo Commission on Trade and Competitiveness

In 1987, New York Governor Mario M. Cuomo established a commission of businesspeople, labor leaders, and academic and public officials. The Commission examined and prepared a report on the U.S. economy. In the following viewpoint, excerpted from their 1988 report, the Commission argues that future economic growth is threatened because the U.S. has lost its competitive position in world trade. They point to seven warning signs of economic trouble, and argue that U.S. economic power will decline if these trends remain unchecked.

As you read, consider the following questions:

1. What are the seven warning signs the Commission describes?
2. According to the authors, what impact would a U.S. economic decline have on the global economy?
3. Which group of Americans will be most affected by a U.S. economic decline, according to the Commission?

America has failed to adjust to the new reality of a global economy, and we are beginning to pay the price. The price of failure will not be just economic; the consequences in the next decade will be more than a slower rate of economic growth or a stagnation in living standards and opportunities. Just as any debtor is at the mercy of its creditors, if the U.S. continues to sink into debt, our foreign creditors will eventually have undue influence over our future and the policies of our elected government. And if America fails to grow—and it cannot grow without becoming more competitive in markets at home and abroad—it will be unable to sustain national security commitments and the network of alliances and institutions that has preserved America's place in the world for the last forty years. Without a growing American economy whose growth is earned, not borrowed, the world will be a poorer and more dangerous place, not only for Americans, but for all those in Europe, Japan, and the developing world who depend on our markets to keep their own economies healthy and growing.

These are the conclusions of Governor Cuomo's Commission on Trade and Competitiveness, reached after more than a year's study of the relationship between the American and the world economies. . . .

Seven Warning Signs

As the Commission reviewed the long-term picture of America's economy we identified seven warning signs of serious economic trouble. While any one of these signs might not be dangerous by itself, together they constitute a tangible threat to our economic system and our way of life. Left untreated they will seriously weaken, even undermine, our economy in the next decade.

1. *The Trade Crisis*

For most of this century America has been a surplus nation, selling more goods abroad than we purchased—but no longer.

• The U.S. has not had a surplus in the trade of merchandise since 1975.

• Our trade deficit has grown steadily—from a few billion dollars per year in the 1970s to more than $156 billion in 1986 and $171 billion in 1987.

• In 1987 imports reached a record 22.7 percent of all goods consumed in the U.S. (excluding oil)—up from 16.0 percent as recently as 1982, over a 40 percent increase.

• The U.S. has lost 30 percent of its market share of total world exports since 1950. . . .

2. *A Nation in Hock*

If there is one word which captures the feeling of anxiety among Americans, it is debt. Total household, corporate, and consumer debt has risen 60 percent in five years, rising from $4.9 trillion in 1982 to $7.9 trillion in 1987. It is true that rising levels of private and public debt have helped maintain high levels of consumption and spurred growth. There are also signs that the worst years of the "debt explosion" are over, since the rate of debt growth has slowed. But once the economic expansion ends, the weight of the debt burden will surely increase and in the next recession will drag us even farther down. And under any circumstances, it will depress growth and the nation's standard of living. . . .

Bert Dodson. Reprinted with permission

3. *More Risk, More Volatility*

Closely related to the increase in debt has been an increase in risk in the economy and volatility in financial markets around the world.

• Business bankruptcies have soared. In the worst years of the worst recessions since World War Two, an average of 49 businesses out of every 10,000 failed. But in 1982 that number climbed to 88 and in 1986 it reached 120 before dropping off slightly in 1987. . . .

• Volatility—the rate at which interest rates change—is also up from previous years. The prime rate, which once remained stable for years at a time, has been on a roller coaster in the 1980s, rising as high as 21 percent in 1981. Bond prices, which reflect interest rates, have also plunged and soared. These volatile rates vastly complicate the work of banks and corporations that need to decide on long-term investment strategies in an unpredictable environment. Stock price volatility is also high; 50-point rises and falls in the Dow Jones Industrial Average have become almost commonplace.

4. *Slow Growth*

The U.S. economy is still growing, but ever more slowly. In the 1960s the annual average GNP [gross national product] growth rate was 3.8 percent. In the 1970s, it fell to 2.8 percent. From 1980 through 1987 it slid even further to 2.2 percent.

5. *A Less Innovative Economy*

Long-term trends show that our economy is losing its dynamism. Investment, productivity growth, and savings are weak; in education and innovation we have lost our lead.

• Weak Investment: Low levels of capacity utilization have accompanied a drop in private investment. Annual average investment (as a percent of the GNP) was 34 percent less for the period 1980-1986 than it was, on average, during the three preceding decades.

• Diminished advantage in productivity: Are we losing our edge? Investment in plant and equipment is essential if the nation is to raise productivity, a key ingredient for improving the competitiveness of U.S. industry and stimulating incomes. Partly because investment has slowed, the rate of growth of American productivity has failed to match that of its major competitors. While manufacturing productivity growth improved substantially to an average rate of 4.25 percent, the U.S.'s traditional advantage over its key competitors continues to shrink.

• Too few savers: The availability of funds for investment depends largely on national savings. Here, again, we have witnessed decline. The internal savings of businesses, which previously made possible a high degree of self-financing, have been shrinking. Indeed, private savings overall have fallen. Net private savings (as a percentage of GNP) were 25 percent less in the 1980s than in the 1970s. . . .

Foreign Competition

6. *Increasing Exposure to Tough Foreign Competition*

More American industries than ever are exposed to foreign competition. Today the effect of that competition can be seen across our nation's landscape.

• In New England and the Southeast, the textile industry competed successfully in world markets throughout the 1960s. But as textile technology was disseminated abroad, producers from low-wage countries seized their opportunity, and the growth rate of textile imports exploded. Between 1980 and 1984 imports grew at an average annual rate of 18 percent. Since 1981 nearly 100,000 U.S. textile jobs have been lost. . . .

• Detroit has lost its position as the auto capital of the world. In 1960, American automakers produced more than 75 percent of the world's automobiles. Today the U.S. produces less than 25 percent of the world's autos. In 1986, the auto industry employed 140,000 fewer workers than it did in 1978.

• In Iowa and the rest of the farm belt, agriculture suffers from tough foreign competition. The Green Revolution made more of the Third World self-sufficient for its food, a worthwhile goal by any standard. But this has reduced U.S. exports and placed the nation in direct competition with farmers around the world scrambling for shares of the shrinking export market. Since 1982 the number of American farms has dropped by nearly 10 percent.

• In California's Silicon Valley, the high-technology companies told themselves for years that "it can't happen here" and heralded themselves as America's manufacturing future. But in the mid-1980s, the semiconductor industry lost $2 billion, and laid off nearly 25,000 employees. Conditions for semiconductor manufacturers have improved somewhat, but are still difficult. Not surprisingly, manufacturers have come to the forefront of the battle for reform of U.S. trade laws.

7. The End of a Rising Standard of Living for Many Americans

One of the key features of life in postwar America, a rising standard of living for most people, has virtually disappeared. Real income levels for many Americans have declined since the early 1970s, not coincidentally just at the time the U.S. began importing more goods than it exported.

Hourly income for production workers, as measured by real spendable earnings, rose 56 percent from 1948 to 1972. The long upward trend in wages has stopped; real hourly wages have stagnated since 1973.

Between January 1981 and January 1986, more than 13 million Americans lost their jobs. One-third of those workers have remained unemployed or have given up and left the work force. Almost half of those who did find new jobs earn less than they did before. . . .

A Phony Prosperity

What's wrong is no secret: We are living on borrowed time. These are days of phony, soap-bubble prosperity. Wall Street is America's Potemkin village. A paper-thin veneer of economic well-being covers over the deep structural problems of an economy burdened by too little real productivity and too much assumed debt.

Alan M. Webber, *Los Angeles Times*, October 18, 1989.

The outlook for our economy suggests a future with a stagnant or falling standard of living for many and a rising standard for some. If allowed to continue, this trend will destroy one of America's greatest strengths—an economy which produced a rising standard of living, and increasingly offered equal opportunity to all.

The Commission thinks these seven warning signs, taken together, lead to a single conclusion: the nation is not keeping pace with changes in the world economy and has a serious competitiveness problem. . . .

The word ''crisis'' has been cheapened by too frequent use, but no other word so well describes America's present situation. Originally, ''crisis'' meant turning point, which is precisely where America stands today. Either we pursue reforms that both strengthen the international trading system and make us more competitive at home, or we risk a long, slow national decline.

The majority of today's Americans grew up after the last great turning point in our history—the fifteen-year period encompassing the Depression, World War Two, and postwar reconstruction. In the long peace and prosperity that followed, many of us came to take the good life for granted, believing that our lives would contain few hard choices and that there would be no serious penalties for national mistakes. America was on an economic escalator.

But today the escalator has slowed, and in some respects begun going backward. Tough choices *do* confront us, and the greatest mistake would be to minimize their seriousness. Unfortunately, political leaders in both parties have for too long ignored the warning signs, squandering irreplaceable assets and precious time for the sake of short-term political gain. Indeed, some say that any political leader is doomed to defeat if he or she tells the American people the truth about the difficult things we must do to secure a prosperous future. Our political system, it is said, rewards only the bearers of glad tidings. . . .

Envisioning the Year 2000

To convey the urgency and opportunities of our condition, we . . . envision America as it may be when the next century begins . . . if we accept our current policies as adequate and do little in the way of fundamental change. . . .

Assume that present long-term trends continue. The year 2000 will see a United States dependent on imported goods in most of its vital industries. Forty-one percent of all goods sold in the U.S. will be imports, including 42 percent of all cars. Thirty percent of our telecommunications, one-third of our steel, and a full 90 percent of all consumer electronics will come from other countries. Unless we can reverse the trend, by the year 2000 we will no longer be a major producer of computers. In 1985 we produced 30 percent of all the computers made in the world; by the year 2000 our share may be as little as 8 percent.

This continuing loss of competitiveness will trigger a decline in our standard of living. Over-the-decade average rates of growth have been sliding downward; another decade of decline will leave our average annual growth in the late 1990s at a slow 1.6 percent. This slowdown will ultimately put our standard of living far behind not only those of Germany, Japan, and Sweden, but those of many other industrial societies as well.

If the national debt continues to grow as it has—11 percent per year—at present rates of population and GNP growth, interest payments on the national debt would amount to more than 10 percent of our GNP in the year 2000—or about $2,600 per year for every man, woman, and child in the United States. The federal debt would be $9 trillion by the year 2000 and interest payments would consume $750 billion per year. This is clearly not possible, but a doubling of the federal debt to $4 trillion is, unfortunately, not impossible. Annual interest payments on that debt will be over $300 billion. Assuming that foreign holdings grow 1 percent per year, to 25 percent of our national debt, interest payments to foreigners will reach $75 billion a year.

Economic Malaise

At the risk of being called a messenger of gloom and doom, I will go out on a limb and predict that the artificially sustained and illusory state of well-being is coming to a rather abrupt end. For millions, the illusion—and with it the American dream—is going to turn into a nightmare. There are both short-term and long-term reasons for the economic malaise.

Gus Hall, *Political Affairs*, December 1988.

We will lose a large measure of control over our future to foreign investors. Already, average annual foreign direct investment in the United States has risen to record levels. If this trend continues, foreign investors will control many firms in key industries and decide what new investments will be made. America may increasingly look like an economic colony, which is where we came in 212 years ago. Foreign interest groups, backed by enormous wealth, will form powerful lobbies that will influence political decisions at every level of government. The spectacle of Toshiba Corporation mobilizing a lobbying campaign to try to stop our government from punishing it for giving secret technology to the Soviet Union will be repeated many times.

Lower Wages

Our slow growth and foreign debt will result in lower real wages for American workers. By the year 2000, the average real weekly pay of American workers will be lower than at any time since the Korean War. Unemployment will vary between 11 and 12 percent during recessions and between 7 and 8 percent during expansions. One out of six American families—and one out of every four American children—will live below the poverty line. In 1973, almost half of American families earned enough money to afford what the Census Bureau considers a middle-class standard of living. By the year 2000, if present trends continue, only one-third of our families will still be middle-class. By that year, the monthly mortgage payment for a median-priced home will equal one-half of the median monthly income for a 30-year-old man, up from 21 percent in 1973. We can expect homeownership rates to fall until more than 40 percent of American families cannot afford to buy a home, and homelessness will reach uncontrollable levels. One-third of the population will have no health insurance at all.

Family life will suffer. Falling real wages in the last fifteen years have made common the two-income family. Mothers of preschool children have entered the labor force in ever-increasing numbers—too often out of necessity. But by the year 2000, two incomes will not be enough. Three- and four-income families will multiply as more parents seek second jobs and more children work after school. Over 60 percent of American teenagers aged 16 to 19 will be employed while still enrolled in high school, up from 30 percent in 1960 and 45 percent in 1987. . . .

Consequences

What will be the consequences if these forecasts prove accurate? America will not be able to keep its promises to retirees; Social Security and Medicare will surely be undermined as domestic spending programs are cut to the bone. As our hard-pressed cities and towns reduce their education funding, the gap between the quality of American education and that of our competitors' education will widen.

The brunt of an American decline will fall on the middle class. A government saddled with immense debts and crushing interest payments will desperately seek to raise revenues, and the largest portion of these will have to come from the middle class; the poor have too little money and there are not enough wealthy people to carry the burden. Even now we are hearing proposals to cut the tax benefits that make middle-class life possible, including the deduction for single-family home mortgage loans. In effect, the middle class will pay more to government and get less from it. Government benefits and services that provide social security for middle-class recipients will be slashed. We can expect major cuts in police, sanitation, mass transit, and education—services the middle class needs to get from state and federal government—if the budget crisis persists. Increasingly, "user fees" will pay for services once regarded as basic. In addition, as the number of older Americans reaches record levels, the demand for government services will rise—without the resources to meet it.

Economic decline will make it harder, not easier, to take the actions necessary to correct the crisis. Austerity and cutbacks will sharpen political competition among society's interest groups and make compromise more difficult. . . .

The economic decline and retreat of our nation will have consequences far beyond our own borders. A poorer America will mean a poorer and more dangerous world. The success of democracy in the Philippines, for example, is fundamentally linked with the success of the Philippine economy, and that economy needs substantial, long-term assistance from the U.S. It is improbable that a declining America can provide that aid when we are forced to cut essential programs at home. Israel, Egypt, Latin America, sub-Saharan Africa, and other regions that look to us for assistance cannot expect to receive the aid they need if we fall into economic decline. Our commitments to NATO [North Atlantic Treaty Organization] and Japan are also jeopardized unless we alter our course. Professor Paul Kennedy's warnings about "imperial overstretch"—the growing gap between our obligations and our resources—will become more apparent.

The Locomotive of Growth

Since World War Two the American economy has been the locomotive of world growth; our consumers have provided demand for products around the world, and, until recently, our savers provided much of the capital. Without a strong and growing American market, even the rapidly growing NICs [newly industrializing countries] of East Asia will slip into recession and stagnation. Although we are no longer the only important market economy in the world, we remain the most important source of demand. Our failure to grow will have disastrous consequences for our neighbors and for trading partners around the world. The Third World will suffer the most, as economic problems and political instability will rock governments and societies around the world. This instability will create new threats to America's military security at the same time that our economy will be unable to bear the strains of high defense budgets. The result is likely to be an unpleasant and dangerous world, haunted by a growing threat of war.

This scenario of American drift and decline does not require any dramatic changes to become a reality. We do not need another 500-point crash on the stock market or a collapse of the international banking system in order to see a long-term, gradual decline in our standard of living. This is the kind of future toward which we are currently headed, and unless we carry out major reforms, this is the future that we will reach.

3 VIEWPOINT

"The only certainty is that nothing is certain."

America's Economic Future Is Uncertain

Murray Weidenbaum

Murray Weidenbaum chaired the President's Council of Economic Advisors from 1981 to 1982. He is now a Distinguished Scholar at the Center for Strategic and International Studies in Washington, D.C. In the following viewpoint, he describes three possible scenarios for the U.S. economy. He argues that America's economic strengths and weaknesses will most likely offset each other, and that the future of the U.S. economy will probably feature neither boom nor decline.

As you read, consider the following questions:

1. What three economic scenarios does Weidenbaum describe?
2. According to the author, what primary differences exist between the first and second economic scenarios?
3. What basic feature of the American economy makes it resistant to drastic changes, according to Weidenbaum?

You may wonder why credence should be given to the views of any economist, including the well-intentioned author of this viewpoint. Let me offer some explanation of why economists continue to make forecasts and, more particularly, why the public should pay attention to them. Although highly publicized forecasts of the next month or quarter of the year have been off the mark frequently, economists have done much better with annual prognostications. Over a period of a year, many specific economic crosscurrents offset one other. That is why humorists in the economics profession (and there are some) contend that St. Offset is the patron saint of economic forecasting. . . .

Those who anticipate pinpoint accuracy in economic extrapolations will be disappointed. But the standard economic projection has been helpful in indicating general directions and trends for the year ahead. Indeed, over the past ten years, the prevailing annual forecasts of economic growth and inflation were within 1.2 percentage points of the actual result. Not bad, but admittedly these prognostications are not candidates for the *Guinness Book of World Records*.

As we look to the decade ahead, we cannot be certain of the external environment facing policymakers. A useful start can be made by considering three alternative scenarios that citizens and policymakers in the United States might encounter. . . . We must be chastened by the knowledge that in making forecasts, we still face the fundamental limitation, as expressed in ancient times by Pliny the Elder, "The only certainty is that nothing is certain."

A Doom-and-Gloom Scenario

First we conjure up a scenario far different from recent experience. The Reagan presidency is succeeded by an administration dedicated to reversing many of the changes made in the first half of the 1980s. Renewed emphasis on the welfare state leads to substantial tax increases for middle- and upper-bracket taxpayers to help finance expansion of services for and benefits to those in the bottom part of the income pyramid. Adoption of capital budgeting obscures for a while the rise in the budget deficit.

A new wave of social regulation, covering tightened rule making in product and job safety and environmental purity, imposes additional obstacles to the formation of enterprises and to the construction of factories, stores, and office buildings. Antibusiness rhetoric fills congressional hearings and becomes front-page news. Companies respond by cutting back; employment slips, and imports rise.

Financial markets react adversely to these new developments. Interest rates turn up sharply. The inflow of foreign investment slows down and soon halts. Inflation accelerates, but the Federal Reserve System is slow in responding, trying to avoid precipitating a recession. The return to double-digit inflation scares foreign investors, who begin a modest flight of their capital out of the United States. Another rise in interest rates results in downturns in business capital spending and in housing construction.

Social unrest becomes more visible, in urban centers and rural areas alike, as people in distress expect little benefit from the status quo. Waves of nationwide strikes halt the growth of the economy. Inflation erodes the real value of worker earnings, but tough foreign competition keeps managements in most industries from agreeing to more-generous labor settlements. Union-management relations sour, and productivity in manufacturing suffers, encouraging further inroads by foreign producers in U.S. domestic markets. Meanwhile, business profits deteriorate. A wage-price spiral gets under way, further heating up inflationary pressures. Double-digit inflation returns to the American economy.

With the annual budget deficit in excess of $200 billion at the outset of the downturn, Congress is reluctant to stimulate the economy by cutting taxes or voting for new spending programs. To compound the problem, the Federal Reserve belatedly shifts to an anti-inflationary policy of tight money. Once again, it does too much too late. The massive reduction in the availability of credit precipitates a deep recession.

The Changing Economy

Change, not stability, is the chief characteristic of the U.S. economy. Progress always involves change, and change is sometimes unsettling. Throughout American history there have been periods that seemed like a hurricane of change, yet the nation has always emerged from those periods the stronger for having weathered the storm.

Malcolm S. Forbes Jr., *Cato Policy Report*, May/June 1988.

The overseas reaction is severe. More foreign capital is pulled out of the United States. The combination of rising budget deficits and the domestic refunding of maturing debt (previously held overseas) puts further upward pressure on U.S. interest rates. The combination of reduced earnings and higher interest rates forces many highly leveraged firms to the wall. Banks bear the brunt of the rising bankruptcies of American companies that they financed. Some of the weaker financial institutions go under. Confidence of investors, both at home and abroad, is eroded very substantially. The prices of gold, silver, and other precious metals shoot up rapidly, as American investors join the exodus of capital from the United States. Panic selling forces stock exchanges to halt trading. The President calls the Congress into emergency session.

At this point, readers may anticipate the alarm clock ringing, awakening us all from this economic nightmare. To be sure, I do not attach the same degree of likelihood to this doom-and-gloom scenario as to the other outcomes I will be presenting. But the point needs to be made that, with some bad luck and stupid policy-making (a combination that cannot be ruled out), the underlying problems facing the United States could become quite severe and even get out of control.

An Upbeat Scenario

On the other hand, we can think of a time when Americans take a more positive attitude toward the problems facing the nation. The administration in Washington sets a different policy emphasis for the federal government. It focuses on ways of improving economic performance by strengthening the competitive position of the United States in world markets. Regulatory burdens are reduced. The Congress votes down new compulsory fringe benefits. A sustained period of economic growth gets under way. The rise in tax collections—and concomitant reductions in unemployment compensation and other transfer payments—yields a steady decline in the budget deficit.

In this scenario, the United States finally makes many of the tough choices that have been postponed during the 1970s and 1980s. The composition of federal spending is shifted substantially from politically attractive consumption-oriented expenditures (welfare, farm subsidies, retirement, and other handouts) to economically important investment-oriented outlays, such as education, research and development, and new roads and airports (infrastructure). A secondary shift occurs, within the broad category of aid to producers, away from farm price supports and other subsidies that reduce output and to incentives for new investment and hence rising output.

In this picture, the pace of economic growth in the United States quickens, to an average of more than 3 percent a year. Rising productivity holds down inflationary pressures. Unemployment declines to about 5 percent. Strike activity remains close to the current all-time low. Wage and benefit increases, on the average, match the rate of inflation.

The numbers describing such a decade of growth are very impressive. The gross national product [in this scenario] more than doubles in the course of ten years, from $3.8 trillion in 1986 to $8.0 trillion in 1996. Even after the effects of inflation have been boiled out, the real GNP shows a rapid rise over the decade, from $3.7 trillion to $5.2 trillion.

A good indicator of the underlying health of the economy is the expectation that total saving rises from $536 billion in 1986 to $800 billion in 1996. This money finances new factories and other pro-

The U.S. Economy over the Coming Decade
1987 Survey of Executives of Major Corporations

POSSIBLE EVENT	LIKELIHOOD
High Probability (60 percent or more)	
U.S. industry will become increasingly price competitive.	69
Severity of taxation will increase to deal with the deficit.	68
Low saving rate of U.S. will continue.	65
The educated baby boomers will have a positive influence on U.S. economy.	64
U.S. share of world markets will erode.	64
Environmental regulation will intensify.	62
Direct foreign investment in U.S. will rise rapidly.	61
Medium Probability (41-59 percent)	
Problems of farmers will not have a major adverse impact on the U.S. economy.	54
Per capita standard of living in U.S. will trend upward.	52
U.S. import restrictions will increase considerably.	52
No major depression will occur during coming decade.	50
U.S. will suffer a major financial crisis.	49
The decade will be generally deflationary.	47
High debt will precipitate greatly increased inflation.	47
Regulation of industry will increase.	44
U.S. interest rates will be lower than today.	43
Social problems will slow the growth of the U.S. economy.	41
Low Probability (0-40 percent)	
An energy shortage will occur.	39
The budget deficit will fall below $50 billion a year.	32
Advancing technology will eliminate jobs.	29
A major shortage of labor will occur.	27
U.S. manufacturers will win back most of the market share recently lost to foreign competition.	26

Source: *Conference Board Perspectives,* 1987, no. 6.
Reprinted with permission.

ductive facilities. The number of civilian jobs expands steadily, from 110 million in 1986 to 130 million ten years later. These and the other statistics portray a healthy, dynamic economy. Abroad, confidence in American leadership is strengthened.

Nevertheless, Pollyanna does not rule the land. Serious problems continue to bubble below the tranquil surface. Further polarization occurs between upper- and lower-income groups, with continued bitterness on the part of those whom prosperity passes by. Trouble spots include portions of the farm belt, the oil country, some central-city ghettos, and rust bucket towns. Nevertheless, a growing number of areas participate in the expanding economy, and hope keeps a lid on potential social disruption.

The possibility of unpredictable crises always has to be considered. Terrorists or revolutionaries might knock out the Saudi oil capability. A Bhopal-type explosion might occur in North America. The President of the United States might die in office. The United States might get involved in a shooting war in Central America, on the order of our earlier commitments in South Korea and in Vietnam. But, in the upbeat scenario, concerns over these remote possibilities are assigned merely to contingency planning.

Muddling Through

Finally, let us consider a third scenario, which basically extends the status quo. The federal government continues to be bedeviled by the twin deficits of foreign trade and domestic budget. But no significant departure is made from current policy, so little additional progress can be anticipated. In effect, the country follows a "muddle through" approach. Given its tremendous resource base, in both material wealth and educated people, the United States is likely to succeed in muddling through. Some close calls, however, may well occur in this third scenario.

Real growth in the economy as a whole peters out, and more talk is heard about recession. Inflation starts to rise more rapidly, while unemployment stops declining. The term *stagflation* is used once again to describe the combination of rising inflation and sluggish economic growth.

Trouble spots in society are allowed to fester. The national attitude sounds like "Do not do anything today that can be postponed until tomorrow—or the day after." Fortunately, the national luck holds out. The characteristic sign of the times is the one proclaiming, tongue in cheek, "The end of the world has been postponed." This muddling-through attitude currently pervades a large portion of business thinking. A 1987 survey of the chief executives of America's largest companies typifies this outlook (see table).

The heads of major companies anticipate a crosscurrent of forces to be operating over the coming decade: increasing taxation and government regulation at home and erosion of the U.S. share of world markets overseas; American industry becomes more price competitive but has little chance of winning back the shares of world markets lost in recent years. The education and work experience of the huge post-World War II baby crop has a very positive influence on the U.S. economy. Yet, a continuing negative factor is the slim chance that the budget deficit will be cut to less than $50 billion ten years from now.

In sum, American business executives estimate a fifty-fifty possibility that the United States will avoid a major depression during the coming decade—which is a good statistical approximation of the odds of successfully muddling through. But none of this is foreordained.

It is unlikely that any of the three scenarios will occur in the 1990s exactly as I have described them. A combination or variation is more probable, depending on future decisions to be made in both the public and the private sectors. Some of the tough choices leading to the upbeat scenario will probably be made, but very likely not enough to avoid all of the ugly situations that occur in the doom-and-gloom scenario.

Offsetting Trends

It is useful to emphasize the basic continuity of American institutions. We do not live in a linear world. Trends do not continue unfolding in a straight line indefinitely. Counterpressures arise to arrest or modify or even reverse the most durable trend. In a real sense, the American economy is Newtonian—the more important actions generate counteractions. Talk about megatrend shocks, negative-sum economies, and other melodramatic use of buzzwords needs to be taken with more than the proverbial pinch of salt.

4 VIEWPOINT

"We need an improvement of about $200,000,000,000 in the U.S. trade balance to assure a stable future for our domestic economy."

America's Deficits Threaten Its Economic Future

C. Fred Bergsten

U.S. budget and trade deficits increased enormously in the 1980s. In the following viewpoint, C. Fred Bergsten argues that the two deficits indicate that the U.S. buys more than it sells, and consumes more than it produces. Such trends, he believes, leave the U.S. in a precarious economic position, and should be reversed to restore America's economic security. Bergsten is director of the Institute for International Economics in Washington, D.C. and has written fifteen books on economic issues.

As you read, consider the following questions:

1. How might the trade deficit start a U.S. recession, according to Bergsten?
2. What does Bergsten believe to be the secret of "supply-side" economics?
3. According to the author, why must the federal budget deficit be reduced?

C. Fred Bergsten, "Debtor America and the Budget Deficit." Reprinted from USA TODAY MAGAZINE, July 1988. Copyright 1988 by the Society for the Advancement of Education.

The most profound and enduring legacy of the Reagan Administration is its conversion of the U.S. from the largest creditor country in the world to the largest debtor. As recently as 1983, we retained the strongest international balance sheet of any nation. At the end of 1987, our net international debt stood at about $400,000,000,000—more than the external red ink of the next three largest debtors combined (Canada, Brazil, and Mexico). Under the most optimistic adjustment scenario, that number will rise to $750,000,000,000 before it could possibly level off, and a more likely outcome is much closer to one trillion dollars.

The proximate cause of this historically unprecedented deterioration—which will render both American economic and foreign policy exceedingly vulnerable to decisions made abroad for the indefinite future—is, of course, our massive trade deficit. . . . The trade deficit and its financial consequences hang like a sword of Damocles over the U.S. economy, and provide the context within which budget decisions must be made.

Triggering a Recession

As long as the U.S. has to rely on foreign financing of such magnitude, events could trigger a sharp turndown in our economy at literally any moment. Whenever foreign investors perceive that correction of the patently unsustainable trade imbalance will require another downward move in the exchange rate of the dollar—because of a failure of the authorities both here and abroad to pursue convincingly alternative adjustment strategies—they simply cut back, or totally stop, their investments in dollar assets.

In a self-fulfilling prophecy, the dollar falls. As a result, our interest rates rise until the combination of a cheaper dollar and higher yields again attracts the essential foreign money. My colleague, Stephen Marris, has calculated that such an "investment strike" by foreigners could produce a rise in real U.S. interest rates of as much as three-five percentage points, which, in the current state of the economy, almost certainly would push it into a sharp recession.

This is not theory. It is a reality which already occurred partially on two occasions in 1987, when bad monthly trade numbers focused the attention of the global investment community on the huge American external deficit. In the early months of 1987, the dollar plunged anew and U.S. interest rates soared by about three percentage points when Japanese and other foreign investors stopped buying dollars. (It was this run-up in interest rates which forced Treasury Secretary James Baker to call a halt to the Plaza strategy of pushing down the dollar and to substitute the Louvre accord in an effort to stabilize it instead.) In the autumn, widespread fears of a repeat performance passed through to the equity markets and were the primary underlying cause of Black Monday, the October, 1987, stock market crash.

Foreign central banks ultimately filled the financing gap on both occasions with massive intervention, but much damage obviously was done before they arrived. However, there are also limits to their involvement. Such intervention expands their domestic money supplies and thereby ignites inflationary fears (which can drive up interest rates, as occurred in Japan and Germany in mid-1987), exposes them to sizable additional losses if the dollar falls further, and appears to sanction American deficits and policies which they clearly disapprove of. The foreign officials want to avoid further substantial appreciation of their currencies and global financial instability, but we can not assume that they will bail us out indefinitely and without limit.

The Next Crisis

The next crisis could be much worse. In 1987, foreign central banks reportedly bought about $140,000,000,000 of dollar assets, thereby financing most of our current account deficit. Net private foreign investment in the dollar was quite modest. However, this represents *only* an unwillingness of private foreigners to invest additional sums here. On future occasions, they also might withdraw past dollar investments, of which about 1.5 trillion dollars are now outstanding. Moreover, Americans could begin speculating against the dollar by investing in foreign currencies.

Economic Costs

Our huge Federal budget deficits have not led to either inflation or recession. So why worry about deficits that are smaller? Because deficits, even of the size projected for 1993, carry severe economic costs. Until now the United States, with its low rates of saving, has been able to finance its budget deficits and still meet normal private capital needs by borrowing huge amounts from abroad. This, however, is accompanied by balance of payments deficits.

By continuing to pay debt service to foreigners, we will eventually reduce the growth of American living standards, which are already growing quite slowly. Moreover, foreigners will not continue indefinitely to finance our national profligacy.

Charles L. Schultze, *The New York Times*, March 15, 1988.

Again, this is not theory. During the last period of sharp declines in the dollar, in 1977-78, our external financing requirement was about double the magnitude of the current account deficit because of a sizable net outflow of private funds. Any such occurrence on a similar scale today would mean we would have to borrow

$300,000,000,000 a year from foreign central banks, clearly an impossible task.

This international framework must be *a*, if not *the*, major element in determining fiscal policy for the next few years. The growth in the budget deficit in the 1980's was the primary cause of the trade and dollar problems. A steady and sizable reduction in the budget deficit is the only sure way to remedy these problems without enormous risk and cost to the economy.

The Trade Imbalance

The sharp increase in the budget deficit in the early 1980's, coupled with largely traditional levels of private consumption and investment, simply meant that the U.S. was trying to spend more than it could produce at home. The only possible result was a huge inflow of goods from abroad—the trade deficit.

Likewise, the huge increase in government demand on the capital markets to finance its deficits meant that we were trying to invest more than we could save. (The decline in domestic private savings, contrary to the promises of the so-called "supply-siders," made the situation even worse.) This required the huge inflow of capital from abroad, which has turned us into the world's largest debtor nation.

Indeed, we now know the miracle of "supply-side" economics—foreigners supplied much of the goods and most of the money. As long as they were willing to do so, at exchange and interest rates which were compatible with our economic goals, we could spend and invest more than our domestic resources could support. The budget deficits could continue, without crowding out private investment and/or consumption. The price, however, in addition to the direct costs of the huge trade deficits, was the massive buildup of foreign debt and the inevitable cessation of the needed funding—as began to occur, from private investors abroad, in 1987.

Manipulating the Exchange Rate

The mechanism through which our overspending translated into a trade deficit was the exchange rate. The financing requirements of the budget deficit, coupled with an anti-inflationary monetary policy at the Federal Reserve, generated U.S. interest rates that sucked in capital from around the world, driving the value of our currency far above a level compatible with our international competitive position. Hence, we priced ourselves out of world markets, the trade deficit soared, and our debt to the rest of the world soared with it.

Since early 1985, however, the dollar has declined sharply against the currencies of most of the other industrial countries (and more modestly against many of our other key trading partners, including Canada, Korea, and Taiwan). American firms thus have recouped much of their competitiveness. . . .

Lurie, Cartoonews International, Inc.

However, the trade deficit in nominal terms—and, thus, our external financing requirements—have not come down significantly yet because domestic demand has continued to grow rapidly and suck in imports. As the Group of 33 economists put it, "currency depreciation that is not accompanied by strong action to slow down domestic demand simply leads to inflation and paves the way to future currency depreciation."

Over the course of the current economic expansion, domestic demand in the U.S. has grown by about four percent per year, while real output (the GNP [gross national product]) has grown by about three percent. The difference represents the steady growth (until 1987) in the trade deficit. The only way to reduce this deficit is to reverse this relationship. The growth in domestic spending will have to be slower than the growth in domestic output, to make room for a substantial shift to net exports. Three crucial issues arise: What is the magnitude of the needed reduction in the deficit? How fast must it occur? By what means can it best be achieved?

What the U.S. Needs

We need an improvement of about $200,000,000,000 in the U.S. trade balance to assure a stable future for our domestic economy and the world as a whole. The current account deficit presently is running at about $150,000,000,000. The additional cost of servicing the rapidly growing foreign debt will be close to $50,000,000,000 by the early 1990's. There probably will be a further increase in our oil imports because of the decline of about 1,000,000 barrels a day in domestic production in 1986-87, let alone any future increases in the world price.

Hence, we will need an improvement of at least $200,000,000,000 in our non-oil trade simply to restore balance in the current account and stop the further buildup of net debt abroad, let alone return to our traditional surplus position and start reducing the external red ink (as strongly advocated by the Joint Economic Committee). A reasonable, if somewhat optimistic, target would be to achieve this adjustment over a period of four-five years. If policy could maintain the growth of real domestic demand at about two percent annually, output growth could continue at around three percent as in 1985-87. . . .

Three Methods

There are basically three ways in which this outcome could be pursued. One, perhaps the most painless, would be an autonomous cutback in consumer demand, perhaps because individuals felt a need to rebuild financial positions after their extensive use of credit. This would increase domestic savings and reduce our need for foreign capital. The data suggest that such a phenomenon may have started to occur. If it were to continue for several years, it could contribute a bit of the needed adjustment.

Consumer demand growth would be cut more painfully if we suffer further market hits of the type experienced in 1987. Their effects on individual wealth and, hence, on spending also could produce a significant reduction in consumption. Failing alternative adjustment methods, such hits virtually are certain. This is obviously an inefficient, as well as painful, way to achieve adjustment, however. Avoiding it is a major reason why every effort must be made to pursue more constructive approaches.

A second alternative is to cut private investment. This, too, would be an inexorable element of adjustment if left wholly to market forces without conscious policy action, because higher interest rates would result from a cessation of new foreign investment in—or foreign withdrawal from—dollar assets.

However, we need more, rather than less, private investment. This is not only to provide productivity growth, but to create the additional capacity needed to generate enough exports and replacements for imports to correct the trade deficit. Many of our highly competitive industries already are running at or near full capacity, and must expand their plants domestically to achieve the trade swing.

The Federal Budget Deficit

Accordingly, the focus must return to the Federal budget deficit. We can assure elimination of the external deficit, and the financial sword of Damocles which it holds over the entire economy, only by cutting the budget deficit by $150-200,000,000,000. . . .

It would be neither realistic nor desirable to achieve such cuts all at once. It is essential, however, to set a course as soon as possible that will assure achievement of the full goal within a plausible period of time, say four-five years. Markets undoubtedly would respond favorably and provide the needed financing during even a rather long transition period, if they are convinced that the problem is on its way to resolution. . . .

The most promising prospects are changes in benefit formulas under some of the entitlement programs, in major weapons systems in the defense budget, and on the revenue side via new taxes that primarily hit consumption (which needs to be dampened).

This is obviously a politically difficult agenda, though it should be achievable with effective leadership from the White House. Its realization would eliminate the pervasive threat to the economy now stemming from the massive trade deficit and constant vulnerability of the dollar. With such a program, and supportive action by the major countries abroad (more likely with such steps by the U.S.), the exchange rate of the dollar would require modest, if any, further depreciation (except perhaps against the Asian newly industrialized countries, which, until recently, had followed the dollar down against the yen and the European currencies).

In the absence of such a program, by contrast, the dollar will remain under constant pressure. Forecasts of its falling another 20-30% easily could be realized. American interest rates could rise sharply. We might fall into a deep recession, with no ready way to combat it. Fiscal policy would be immobilized by the huge budget deficit already in place, and monetary policy largely would be impotent because of the continuing lack of confidence in the dollar.

5

VIEWPOINT

"[Some people believe] the federal budget deficit and the foreign trade deficit are time bombs that will sooner or later undermine our prosperity. . . . Nothing could be farther from the truth."

America's Deficits Do Not Threaten Its Economic Future

Milton Friedman

Milton Friedman is a Nobel Prize-winning economist and a professor emeritus at the University of Chicago. In the following viewpoint, he argues against the idea that budget and trade deficits pose a future danger to the U.S. economy. He states that because the U.S. is a wealthy country with a diverse economy, it is more able to carry deficits than poorer countries, such as Mexico and Brazil. Friedman argues that focusing on U.S. trade and budget deficits diverts attention from what he believes to be the real problem: excessive government spending.

As you read, consider the following questions:

1. What motivates the people who argue that the budget deficit should be reduced, according to Friedman?
2. Why does the author argue that the size of the budget deficit has been exaggerated?
3. According to Friedman, why have many foreigners invested money in the U.S.?

Milton Friedman, "Why the Twin Deficits Are a Blessing," *The Wall Street Journal*, December 14, 1988.

The media and the public have been sold a bill of goods. They have become convinced that the so-called twin deficits—the federal budget deficit and the foreign trade deficit—are time bombs that will sooner or later undermine our prosperity and prospects for growth. Nothing could be farther from the truth. True, budget deficits and foreign-trade deficits can be disastrous under some circumstances—witness Brazil, Argentina, Mexico, or Chile under Allende. But they can also be beneficial under other circumstances. And I submit that those "other circumstances" prevail in the U.S. today, and have prevailed for some years.

Do you really believe that the liberal Democrats who told the country for decades that deficits were an effective tool for stimulating and stabilizing the economy have seen the light and become born-again budget balancers? Or that people like myself who were lonely voices maintaining that deficits were not effective for such purposes have become born-again inflationists and reckless spenders?

Spending Other People's Money

The explanation for the apparent reversal of positions is much more straightforward. . . . Politicians who have prospered spending other people's money are frustrated because the tax revolt plus the public outcry against deficits has made it harder to spend still more of other people's money. They are rattling the scarecrow of deficits to frighten the public—and not least, the president—into accepting higher taxes. But higher taxes will not eliminate the deficit. They will, after a brief delay, simply increase spending. Taxes have been going up for 50 years without any apparent success in eliminating deficits. That experience suggests Congress will spend whatever the tax system yields plus the highest deficit the public will accept.

Those of us who have opposed higher taxes believe government spending is already too high, that the public is not getting its money's worth from the more than 40% of its income currently being spent, supposedly on its behalf, by government—federal, state and local. We believe the deficit has been the only effective restraint on congressional spending.

We would much prefer a constitutional amendment that requires a balanced budget and limits spending. Relying on the deficit to check spending is admittedly a second-best solution—but it is better than nothing.

Scare Tactics

As to the scare tactic that the deficit, and the growing debt, are stealing from future generations, that is simply rhetoric. The amount government spends, not those government receipts labeled taxes, is the real burden imposed on the public. If the national income is four trillion dollars, and the federal government spends a trillion dollars, that leaves three trillion dollars for state and local governments, private individuals and institutions to spend or invest as they separately wish, whether the government finances its spending by explicit taxes or by borrowing. The part of government receipts labeled "deficit" is a hidden tax. It is a bad tax. Nonetheless, it is currently preventing the imposition of a still larger and still worse tax.

Deficit Hysteria

Deficit hysteria has become a dangerous national pastime. Fixing on these arbitrary numbers could lead to irrationally tight fiscal policies and damaging trade restrictions. We need to consider more meaningful measures of fiscal policy, and to drop our obsession with official deficit numbers.

Laurence J. Kotlikoff, *The New York Times*, November 2, 1987.

As to the so-called debt burden we are piling up, the federal debt is a smaller fraction of the national income today than it was in any year from the end of World War II to 1960. Where were the doom-and-gloomers then? Certainly not among the congressional big spenders.

Finally, the size of the deficit has been exaggerated by use of such adjectives as "tremendous," "monstrous," "gigantic," "obscene." As a percentage of the national income, the deficit is not out of line with levels frequently reached in the past. Indeed, if the surplus at state and local levels is subtracted, the combined government deficit is considerably lower than in many past years and lower than in Japan, West Germany, and France—whose pundits have been among the loudest in decrying the U.S. deficit.

The Trade Deficit

What about the other twin? Isn't our balance-of-payments deficit condemning us to tightening our belt and lowering our standard of living in order to prevent bankruptcy? Isn't our financial stability threatened by the danger that foreigners will suddenly decide to take their money out of the country?

The short answer is: arrant nonsense. There are circumstances under which such fears are justified, but they are not ours. If you as an individual borrow to engage in riotous living beyond your means, you are headed for trouble, whether you borrow in your own country or abroad. On the other hand, if you borrow to finance an enterprise you expect to be profitable and you are right, you are headed for wealth, whether you borrow in your own country or abroad, especially if you borrow in your own country's currency to avoid exchange risk. These propositions are just as valid for a country as for an individual.

The doom-and-gloomers would have you believe the U.S. is in the first category. That is not the case. Throughout the 1980s, total consumption in the U.S., including all government spending, has been less than domestic national income. Domestic savings have throughout been larger than the net government deficit. The balance available to finance private net investment, though a smaller fraction of the national income than in many past years, has been positive. However, prospects for domestic investment have been sufficiently bright to make investment in the U.S. more attractive than investment elsewhere. U.S. banks and other entities decided to invest less abroad and more in the U.S., and foreigners decided to do the same.

A Matter of Arithmetic

It is a matter of arithmetic that the number of dollars spent by foreigners on U.S. goods, services and assets must be equal to the number of dollars U.S. residents spend on foreign goods, services and assets. It follows that foreign investors can get dollars only by generating a U.S. balance-of-payments deficit on current account. That deficit provides the dollars for them to invest and has as its opposite side an equal U.S. surplus on capital account. There is no way of having the one without the other—no matter how much some commentators may deplore the deficit on current account while welcoming the surplus on capital account.

The improved investment possibilities in the U.S. after the implementation of Reaganomics induced holders of foreign assets—both U.S. and foreign holders—to add to their dollar assets. This inflow of capital drove up the dollar exchange rate to generate the necessary current-account deficit. As holders of foreign assets have reduced the rate at which they want to add to their dollar holdings, dollar exchange rates have declined. Both the rise and subsequent decline in the dollar have probably been overdone, a not unusual phenomenon, but one that was exacerbated in this instance by unwise intervention by central banks in the exchange market—intervention that is proving costly to Japanese, German, U.S. and other countries' taxpayers.

A Sign of Strength

It is a mystery to me why, to take a specific example, it is regarded as a sign of Japanese strength and U.S. weakness that the Japanese find it more attractive to invest in the U.S. than in Japan. Surely it is precisely the reverse—a sign of U.S. strength and Japanese weakness. The capital inflow that is the other side of the current-account deficit has enabled productive investment in the U.S. to be higher than the amount U.S. residents were willing to finance. It has thereby contributed to a higher national output and a more rapid rate of growth. That is precisely how the U.S. managed to grow so rapidly in the 19th century—by financing investment with funds from Britain and elsewhere. It was a good deal for the foreign investors—but also for the U.S.

What if foreign investors suddenly decided to take their money out? Their "money" is in the form of stocks, bonds, factories, land, etc. How can they take it out? First, they have to sell their assets. That would drive prices down, creating bargains for purchasers who have confidence in the U.S. Who would lose in that process? The sellers, not the buyers.

Myth and Reality

The budget deficit causes the trade deficit, and thus exports American jobs to foreign workers. First of all, the trade deficit is not caused by the budget deficit; it is caused by America's economic strength, as foreign countries invest in the U.S.'s booming economy and export goods to America's prosperous consumers. Economist George Gilder put it best when he said America has a trade deficit because it's the only country in the world that can't export to America.

The trade deficit hasn't caused Americans to lose their jobs, either. There are 15,000,000 more jobs for Americans today than there were before the U.S. became a "debtor nation." We need to stop listening to scare stories and start looking at the numbers. The "Great American Job Machine" is chugging along better than ever before.

Robert W. Kasten Jr., *USA Today*, July 1988.

Once the foreign investors have dollars, what then? They don't want dollars; they want pounds or marks or francs or yen. How do they get them? Only by bidding up the dollar price of those currencies, which means further losses to them. Who gains this time? Mostly, the foreigners who use their domestic currencies to buy dollars, with which they buy U.S. goods and services, thereby generating the current-account surplus in the U.S. balance of payments that is the other side of the outflow of capital. All in all, not a likely scenario.

Hostages to Fortune?

What about the claim that foreign investors in the U.S. gain political power over us. Again, how? What happened to German enterprises in the U.S. during World War II? They were expropriated and taken over by the alien property custodian. Or what happened to U.S. oil investments in Mexico? Expropriated when Mexico nationalized the production of oil. In building factories, buying land or other assets in the U.S., foreigners are giving hostages to fortune. They are putting themselves at the mercy of the government. They are gambling that the U.S. will not expropriate their assets, or prevent them from benefiting from their dollar earnings.

Let us put aside the scarecrows of the twin deficits and face up to the real problems that threaten U.S. growth and prosperity: excessive and wasteful government spending and taxing, including in particular the real time bomb in Social Security, Medicare and Medicaid programs; concealed taxes in the form of mandated expenditures on private business; excessive and misguided regulation of individuals as well as businesses; the changes in tort legislation that are discouraging innovation; and not least, the increase in protectionism and the threat of a further major increase. We should and can do something about these problems, not allow ourselves to be diverted by politically convenient scarecrows.

6 VIEWPOINT

"A growing dependence on foreign investors will inevitably lead to a loss of freedom as foreigners gain economic and political leverage over the lives of Americans."

Foreign Investment Is a Threat

Martin Tolchin and Susan Tolchin

In 1985 the United States became a net debtor nation. For the first time since World War I, the total value of U.S. assets owned by foreigners exceeded the value of foreign assets owned by Americans. Foreign investors own over one trillion dollars in U.S. businesses, banks, government bonds, and real estate. In the following viewpoint, Martin and Susan Tolchin argue that foreign investment poses a potential threat to America's economic future. As more U.S. assets fall under foreign ownership, they argue, the U.S. will lose control of its own economy. Martin Tolchin is a correspondent in the Washington Bureau of *The New York Times*. Susan Tolchin is a professor of public administration at George Washington University in Washington, D.C.

As you read, consider the following questions:

1. According to the authors, why is the amount of U.S. foreign investment hard to estimate?
2. How does foreign investment today differ from foreign investment in the past, according to the Tolchins?
3. What do the authors believe to be some of the harmful effects of foreign investment?

Foreign money is changing the face of America, the lives of Americans, and the nature of our political processes. A surge of foreign investment in the United States is rebuilding the nation's cities, reshaping rural America, and building manufacturing and assembly plants that are creating jobs for millions of Americans. Mayors, governors, and cabinet officers are circling the globe in quest of foreign funds, with the intensity of third-world ministers trying to stave off the financial collapse of their shaky governments. Treasury officials have designed securities offerings with a view toward wooing foreign investors, cities and states maintain offices abroad for this purpose, and the U.S. Conference of Mayors holds semiannual conferences in Asia and Europe to help cities attract foreign money.

For much of our history American businessmen went around the world investing in overseas ventures, exporting their culture, and intervening in foreign governments. During the past decade, however, the trend has steadily reversed. Foreign investors have found a haven on U.S. shores, enriched our lives by bringing us their cultures, and protected their investments by becoming increasingly involved in our political processes.

In the most pragmatic nation in the world, most Americans don't care where the money comes from as long as it provides jobs and stimulates economic growth. Most Americans don't care whom they work for provided their salaries and working conditions are good, and sometimes even when they are not. Most mayors and governors don't care who pours money into their financially beleaguered cities and states to revive their failing economies, and most federal officials don't seem to care who finances the national debt. Under pressure to bring home the bacon, politicians have paid scant attention to the long-term economic, political, and social effects of their country's deepening dependence on foreign money. . . .

Warnings

But others are less sanguine. They warn that the United States is becoming "addicted" to foreign capital. They fear that this overdependence has made us vulnerable to the vagaries of foreign investment and that the withdrawal of foreign investment could wreak havoc on the economy. They lament the loss of profits that are taken out of the country and say that some foreign investors treat their American hirelings with the tenderness that imperialist powers reserved for the colonies. Mostly, they fear that the surge of foreign investment is eroding the nation's independence, both political and economic. They warn that major decisions affecting the lives of Americans and, possibly, the security of the nation, are now being made in Tokyo, London, Riyadh, and other foreign capitals.

"They make us dance to a tune played afar," said Richard D. Lamm, former governor of Colorado, adding that Westerners were sensitized to the problems of absentee ownership because they had suffered from Eastern ownership of the West in the last century. "There's all kinds of Faustian bargains made in economic development. Even though you get 250 jobs, the net effect on your community is negative because you've given away the show."

Thoughtful critics do not blame the foreign investors, who are putting their money into a politically safe haven, where they can get the best returns on their yen, francs, pounds, riyals, deutsche marks, and guilders. Instead, these critics blame Americans' own rapacious need for foreign money to finance a standard of living undreamed of in the rest of the world. . . .

How Much Is There?

Nobody knows the full extent of foreign investment in the United States. Much of it comes across U.S. borders with the stealth and anonymity of illegal aliens. Lax reporting requirements, hidden ownerships, and other circumventions of the laws have made it virtually impossible to keep track of the flood of foreign money.

Reduced Autonomy

The most pervasive concern about foreign investment is that it will reduce America's economic and political autonomy. Foreign-held debt and foreign ownership imply dependence and vulnerability. With ownership goes control over economic decisions and influence over political ones. Senator Frank Murkowski (R-Alaska) summed up this view bluntly in the December 30, 1985, *New York Times*: "Once they own your assets, they own you."

Thomas Omestad, *Foreign Policy*, Fall 1989.

Most experts agree, however, that more than $1.5 trillion in foreign investment has poured into the United States from around the world, a significant increase from $196 billion in 1974. About 80 percent of this foreign investment is in government and private securities, so-called portfolio investments, with foreign investors now holding more than $200 billion—or one-tenth—of America's $2 trillion national debt. Some experts put the foreign share of the national debt at between $300 billion and $400 billion, or between 15 and 20 percent. In addition, foreign investors own close to $445 billion in U.S. bank assets, more than $300 billion in diversified stocks and bonds, more than $100 billion in real estate, and $200-$300 billion in direct investments of factories, warehouses, and assembly plants.

Foreign companies are buying up American oil and gas companies at a rapid rate and are making significant inroads into the construction industry, machine tools, automobiles, auto parts, and a host of other industries. More than half of the nation's cement industry and four of the nation's top ten chemical companies are foreign owned, while a French company will soon become the leading manufacturer of television sets in the United States. Foreign investors have bought land, skyscrapers, and shopping centers in virtually every state of the union, to the delight of real estate agents and the dismay of some developers and other groups. Foreign governments also play a large role in the investment business, holding 20 percent of all the foreign investment in the United States. . . .

A Debtor Nation

The United States often has borrowed to finance investments vital to its national interests—from its early need to industrialize to its periodic need to arm itself for military conflicts. But critics contend that it is one thing to borrow to industrialize and then repay out of a newly industrialized economy, and quite different for the most industrialized nation in the world to go on a borrowing spree to finance its burgeoning budget deficit. Their warnings increased when the United States suddenly became a net debtor nation in 1985 for the first time since World War I. This meant that the value of assets owned by foreigners in the United States exceeded the value of assets owned by Americans abroad. The figure, known as the current-account deficit, widens every year; by the end of 1986, it had reached $263.6 billion.

"The real thinkers around here are concerned about the long-term cost of the capital inflows," said Representative Don Bonker, Washington State Democrat and chairman of the House Democratic Trade Task Force and chairman of the Subcommittee on Economic Policy and Trade of the House Foreign Affairs Committee. "It's subsidizing the present with the hardships of the future."

Critics fear that a growing dependence on foreign investors will inevitably lead to a loss of freedom as foreigners gain economic and political leverage over the lives of Americans. Foreign investors, who now hold more than 10 percent of the outstanding U.S. treasury bills, for example, could exercise this leverage on behalf of a foreign government and shape national decisions. The late representative Benjamin S. Rosenthal, a Queens Democrat, referred to such holdings of U.S. securities by foreign governments as "the money weapon."

The Power of Foreigners

Treasury officials panicked in May 1987 when foreign investors temporarily declined to bid on the sale of $29 billion in T-bills, needed to finance the deficit. After two days of nervous waiting,

Danziger in The Christian Science Monitor © 1989 TCSPS

the treasury reduced the price of the thirty-year bills and raised their yield, prompting foreigners to return to the market. The Japanese alone bought nearly half the $9.3 billion in thirty-year bonds offered to the public.

"The message of the bond sale was clear: Foreigners are our bankers," wrote Jeff B. Copeland and Rich Thomas in *Newsweek*.

"The era of American economic independence is gone, thanks to a trade deficit too big to fund ourselves. Foreigners increasingly influence inflation and recession in the United States."

There was mounting evidence, moreover, that private foreign investors were being replaced by foreign governments as major purchasers of government securities. Economist Alan Greenspan calculated that in the first three months of 1987, the central banks of Japan, Western Europe, and Canada provided most of the money needed to finance the U.S. trade deficit. The questions that seem to trouble many policymakers are: What will these governments demand in return? And how long will they continue to bail out the United States? . . .

National Security

Questions of national security also emerge from time to time but are quickly dismissed by government officials. The U.S. government's interagency Committee on Foreign Investment in the United States (CFIUS) reviewed the $110 million sale of New Hampshire Ball Bearings to its chief Japanese competitor, Minooba, on national security grounds and then allowed the sale. CFIUS is known around government circles as a "paper tiger": It rarely meets and has never, to anyone's knowledge, blocked a foreign investment. Considering that CFIUS is the only foreign-investment review mechanism in the executive branch, its inactivity speaks volumes about government complacency toward foreign investment.

There is persuasive evidence that some foreign investors, notably the Japanese, have purchased U.S. companies to acquire their technology and ultimately eliminate U.S. competition in key industries. In this area especially, foreign investment takes on aggressive overtones: a clear attempt to acquire advanced technology in order to dominate industrial markets. The Japanese investment in Boeing, for example, led to widespread alarm about the inevitable loss of the aerospace industry, which many believe to be the last stronghold of American technological superiority. . . .

Costs and Benefits

Foreign investments have become too important to the nation's economy to remain in the shadows of its economic consciousness. Foreign money now finances a substantial amount of all new direct investment and for the last several years has underwritten half the offerings of treasury bills, thereby financing the U.S. budget deficit. Foreign investments in autos, chemicals, and a variety of other industries have created almost three million jobs.

These benefits have so captivated mayors, governors, and treasury officials that many ignore the troubling ramifications, which are now becoming apparent. The most serious threat is America's increasing loss of economic and political independence.

Decisions that used to be made in Sacramento, Albany, and Washington, D.C., are now being made in Tokyo, London, and Riyadh. And although the United States has entered the global economy, where all nations sacrifice a measure of independence, America seems to have gone overboard. . . .

Responsible leaders must take a long, hard look at their country's growing dependence on foreign capital. It is too reminiscent of America's former dependence on foreign oil, and just as we shook ourselves loose from the OPEC [Organization of Petroleum Exporting Countries] cabal, we must reduce our craving for foreign money and practice more selectivity. The United States is sinking deeper and deeper into the condition of a developing country: importing capital when a few short years before it was the world's largest creditor nation. Advanced countries export capital, and that's the company this country should keep.

Retaining U.S. Sovereignty

The forces of the international marketplace have begun to overwhelm America's capacity to deal with them. The surge of foreign investment is only one glaring example. The manner in which the nation's leaders respond will determine how we meet the most difficult economic challenge of our times: to retain U.S. sovereignty in the global economy.

7 VIEWPOINT

"The United States should not be concerned about foreign direct investment."

Foreign Investment Is Not a Threat

Rudiger W. Dornbusch

Many people argue that a large amount of foreign investment in the U.S. is a sign of America's economic strength, not weakness. In the following viewpoint, Rudiger W. Dornbusch contends that the amount of foreign investment and ownership is small relative to the total U.S. economy. He writes that foreign investment enriches the economy and provides employment for Americans. Dornbusch is the Ford International Professor of Economics at the Massachusetts Institute of Technology in Cambridge, Massachusetts.

As you read, consider the following questions:

1. What are the positive effects of foreign investment, according to the author?
2. According to Dornbusch, how would restricting foreign investment hurt America?

Rudiger W. Dornbusch, "Welcome, Foreign Investors," *Technology Review*, April 1988. Reprinted with permission from Technology Review, copyright 1988.

Japan has already taken advantage of the open U.S. market to erode the American ability to compete in manufactured goods. Now foreign firms, the Japanese in the lead, are buying up American assets, ranging from banks and insurers to real-estate and manufacturing operations, at an unprecedented pace. They seem to be establishing a production beachhead in this country to reinforce their inroads, and to forestall the United States from keeping them out with tariffs and quotas. Will all Americans soon be reporting to Japanese managers and deans, and paying rent to Japanese landlords?. . .

Many business and union leaders would like to see more drastic action to restrain foreign direct investment.

But such investment is strictly in the national interest. With this investment comes competition—and nothing is better for established, inefficient, and protected businesses. It is ironic that even as the U.S. business community is trying to open up Mexico and other developing countries to a fresh breeze of competition via direct investment, it laments taking the same medicine at home. But like other countries, we can benefit from foreign technology, management skills, and superior products. Foreign direct investment creates good jobs and benefits consumers.

No Need for Concern

The United States should not be concerned about foreign direct investment now. A number of facts prove my point:

- This country remains the main international investor. Of the entire world stock of foreign direct investment, the United States commands nearly 40 percent, followed by the United Kingdom with 14 percent and Japan with less than 10 percent.
- The total stock of foreign direct investment in the United States amounts to only 1.6 percent of American tangible assets. Of that stock, Japan has a relatively small share. Europe controls 68 percent, with the United Kingdom and the Netherlands each outranking Japan's portion of only 11 percent.
- Of the more than 106 million people employed in the United States, only 3.2 million—3 percent—work for foreign firms.

Firms and workers who oppose foreign direct investment put forth a series of arguments similar to those heard in Europe in the 1960s, when American businesses were investing heavily there.

Labor and management first argue that as foreign companies displace domestic output, they reduce employment. The major reason is supposedly that foreign firms import components from their own factories or suppliers abroad to a much larger extent than U.S. firms would. According to the *Wall Street Journal*, a United Automobile Workers study found that an American-owned auto assembly plant creates 25,000 jobs in U.S. supplier plants, while a typical Japanese assembly plant here creates only 6,700 jobs.

This argument is plausible when we think of firms entering the U.S. market to increase their share at the expense of American companies. But foreign investment halts job losses in industries already facing heavy competition from imports. While domestic companies may close down because of imports, foreigners setting up plants in the United States offer jobs. In a growing economy, a net increase in jobs may well emerge.

In any event, we need to be cautious about overstating differences between U.S. and foreign firms on the issue of importing components. American companies routinely market under their brand names goods produced abroad. And our automakers have discovered that Brazilian engines help reduce model costs.

Unfair Competition?

Another line of attack focuses on the unfair competition that foreign firms, especially those from Japan, are said to bring. They have access to a pool of low-cost capital that is not available to U.S. firms. But that is good news for the consumer who gains in direct access to cheap foreign factors of production.

Critics of foreign direct investment also focus on the fact that many industries, notably the automobile business, have excess capacity. If foreign companies create even more capacity, profitability will drop, especially for the least competitive. Reference to excess capacity calls on the regulatory instincts of our Washington bureaucrats. But why shouldn't Congress think of the situation as increased competition, which has a more positive ring, especially for the consumer?

Nothing to Fear

America has nothing to fear from foreign investment, just as the world's nations have nothing to fear from the multitrillion-dollar assets we hold overseas.

We are entering the age of the global economy—when nations are becoming increasingly interdependent—which will be fueled by a boom in high technology and increased overseas investments. To paraphrase Franklin D. Roosevelt, the only thing we have to fear is fear of the future.

Donald Lambro, *The Washington Times*, May 2, 1989.

Critics also ask what will happen if the foreign firms that do not have a commitment to the United States and its workers find their operations unprofitable. They will simply pack up and return home, leaving behind the shattered lives of workers who placed their careers in the hands of these companies. Yet American companies increasingly move the production of components or entire products abroad and hence are much more suspect than newly arriving concerns. Indeed, foreigners often buy in where U.S. producers sell off.

Two further arguments, commonly made in Europe in the 1960s, have yet to reappear. The first is that foreign firms draw away labor and drive up its costs. It is true that Japanese financial institutions have raided the Federal Reserve, but otherwise such competition has not been an issue. Part of the reason may be that foreign firms have located in parts of the country such as Tennessee where labor is plentiful and relatively cheap.

The Benefits of Foreign Investment

There is, in fact, a positive good that comes from permanent foreign investment in American plant and equipment (including purchases of American companies).

In addition to helping the dollar, such investment generally means new jobs for workers, new taxes for state, local and Federal governments, transfer of foreign management and skills and technology, and, what is least appreciated, the opening up of new markets for American goods and services.

Peter A. Lewis, *The New York Times*, January 21, 1989.

The other argument is that foreign companies, borrowing in the U.S. market, drive up capital costs and crowd out the availability of finance for domestic firms. So far foreign direct investment has been financed primarily by capital from other countries. But we can expect that with further weakening of the dollar, more financing will take place in the American market. And once the U.S. government stops borrowing as much money, investors worldwide will look for new outlets other than financing the American budget. Then we will see Japanese banks in New York attracting local deposits to lend to the U.S. subsidiaries of Japanese corporations. No doubt some people will feel that provides unfair competition in the loan market, but to economists the argument doesn't make any sense. Why should anyone care about the nationality of the lender?

Hurting Ourselves

If we restrict foreign access to the United States, we may well hurt our own interests, present and future, in overseas markets. Our expanding service industry, for example, may find that its foreign investment opportunities will become limited. Consider foreign countries that allow our banks to operate there if we reciprocate by accepting theirs here. Indeed, we should use our leverage over potential foreign investors here to gain better and freer access for our investments abroad.

Moreover, there is no reason why we cannot benefit from the superior performance of Japanese and other foreign firms. All we have to do is buy their shares. Capital markets are wide open, with the largest companies publicly traded. The strict distinction between "theirs" and "ours" no longer applies.

The only sense in which we can think of some firms as ours is that they are predominantly managed by U.S. managers. But here foreign investment will help by demonstrating how we can better produce, market, and sell.

Not only does foreign investment bring industry into underdeveloped regions of the country, but it provides the potential for exports, which we are looking to expand as budget deficits are cut and therefore domestic demand declines. After another 20 percent depreciation in the value of the dollar, the United States may become a cheap-labor country. Foreign firms will want to establish facilities here to produce for their home markets. Foreign firms investing in the United States can help sustain employment at the highest possible wage levels and hence are more than welcome.

a critical thinking activity

Recognizing Statements That Are Provable

From various sources of information we are constantly confronted with statements and generalizations about social and moral problems. In order to think clearly about these problems, it is useful if one can make a basic distinction between statements for which evidence can be found and other statements which cannot be verified or proved because evidence is not available, or the issue is so controversial that it cannot be definitely proved.

Readers should be aware that magazines, newspapers, and other sources often contain statements of a controversial nature. The following activity is designed to allow experimentation with statements that are provable and those that are not.

The following statements are taken from the viewpoints in this chapter. Consider each statement carefully. *Mark P for any statement you believe is provable. Mark U for any statement you feel is unprovable because of the lack of evidence. Mark C for any statements you think are too controversial to be proved to everyone's satisfaction.*

If you are doing this activity as a member of a class or group, compare your answers with those of other class or group members. Be able to defend your answers. You may discover that others will come to different conclusions than you. Listening to the reasons others present for their answers may give you valuable insights in recognizing statements that are provable.

P = provable
U = unprovable
C = too controversial

1. The U.S. trade deficit has grown from a few billion dollars a year in the 1970s to more than $171 billion in 1987.
2. Trade deficits are harmful to the economy.
3. No American company makes VCRs.
4. The federal debt is a smaller fraction of the national income today than it was in any year from the end of World War II to 1960.
5. Arguments about the trade and budget deficits are scare tactics by people who want to increase taxes and government spending.
6. America has failed to adjust to the new reality of a global economy.
7. At the end of 1987, the international debt of the United States stood at about four hundred billion dollars.
8. The United States international debt could well go over a trillion dollars before it declines.
9. After decades of growth, real hourly wages for U.S. workers have stagnated since 1972.
10. Chrysler owns parts of Mitsubishi and Hyundai automobile companies.
11. Foreigners now control the U.S. economy.
12. Manufacturing productivity has grown at an annual rate of 4.3 percent since 1982.
13. America is too rich and powerful to be shutout of the coming global economic boom.
14. Only 3 percent of the 106 million workers in the U.S. work for foreign firms.
15. America has nothing to fear from foreign investment.
16. Most experts agree that over $1.5 trillion of foreign money has poured into the United States.
17. Many U.S. governors and mayors are actively soliciting foreign investment.
18. Foreign investment is beneficial because it creates jobs for Americans.

Periodical Bibliography

The following articles have been selected to supplement the diverse views presented in this chapter.

Barry P. Bosworth and Robert Z. Lawrence	"America in the World Economy," *The Brookings Review*, Winter 1988/1989.
Richard B. Du Boff	"If a Recession Strikes, It Could Be a Whopper," *In These Times*, December 7-13, 1988.
Richard A. Gephardt	"America in the New Global Economy," *USA Today*, May 1988.
J. Peter Grace	"The Deficit Time Bomb," *Vital Speeches of the Day*, April 15, 1989.
Gus Hall	"The U.S. Economy: Time Bomb on a Short Fuse," *Political Affairs*, December 1988.
Robert Kuttner	"Economic Nationalism," *The New Republic*, November 21, 1988.
Walter Russell Mead	"The United States and the World Economy," *World Policy Journal*, Summer 1989.
Ian I. Mitroff	"Why U.S. Business Is in Trouble," *USA Today*, May 1988.
National Review	"The Great Deficit Debate," January 27, 1989.
Robert E. Norton	"The Myths of Foreign Investment," *U.S. News & World Report*, May 29, 1989.
Brian O'Reilly	"America's Place in World Competition," *Fortune*, November 6, 1989.
Jonathan Rauch	"Is the Deficit Really So Bad?" *The Atlantic Monthly*, February 1989.
John Rutledge and Deborah Allen	"We Should Love the Trade Deficit," *Fortune*, February 29, 1988.
Robert J. Samuelson	"America for Sale?" *The New Republic*, June 12, 1989.
Abu K. Selimuddin	"The Selling of America," *USA Today*, March 1989.
Paul L. Wachtel	"The Case Against Growth," *New Age Journal*, November/December 1988.

CHAPTER 3

Is America Falling Behind in Technology?

AMERICA'S FUTURE

Chapter Preface

In 1957 the United States was shocked when the Soviet Union launched *Sputnik*, the first artificial space satellite. The event seemed to signify that the U.S. was falling behind its Cold War adversary in science and technology. Worried about the implications of such a development, the U.S. government increased funding for science education and space research. The resulting "space race" culminated in the United States's successful Apollo mission to the moon in 1969.

Today the U.S. has similar fears of losing supremacy in science—not to the Soviet Union, but, ironically, to its Cold War allies, particularly Japan. In the 1970s and 1980s U.S. steel and automobile industries were eclipsed by foreign competitors with superior technology and quality. Today observers worry about electronics, an industry employing 2.6 million American workers and a key for U.S. economic and military strength. Scholar Charles H. Ferguson argues that America is in danger of becoming dependent on Japan for advances in electronics. He believes the U.S. needs another Apollo-like effort to regain technological supremacy.

The viewpoints in this chapter examine several questions concerning technology and America's future.

VIEWPOINT 1

"Japan has achieved parity with or even superiority over the United States in many information technologies."

The U.S. Is Falling Behind in Information Technology

Charles H. Ferguson

Semiconductors, computer programs, "smart" manufacturing machines, data processing, and nuclear missile early warning systems all fall under the heading of information technology. Since World War II the U.S. has dominated this technology market. In the following viewpoint, Charles H. Ferguson argues that the U.S. is losing its dominance in this area to Japan. Ferguson asserts that U.S. companies, lacking government support, have been too fragmented and disorganized to respond to the Japanese challenge. Ferguson is a research associate at the Center for Technology, Policy and Industrial Development at the Massachusetts Institute of Technology.

As you read, consider the following questions:

1. What are some of the ramifications of the U.S. losing its dominance in information technology, according to Ferguson?
2. According to the author, what two forces contributed to the decline of U.S. technology?
3. What recommendations does Ferguson propose to rebuild U.S. technology?

Technological revolutions often contribute to shifts in wealth and geopolitical influence by changing the sources of industrial and military success. In this respect, information technology is proving no exception. Advanced information technology is profoundly changing global competition, both commercial and military, in such fields as semiconductors, computers, fiberoptic communications, high-definition television, industrial control systems, robotics, office automation, globally integrated financial trading systems, military C^3I (command, control, communication, and intelligence), smart weapons, and electronic warfare.

Eclipsed by Japan

As this transformation progresses, the United States is being gradually but pervasively eclipsed by Japan. In semiconductors, automated machine tools, advanced manufacturing, and mass-produced electronics products, America's problems are already severe. More significant, the long-term structural patterns of U.S.-Japanese interaction in finance and high technology imply a future of U.S. decline and dependence on Japan. Moreover, the behavior of the embryonic though rapidly advancing Japanese defense industry suggests that this prediction holds for military technology as well as for commercial activities. Although a strong U.S. response could soften this decline, the economic and political costs of effective remedial action make some further deterioration almost inevitable.

Although America's nuclear and other military resources assure that it will remain a superpower for some time, Japanese ascendancy will probably have major economic and geopolitical consequences. The combination of financial power and technological primacy could provide Japan not only higher living standards but also the potential for wide influence over international affairs, including U.S. policy, and for the development of Japanese military power. Conversely, these developments could place pressure on American living standards, thereby risking domestic social and political problems. They could also affect America's global posture through trade tensions, declining economic influence, pressure to reduce federal expenditures, and military inefficiency. The U.S. economy might shift toward lower-technology activities in which competitiveness would be maintained through devaluation and wage reduction; industries dependent on high levels of investment, education, and technological progress would decline. Indeed, this process is already under way. . . .

The decline of American high technology involves two distinct classes of forces, neither of which is likely to attenuate. The initial source of U.S. problems was domestic and took the form of shortsightedness and rigidity in U.S. government policies, industrial structure, and corporate strategy. These institutional rigidities included continued reliance upon tax and economic policies biased toward consumption; a fragmented political and economic structure that impeded long-term technological and strategic coordination; policies for basic research, higher education, trade, and military systems that allowed other countries to enjoy asymmetric access to U.S. technological resources; and the entrenchment of outdated techniques within American industry, even in high-technology sectors. Over the past quarter of a century these weaknesses have accumulated as American political and economic decision making has become increasingly shortsighted and the mismatch between U.S. conduct and international reality has grown progressively larger.

Overtaken by Japan

We have been leapfrogged by the Japanese in advanced-generation chip and computer design (the so-called fifth generation), in the production of new ceramics for automobile and aircraft engines, in the areas of fermentation and enzyme technology, cheap chemicals, and even plastics, and in a number of vital areas of metallurgy for making jet engines and high-temperature alloys. The Japanese have also surpassed us in the vital area of process engineering, which is the bedrock of manufacturing, and in robot technology—all very vital areas for the future. In other words, our technological lead has been eroded and seriously undermined.

Joel Kurtzman, *The Decline and Crash of the American Economy*, 1988.

These problems long remained unnoticed because they arose during a period, roughly from 1945 to 1975, in which America dominated global high technology. During this period Japan restricted both American imports and direct investment while massively importing U.S. technology. The United States led in basic research, and its firms typically dominated world markets, except in Japan, for products such as semiconductors, computers, machine tools, and electronic instruments.

However, even before Asian competitors directly challenged U.S. high technology in world markets, U.S. savings rates, capital investment, productivity growth, and commercial technology generation began to decline relative to earlier periods and to other countries. For example, annual U.S. productivity growth declined from 3 per cent in the 1950s to 1 per cent by the early 1980s. Recently these problems have, if anything, worsened; America's underlying macroeconomic condition has deteriorated sharply in the 1980s. Living standards and geopolitical commitments have been temporarily maintained only through unsustainable levels of borrowing and disinvestment.

And now a second source of decline, namely external competitive pressure, has been added. Future U.S. behavior will be seriously constrained by the rapid internationalization of Japanese industry, the discipline of global financial markets, the pace of international technology transfer, the rise of foreign competition, the lower capital and engineering costs of other countries, and the diminishing importance of the U.S. market relative to total world demand. In both high technology and global finance, Japan will clearly be the largest source of these external pressures. . . .

Through both adaptive evolution and strategic calculation, Japan evolved a set of political and industrial arrangements that presented a powerful strategic response to American hegemony. Its production system was superbly adapted to global competition in technology-intensive industries. Japan became a statist, strategically cohesive free rider in the world technology system. Its policies favored technology imports, savings, export-dependent growth, and protectionism in the service of domestic strategic economic planning and long-term competitive advantage. Conversely, Japanese policy discouraged expenditures—such as personal consumption, military spending, basic research, product imports, and capital outflows—that did not yield domestic benefits.

Government policy, as well as the structure of the Japanese financial and tax systems, favored industrial concentration, long time horizons, and domestic cooperation among competitors. Consequently, most Japanese financial and manufacturing activities were controlled by about a dozen enormous, vertically integrated industrial complexes. This structure facilitated domestic coordination of technological development and the control of foreign competition. . . .

Aided by these incentives structures and government policies, Japanese high-technology firms systematically excluded U.S. firms from Japanese markets; imported, copied, and stole U.S. technologies; and eventually launched export drives into the American market. But in addition, Japanese industry developed a unique production system oriented toward rapid product cycles, differentiated markets, continuous integration of new product and process technologies, and flexible—as opposed to rigidly standardized—mass production. . . .

The Rise of Information Technology

Information technology is driving economic and military transformations likely to prove as fundamental as any past industrial revolution. In fact, the technological progress of the information sector is literally unprecedented in economic history. In the major digital information industries—communications, computers, control systems, microelectronics, and software—this growth and progress will continue for another 20 years or more, when information processing will probably be the industrialized world's largest economic activity. Further, information technology affects not only the producing industries themselves but also other areas: the automation of design, manufacturing, and other activities; industrial products ranging from numerically controlled machine tools to consumer electronics; and, finally, military power.

Already these effects are large. The world semiconductor industry, currently $40 billion, is expected to reach $150 billion by the next century. World computer production, now approximately $200 billion, will then exceed $500 billion. Computer software production, already 2 per cent of U.S. gross national product (GNP), will be even larger. Since these industries offer high wages and are heavily dependent on human capital, the direct benefits accruing to successful competitors will include higher GNP, living standards, and wealth. Even so, the indirect effects will most likely be greater. The computerization of design, information management, industrial process control, and manufacturing has yielded productivity gains in many industries and is considered the largest probable source of productivity growth in the industrialized economies over the next several decades. The same is true of product technologies. In a growing number of industries, most notably computers and telecommunications equipment, semiconductor technology has become a major determinant of competitive advantage.

Ed Gamble. Reprinted with permission

The military implications of information technology are, if anything, larger. First, military operations have come to rely heavily on information systems infrastructure for C^3I, surveillance, and management. Second, computerization is at least as important to the design, production, and maintenance of weapons systems as it is to commercial industry. Finally, and analogously to the commercial world, information technology is by far the most important source of current and prospective growth in the capabilities of conventional and nuclear weapons. . . .

Japan's Lead

Clearly, then, the information technology revolution is broad. And although the United States retains leadership in research, in advanced systems design, and in some product markets, Japan must now be considered the world leader in electronics as a whole. Japan's electronics exports currently total about $65 billion and are eight times larger than its electronics imports. Conversely, the United States is now a large net importer of electronics worldwide and a net importer from Japan of advanced electronic materials, computer-controlled machine tools, computers, consumer electronics, robots, semiconductors, and telecommunications equipment.

Japanese efforts began 20 years ago with low-cost consumer electronics. Now Japan holds world leadership in innovation as well as in manufacturing; and consumer electronics has become a large, sophisticated sector with growing linkages to computers, semiconductors, and telecommunications. Moreover, Japanese electronics leadership is now far broader and includes critical industrial technologies.

In the past decade, Japan's share of the world semiconductor market has nearly doubled, to 49 per cent, while U.S. industry's share has declined from 55 per cent to 39 per cent. Japanese industry now has 90 per cent of the world market for the newest generation of semiconductor memories—1-megabit DRAMS (dynamic random access memory chips) that are critical to all computer systems. During the same decade, Japan's share of world computer production has also doubled, to 20 per cent, and exports have risen by a factor of 15. Similarly, between 1955 and 1985 the U.S. share of worldwide machine tool production declined from 40 per cent to 12 per cent, while Japan's rose from 1 per cent to 24 per cent; moreover, by 1984, 67 per cent of Japan's production was numerically controlled, compared with 40 per cent of U.S. production. Japanese firms also now lead in world markets for compact disc systems, computer displays, consumer video systems, digital audio tape, electronic cameras, facsimile systems, laser printers, personal copiers, and videocassette recorders.

A wide variety of evidence suggests that Japan has achieved parity with or even superiority over the United States in many information technologies. For example, between 1975 and 1982, Japanese shares of worldwide patenting activity in integrated circuits, lasers, robotics, and telecommunications grew rapidly while U.S. shares fell, sometimes dramatically.

Similarly, assessments by the U.S. Defense Science Board, the U.S. Japanese Technology Evaluation Program, and various private studies have concluded that although the United States still leads in some areas of R&D [research and development], leadership in engineering, production, and commercial technology has already passed to Japan.

The evidence clearly indicates that Japan's flexible, integrated production system is far more efficient and adaptable than conventional U.S. practices, even without automation. The rise of flexible automation in production further increases the Japanese advantage, and Japan leads the United States in the automation of manufacturing, even in high-technology industries. . . .

A U.S. Response

The United States now faces a challenge more fundamental than any since the cold war: the simultaneous need for internal reform and for the management of a new strategic balance, namely its technological competition with Japan. If America fails it will encounter something approaching an economic crisis, including severe tradeoffs between its global commitments and its domestic living standards. America's goals should include a strong technological position, careful management of its interdependence with Japan, and channeling of Japanese strength into appropriate and stabilizing forms of geopolitical or military burden sharing.

An adequate U.S. response must therefore include three components. First, the United States must improve its own economic environment, productivity growth, and technological performance. Second, it must reform its military procurement system, defense industrial base, and posture toward technological security. And third, the United States must manage its relationships with Japan in a more realistic and sophisticated way.

This challenge derives not only from Japan, but also from America's own mismanagement. Unless the United States restores its own technological and economic vitality, no amount of strategic bargaining, protectionism, or military spending will ensure its future security. However, the United States must also respond to Japan's technoindustrial Prussianism—without xenophobia or hostility, but also without naiveté. Continued U.S. decline is more likely to provoke dangerous social pressures than would any strong but rational policy. In short, the United States must learn that these issues of high technology and Japanese industrial policy, not just

Soviet warheads, will determine the future national security of the United States. . . .

The American high-technology community contains many extremely gifted and imaginative people. With sufficient drive, incentive, and resources there is every reason to expect improvement in the U.S. system's collective management abilities. But the effectiveness of American policy will rest heavily on industrial cooperation, low-cost capital, and rationalization of federal policymaking and administration. Federal policy must support high technology, not control it. Wherever possible, incentive mechanisms should be chosen over direct federal administration. . . .

As Japan grows stronger, its domestic interactions will become increasingly important to the international system and to U.S. policy. The complacency that has led the United States into its current predicament is a luxury it can no longer afford.

VIEWPOINT 2

"The U.S. approach to information technologies has been a supreme success."

The U.S. Is Not Falling Behind in Information Technology

George Gilder

George Gilder is a prominent social researcher who has written eight books, including *Wealth and Poverty* and *The Spirit of Enterprise*. The following viewpoint is excerpted from his 1989 book *Microcosm*. Gilder argues that trends in the computer industry make design and software preeminent, and that the U.S. retains commanding leads in these fields. He concludes that the U.S. can successfully outcompete Japan in developing new computer technologies because its free enterprise system encourages the growth of new companies with new products.

As you read, consider the following questions:

1. How does Gilder describe the "microcosm" and its significance?
2. What lessons does the author derive from Europe's policies to develop its technology?
3. What has caused America's trade deficit in high technology products, according to the author?

The central event of the twentieth century is the overthrow of matter. In technology, economics, and the politics of nations, wealth in the form of physical resources is steadily declining in value and significance. The powers of mind are everywhere ascendant over the brute force of things.

This change marks a great historic divide. Dominating previous human history was the movement and manipulation of massive objects against friction and gravity. In the classic image of humanity, Atlas bears the globe on stooped shoulders, or Sisyphus wrestles a huge rock up an endless slope. For long centuries, humans grew rich chiefly by winning control over territory and treasure, slaves and armies. Even the Industrial Revolution depended on regimented physical labor, natural resources, crude energy sources, and massive transport facilities. Wealth and power came mainly to the possessor of material things or to the ruler of military forces capable of conquering the physical means of production: land, labor, and capital.

Today, the ascendant nations and corporations are masters not of land and material resources but of ideas and technologies. Japan and other barren Asian islands have become the world's fastest-growing economies. Electronics is the world's fastest-growing major industry. Computer software, a pure product of mind, is the chief source of added value in world commerce. The global network of telecommunications carries more valuable goods than all the world's supertankers. Today, wealth comes not to the rulers of slave labor but to the liberators of human creativity, not to the conquerors of land but to the emancipators of mind. . . .

The Microchip

The exemplary technology of this era is the microchip—the computer inscribed on a tiny piece of processed material. More than any other invention, this device epitomizes the overthrow of matter. Consider a parable of the microchip once told by Gordon Moore, chairman of Intel and a founding father of Silicon Valley:

"We need a substrate for our chip. So we looked at the substrate of the earth itself. It was mostly sand. So we used that.

"We needed a metal conductor for the wires and switches on the chip. We looked at all the metals in the earth and found aluminum was the most abundant. So we used that.

"We needed an insulator and we saw that the silicon in sand mixed with the oxygen in the air to form silicon dioxide—a kind of glass. The perfect insulator to protect the chip. So we used that."

The result was a technology—metal oxide silicon (MOS), made from metal, sand, and air—in which materials costs are less than 1 percent of total expense. Combining millions of components on a single chip, operating in billionths of seconds, these devices transcend most of the previous constraints of matter. The most valuable substance in this, the fundamental product of the era, is the idea for the design.

The microchip not only epitomizes but also impels the worldwide shift of the worth of goods from materials to ideas. These transvaluations are not mere luck, to be annulled by some new scarcity. Nor do they reflect only the foresight of one industry, summed up in Moore's parable. The rise of mind as the source of wealth spans all industries and reflects the most profound findings of modern physics and philosophy. The overthrow of matter in economics is made possible by the previous overthrow of matter in physics. All the cascading devaluations of matter in the global economy and society originate with the fundamental transfiguration of matter in quantum science.

A World Leader

The United States has long been and continues to be the world leader in research into computer science. The computer science field has benefited consistently from our continuous program of investment. In spite of the much heralded Japanese Fifth Generation Computer Program and the other Japanese research efforts devoted to computer science, the United States has far larger commitments and a substantial and healthy research tradition that has led to a great American advantage in this field. Further, as a result of over 40 years of experimentation with information technology, the United States has developed a substantial advantage in software technology.

David H. Brandin and Michael A. Harrison, *The Technology War,* 1987.

Max Planck, the discoverer of the quantum, offered the key when he asserted that the new science entailed a movement from the "visible and directly controllable to the invisible sphere, from the macrocosm to the microcosm." The macrocosm may be defined as the visible domain of matter, seen from the outside and ruled by the laws of classical physics. The microcosm is the invisible domain, ruled and revealed by the laws of modern physics. . . .

Futurists and other sages have long agreed that the microcosm would shape the future of nations and industries. They thought it would demand great collective efforts and masses of capital. Both the use and manufacture of computers, they foresaw, would entail huge economies of scale, fostered by the state.

In the 1960s, many observers believed they could discern the pattern already in the United States, then as now the world leader in the use of new technology. In 1967, Jean-Jacques Servan-Schreiber alerted the world to *The American Challenge (Le Défi Américain)*. The challenge as he saw it was the military industrial complex: the combination of American multi-national corporations, government research and development laboratories, Pentagon money and management on the new frontiers of high technology.

The new technologies, the French editor asserted, inherently dictated the kind of capital-intensive and highly collective effort that had put a man on the moon and an IBM mainframe in every data-processing center. Governments not only would need to plan and subsidize the new industries but also would have to protect and support the throngs of expected victims in existing businesses.

Servan-Schreiber experienced an unusual and presumably gratifying success. Not only was his book a best-seller around the world, but nearly all his prophecies were taken to heart and all his prescriptions were adopted. The governments of Europe joined in launching a series of large projects, led by multi-national cartels, to exploit the new technologies. Eureka, Esprit, Prestel, Teletext, Informatique, Antiope, Airbus Industrie, Alvey, JESSI, the Silicon Structures Project, and other major government initiatives focused on answering the American challenge with a colossal *défi Européen*. . . .

Servan-Schreiber's industrial policies left European technology aswim in an alphabet soup of acronyms while European entrepreneurs negotiated with bureaucrats and union bosses for the right to fire a saboteur or close down an obsolete plant. Trying to enter the microcosm clutching macrocosmic institutions and technologies, the parts of Europe where Servan-Schreiber's views were adopted suffered the worst slump of the post-World War II era. In nearly twenty years after the publication of his book, no net new jobs were created on the continent. During that period Europe fell even farther behind in the very information technologies that were targeted by national industrial policies. Their small share of the microchip and computer industries, for example, fell some 20 percent between 1967 and 1987.

Two Approaches

Meanwhile the United States followed totally different policies. Rather than extending national regulation and control over the "central nervous system" of finance, transport, and communications, the United States deregulated finance, telecommunications, energy, trucking, and air transport. Rather than increasing taxes on individuals and subsidizing corporations as Europeans did, the United States drastically lowered tax rates across the board, to an eventual top rate under 30 percent for individuals and closely held businesses, and under 35 percent for normal corporations. Rather than concentrating investment in industrial conglomerates, the United States liberated pension funds and other institutions to invest in venture capital for risky new companies.

These policies, beginning in the late 1970s, fostered a massive upsurge of entrepreneurship and innovation. Not only did venture capital outlays rise by a factor of 200 but new public issues of shares on the stock market rose some tenfold; small business starts nearly tripled, from 270,000 in 1978 to some 750,000 in 1988. The result, contrary to predictions of rising unemployment, was a total of some 15 million new jobs, with a record of some 67 percent of adults in the labor force in 1988 (compared to 58 percent in Europe). Real per capita disposable income rose 20 percent. Surging 30 percent between 1981 and 1989, even industrial production rose three times faster in the United States than in the European realms of industrial policy.

Ignoring all this history, many experts now urge the United States to reverse policy and embrace the Servan-Schreiber code. They declare that the new technologies demand drastically more government guidance and aid rather than less. They point to Japan's Fifth Generation Computer Project and to similar European schemes; they decry the imbalance in U.S. trade accounts; they panic at the Japanese lead in DRAMs [direct random access memory] and in HDTV [high definition television]; and they predict a steady decline in the international position of the United States on the frontiers of technology.

Once again these voices are wrong, victims of a common nostalgia alien to the meaning and prospects of the quantum era. They are wrong first of all on the facts, misreading the recent history of the computer and semiconductor industries. More importantly, they are wrong on the future, deeply misunderstanding the meaning of the microcosm.

U.S. Regains Lead

If the doomsayers were correct, the United States would still be losing global market share in electronics. But since 1985, U.S. companies have been steadily gaining market share in most parts of the computer industry and more than holding their own in semiconductors. In mid-1987, the U.S. semiconductor open market (excluding IBM and other captive producers that consume a third of U.S. output) again exceeded the total Japanese market in size (the Japanese have no companies categorized as captive).

George Gilder, *Harvard Business Review*, March/April 1988.

American companies hold some 70 percent of the worldwide computer market and in many ways are increasing their lead in the technology. With accelerating technical progress, the value added in the industry has shifted rapidly from hardware to the software that makes the hardware useful. Summing up the situation is Intel's 32-bit microprocessor, the 386. Intel invents it, IBM and scores of other firms adopt it, and all must wait for some three years for Microsoft, a relatively new firm headed by thirty-three-year-old Bill Gates, to produce the software to exploit its full powers.

Gates's firm is now worth several billion dollars and the value of its software to the users is far more. Yet the most complex and expensive capital equipment used in this enterprise, other than Bill Gates's mind, are desktop computers. This is typical of the industry.

Software is chiefly a product of individuals working alone or in small teams with minimal capital. Between 1975 and 1985, some 14,000 new software firms rose up in the United States, lifting the U.S. share of the world software market from under two thirds to more than three quarters. Since 1985, U.S. software output has grown faster even than Japan's. Software comprises a four times greater share of computer industry revenues in the United States than in Japan, and the United States produces more than four times more marketed software.

Mostly created since 1981, the new U.S. software firms transformed the computer from an esoteric technology into a desktop appliance found in 20 percent or more of American homes and ubiquitous in corporate workplaces. In the per capita application of PCs [personal computers], the United States in the late 1980s led Japan by approximately three to one.

Analysts focusing on "Fifth Generation computer projects," on mainframe systems, and on supercomputers, swoon worshipfully before HDTV screens and dismiss these PCs as toys. So did the experts at IBM a few years ago. But at the same time that the United States moved massively into microcomputers, small systems surged far ahead in price-performance. In cost per MIPS (millions of instructions per second, a very rough but roughly serviceable measure), the new PCs are an amazing ninety times more cost-effective than mainframes. With the ever-growing ability to interconnect these machines in networks and use them in parallel configurations that yield mainframe performance, microcomputers are rapidly gaining market share against the large machines. . . .

The Future of Computing

The future of computing lies not in the Cray 3 or the IBM 3090 supercomputers or all the IBM imitations in Japan but in the Intel 386, 486, and the Motorola 68000 family of chips. It lies in their array of networking co-processors, and in reduced instruction set (RISC) processors optimized for parallel use. These devices are creating entire new businesses in computer-aided engineering workstations, in specialized semiconductors, in embedded microprocessors, in superminicomputers, in graphics computers, and even in minisupercomputers. Yet large machines still dominate data processing in Japan and most of Europe and the Japanese hold under 10 percent of the U.S. microcomputer market. During the late 1980s, even their chip designers were still doing the vast bulk of their computer-aided engineering on mainframe terminals.

Japan Depends on the U.S.

Japanese technology depends on American research. Supercomputers, personal computers, the latest superconductors, and bioresearch, the whole spectrum of technological development, carries the "Made in the USA" label. The Japanese have structured their economy according to US blueprints, and they have made it an appendix to the US economy.

Tas Papathanasis and Chris Vasillopulos, *The Christian Science Monitor*, April 27, 1989.

Driven by the proliferation of software packages, the more rapid diffusion of computer technology to individuals in American homes, schools, and workplaces is as important a source of future competitiveness for the U.S. economy as the Japanese lead in robotics and manufacturing is for Japan.

In fact, it was the U.S. software lead, not a hardware lag, that caused the high-technology trade gap. Most of the imported hardware was components and equipment needed to respond to the unexpected impact of a booming U.S. software industry. . . .

Nonetheless, preoccupied with the balance of trade as an index of competitiveness, many analysts were full of fear and trembling. Americans import far more computer products than any other country and run a large trade deficit with Asia in both systems and components. Trade deficit fetishists prophesied doom.

America's Lead

The trade deficit with Asia in computers and semiconductors, almost entirely the result of a booming computer market, mostly stems from overseas manufacturing by U.S. firms and comprises less than 4 percent of U.S. computer industry revenues. U.S. companies still hold more than two thirds of the total world market even for peripherals. In 1988, U.S. producers of hard disk drives, largely manufactured by wholly owned branches and subsidiaries in Asia, took between 70 and 80 percent of the world market.

In the broader electronics industry, U.S. companies produced more than $195 billion of electronic equipment in 1988, some 80 percent more than Japan. Even excluding some $50 billion of defense electronics, the United States substantially outproduced Japan. Indeed, during most of the 1980s, U.S. electronics production firms may well have grown faster than Japanese output, which was vastly inflated in the data by an 80 percent rise in the value of the yen. Including the fourfold U.S. edge both in software and in telecom equipment revenues, the United States continues to hold the lead in the keystone products of the age.

The computer industry is not a special case. It exemplifies the new technologies of the quantum era. But the lesson is deeper than a mere failure of insight by economists and other experts. The lesson is that the United States made gains in competitiveness during the 1980s chiefly by ignoring nationalist fears and fetishes and statist industrial plans. Instead, the United States pursued strategies suited to the global microcosm.

Rather than trying to become self-sufficient in computing by some massive national project in defiance of the market, the United States paid for imports by adding enormous new value to them. Shopping in the farthest corners of the globe to find the best suppliers of components to implement their systems and software, U.S. entrepreneurs ended up making America the center of the industry and the prime source of world economic growth.

Will the Future Be Different?

Ignoring a few failed sallies into industrial policy, the U.S. approach to information technologies has been a supreme success. But the Cassandras have an answer. They say the future will be different. Computer technologies are now allegedly maturing. As growth slows and large firms marshal their forces to achieve market share, America's dependence on Japan will gradually cripple and destroy the U.S. industry.

This view has even less merit than the claims of U.S. failure. It entails an acute misreading of the technology. Computer industry growth is not slowing, the technology is not "maturing" (they mean ossifying), and large companies are not gaining ground (although new firms are growing large). The pace of progress in computers is now on the verge of a drastic acceleration. Summoning these advances is a convergence of three major developments in the industry that also play to American strengths in the microcosm. Indeed, pioneering in silicon compilation, artificial intelligence, and parallel processing, U.S. entrepreneurial startups are already in the lead in shaping the key technologies of the coming era.

Contrary to the analysis of the critics, the industry is not becoming more capital-intensive. Measured by the capital costs per device function—the investment needed to deliver value to the customer—the industry is becoming ever cheaper to enter. The silicon compiler and related technologies move power from large corporations to individual designers and entrepreneurs. . . .

In a sense the Cassandras are right: the U.S. semiconductor industry will disappear. It will become a different kind of business, dominated by design and systems. Semiconductor companies no longer are chiefly making components. In the future, components will be almost entirely part of the chip. Even while losing market share in the remaining commodity chips, the United States can continue to lead the move into the microcosm. Most important, U.S. companies can still dominate the computer industry and its software, which is what the contest was all about.

The Lessons of Success

While American economists ululated about declining competitiveness, we won the first phase of the competition. Whatever happens in the future, we should learn the lessons of this success, not forget them in a hypochondria of decline. We won because we dispersed power among thousands of entrepreneurs rather than concentrated it in conglomerates and bureaucracies. We won because we went for growth opportunities rather than for trade surpluses. We won because we didn't try to do everything at once. We won because we were not afraid of the international division of labor. We had a global orientation rather than a national industrial policy.

It is the power of the microcosm that ultimately confounded the policies and predictions of Servan-Schreiber. . . . During the very period that the Europeans placed their reliance increasingly on the state's ability to gather capital and experts, the balance of power in the world shifted massively in favor of the individual. For Servan-Schreiber was right. The organization of world industry would indeed be shaped by the nature of the new technology.

The new technologies of the microcosm—artificial intelligence, silicon compilation, and parallel processing—all favor entrepreneurs and small companies. All three allow entrepreneurs to use the power of knowledge to economize on capital and enhance its efficiency: mixing sand and ideas to generate new wealth and power for men and women anywhere in the world.

3 VIEWPOINT

"The crux of America's problem is manufacturing—translating ideas into products good enough to be sold on international markets."

U.S. Manufacturing Is Declining

Otis Port

Many Americans are worried that the U.S. is no longer technologically supreme because they notice that most hi-tech consumer goods, such as automobiles, computers, and television sets, are made by foreign companies. In the following viewpoint, Otis Port argues that while the U.S. continues to be a world leader in scientific research, it has fallen behind other countries in adapting technology to manufacture products. Port argues that for too many years U.S. corporations have concentrated on financial transactions at the expense of manufacturing. He concludes that U.S. corporations must be restructured to emphasize technological innovation. Port is an associate editor for *Business Week*, a national business magazine.

As you read, consider the following questions:

1. According to Port, why do many foreigners believe the U.S. has fallen behind in manufacturing?
2. In what areas does the U.S. trail its major economic competitors, according to the author?

James Fallows, an American author living in Japan, was having a convivial beer with an English friend. After taking a long drink, Fallows' companion put down his glass and said: "Why don't you just face the fact that you're second-raters, like us?"

That question reveals just how far the U.S. has slipped in the eyes of the world. Even the British are wondering if the time has come for their former colony to pass the baton—to Japan. Incredulous at the U.S. retreat in market after market for the last two decades, other countries have come to believe that America has lost its spirit of enterprise. Today, as Fallows notes in his book, *More Like Us: Making America Great Again*, the phrase "lazy American" has become a cliché.

What happened to the mighty U.S. innovation machine? This is the system that invented the phonograph, the color television, the tape recorder (audio and video), the telephone, and the integrated circuit, to name a few milestone products. Yet today, U.S. producers account for only a small percentage of the U.S. market for most of those products—and an even smaller share of the world market.

Since 1987 the Tokyo government has been prodding companies and consumers to buy more imported goods. Purchases of European products have jumped substantially. But not American imports. The Japanese, it seems, have no more use for things stamped "Made in the USA" than Americans did for the knickknacks exported by Japan in the 1950s.

Laziness seems the only logical explanation to many people in Asia and Europe. By nearly all measures, the U.S. should be unbeatable. America has 15 million companies; no other nation comes close. It has 5.5 million scientists and engineers—double the number in Japan—and they have won more Nobel prizes than the rest of the world put together. Plus, the U.S. spends almost twice as much on research and development as Japan and Germany combined.

There's more: Students from around the globe flock here for the world's best training in advanced science, mathematics, and engineering. The U.S. remains a hothouse of ideas and technology: California's Silicon Valley and Boston's Route 128 serve as perennial models for other governments' thrusts into high tech. And America's venture-capital and job-generating engines are the envy of the world. "We have everything in spades—if we can just get our act together," says D. Bruce Merrifield, until recently the Assistant Secretary of Commerce for Productivity, Technology & Innovation.

But as is now painfully clear, there's more to innovation than Nobel prizes and fat R&D budgets. "The Japanese would gladly give us all the Nobel prizes," says H. John Caulfield, director of the Center for Applied Optics at the University of Alabama in

Huntsville. "They're not worth a damn thing unless they're converted into products."

The problem is that most Americans, including managers and government leaders, believe that invention and innovation are synonymous—or at least that one flows inevitably from the other. That is reflected in Washington's standard recipe for boosting innovation and competitiveness: Throw more resources into basic research and education.

But this knee-jerk response is "a devastating error," says Rustum Roy, director of the Science, Technology & Society Program at Pennsylvania State University. In April 1989, he told a congressional committee that Japan's "awesome machine for converting new scientific discovery into marketable products is living proof of that." Roy's discouraging conclusion: The more inventive ideas the U.S. dreams up, the farther it will fall behind. Each one will be just another opportunity for a foreign rival to out-innovate a U.S. company in producing it.

Mismanagement

The problem of U.S. competitiveness is partly attributable to the way in which American corporations have been managed.

For one thing, some corporations have been slower than they should have been in applying new technology. Japan, for example, now has more than three times the number of robots in operation on factory production lines as we do. And consider what happened to the American steel industry. For many years, no other country's steel industry came close to it. We were the undisputed leader worldwide. But then we failed to implement modern, highly automated process manufacturing systems as our international rivals were doing. Instead, we continued to make steel in the old, inefficient open-hearth way. The American steel industry has since fallen on hard times, and is now hard-pressed to sell its product beyond small niche markets.

Richard A. Voell, *Vital Speeches of the Day*, August 15, 1987.

So the crux of America's problem is manufacturing—translating ideas into products good enough to be sold on international markets to pay the country's import bills. "American companies don't like to build things—they like to make deals," says C. Gordon Bell, R&D vice-president of Ardent Computer Corp. and formerly with Digital Equipment Corp., where he engineered the hugely successful line of Vax minicomputers. "Our large organizations have become purchasing agents."

It wasn't always so. Before World War II, the factory was the cornerstone of American industry. But U.S. managers started to ignore manufacturing in the postwar years, when companies sold everything they could produce. The U.S. had no competition then, so the job of running the factory could safely be delegated to second-rate managers. Just keep the plant churning out widgets, they were told, and don't fix anything that works.

In that static environment, manufacturing quickly ceased to be a source of innovation. Companies began to focus all of their creative support on product designers. Those technicians knew nothing about production and therefore focused on developing brand-new products from scratch. Unfortunately, of the two main routes to innovation, that's the less fertile one.

That kind of product innovation tends to be like a ladder, says Ralph E. Gomory, formerly IBM's chief scientist and now president of the Alfred P. Sloan Foundation. Climb, and you acquire new knowledge that confers a competitive advantage—but only until rivals join you at the top. Then you have to build a new ladder—a very slow and expensive process.

A more productive route, called process-oriented innovation, resembles the wheel in a hamster cage—a ladder wrapped into a cylinder, with no beginning and no end. Each turn of the wheel improves an existing product and its production methods. Year after year, the company unveils not-entirely-new products that keep getting better, more reliable, and cheaper. "It sounds dull," Gomory admits, but the cumulative effect can be exhilirating. It was constant cyclical refinements, for example, that took the semiconductor and computer industries from memory chips that stored 1 bit of data each to today's 4-million-bit designs.

Similarly, auto makers don't try to reinvent totally new forms of transportation every year. It was incremental innovation that replaced manual transmissions with automatics and resulted in power steering and power brakes. "The cumulation of a large number of small improvements is the surest path, in most industries, to increasing your competitive advantage," says John P. McTague, research vice-president at Ford Motor Co.

The Japanese have become masters at that. When they were preparing their assault on the U.S. market, they spotted a glaring weakness in U.S. manufacturing. Because it depended on economies of scale from long production runs, it was vulnerable to a system that could whip out a constant barrage of incrementally better products. Even today, "we put twice the resources into product innovation as we do into process innovation," notes Arden L. Bement Jr., TRW Inc.'s vice-president of technical resources. "Japan does the opposite."

Japan's strategy was brilliant: It yanked the economic rug from under U.S. industry. It has been so successful that U.S. manufacturers still find themselves unable to compete, even with lower-cost labor. "Over half our trade deficit now comes from foreign

Danziger in The Christian Science Monitor © 1989 TCSPS

industries that pay their workers higher wages than we do," emphasizes Ira Magaziner, a Providence management consultant. "They don't beat us with cheap labor. They beat us with technology and skilled labor."

The results are glaringly apparent in America's balance of trade. Since 1980, the U.S. has sunk from a positive trade balance to the world's biggest debtor. And no end is in sight. DRI/McGraw-Hill Inc. projects that the trade deficit will ease just slightly in coming years, dipping from 1987's $154 billion to "only" $111 billion in 1995. Then, with a united Europe flexing its new-found economic muscle, the deficit could head upward again, hitting an all-time high—$160 billion—in the year 2000. "It really threatens our future," said U.S. Trade Representative Carla A. Hills at a Senate hearing.

Plot almost any index of national well-being, from adult literacy to per-capita gross national product, and the U.S. trails its major competitors. Take the rates for savings and fixed investment: During the 1980s, Japan and Germany have been outstripping America by two, three, four, or five to one. Even in the bellwether area of industrial research, Japan has been progressively outspending the U.S. (as a percentage of GNP) since 1971. By 1985, the disparity had swollen to 47% (1.9% of GNP for the U.S. vs. 2.8% for Japan). And the U.S. no longer has the world's highest per-capita GNP.

It has taken a long time, but America's leaders are finally beginning to see that manufacturing is indispensable. Several studies have detailed the reasons why, the latest being *Made in America*, conducted by the Commission on Industrial Productivity at Massachusetts Institute of Technology. It points out that the U.S. consumed roughly $1 trillion in manufactured goods in 1987, while total exports of services that year amounted to only $57 billion. Thus, if the U.S. imported half of its manufactured items, exports of services would have to increase nearly 10 times to pay the bills.

That is highly unlikely. Experience shows that when manufacturing moves offshore, many related services soon follow, including high-value-added functions such as design and engineering. Moreover, manufacturers account for virtually all of the basic research sponsored by industry. This generates the bulk of the technological innovation that fuels long-term economic growth, inside and outside the industries that funded the research.

Even the business schools now recognize that the U.S. cannot go on ceding markets to foreign competitors. "We've got to fight it out in the trenches," says Lester C. Thurow, dean of MIT's Sloan School of Management. "Once you start retreating, you end up retreating into oblivion."

That's quite a turnaround. After World War II, when the U.S. was unconcerned about overseas competition, Harvard and other business schools introduced portfolio theory to contend with vacillations in the domestic market. The idea was to diversify into counter-cyclical businesses so total profits wouldn't be dragged down by a slump—or intense price competition—in one market.

But diversification meant that top management could no longer be intimately familiar with all its businesses. So the schools devised various manage-by-the-numbers formulas that supposedly enabled an executive to run any business. As a result, U.S. industry today is saddled with people in important positions who don't understand technology, notes Richard M. Cyert, president of Carnegie Mellon University.

To corporate technologists, the financial guidelines imposed by these managers seem designed mainly "to tell you why what you need to do won't pay," says Robert A. Frosch, vice-president for research at General Motors Corp. "I'm not a big booster of the MBA analysis system," he adds.

Because the bean counters impose such high payback expectations on capital investments, research departments feel forced to swing for home runs rather than slap singles. And since the payoff from basic research rarely falls through to the bottom line in fewer than six or seven years—too long to be factored into Wall Street valuations—most companies have stopped doing it altogether.

But the top brass and Wall Street are not solely to blame. There's also the high cost of U.S. capital, says Joseph P. Martino, senior research scientist at the University of Dayton Research Institute. The difference between a long-term interest rate of 11% in the U.S. and 4.5% in Japan, compounded for 5 to 10 years, becomes a high hurdle. "So it's easy to see why Japanese industrialists look farther ahead," says Martino. "They can afford to."

Another factor is the soaring cost of doing leading-edge research. Just to develop the next-generation chipmaking method, which will use X-rays instead of light to "print" circuit patterns on silicon, IBM is spending $435 million, according to recently named President Jack D. Kuehler. Tack on the cost of production equipment, and that price tag will more than double.

How many other U.S. chipmakers will be able to afford similar programs? Only a handful—five at most. Yet in Japan, 19 such projects are already under way. Suggesting that typical U.S. companies can compete on their own against the likes of Hitachi, Matsushita, Sumitomo, and Toshiba "brings only a wan smile" to anyone who knows the current state of industrial research on both sides of the Pacific, says Penn State's Roy.

Don't write off America as a rust-bucket case just yet, however. There are signs of brighter days ahead. Harvard business school, for example, is trying to shift gears, says Thomas R. Piper, senior associate dean for educational programs. "In the past three or four years, there has been a change to where faculty are raising public-policy questions on takeovers, leveraged buyouts, and the short-term focus of management." And the school no longer requires students to take a course in quantitative management.

Companies are struggling to do a better job of managing innovation, and more products are being designed with an eye to manufacturability. In many industries, competitors big and small are banding together into research consortiums—and pushing for changes in antitrust laws so they can collaborate on manufacturing as well. While they are asking for government support, it's not a handout, says Robert N. Noyce, chairman of Sematech, the semiconductor consortium. If it helps the U.S. chip industry grow just 5%, he says, corporate taxes on those added revenues will repay the investment.

Size needn't be a prerequisite for competing with Japan's huge conglomerates. "The Germans and Italians do it well without being raised on a sushi diet," quips John Zysman, codirector of the Berkeley Roundtable on the International Economy. There are standout performers in the U.S., too. The MIT productivity commission found one or two in every industry it studied. "So why don't more companies copy what the good performers are doing?" asks commission Chairman Michael L. Dertouzos.

One reason, he says, is that it calls for a disruptive, wrenching restructuring of the entire corporation, from the very top on down.

Organizing for innovation means flattening the hierarchy, giving more responsibility to the lower levels, and scuttling discipline-oriented departments in favor of ad hoc mission-team groups. "Forget the organizational structure we've used for 300 years," says Robert L. Callahan, president of Ingersoll Engineers Inc. "Simply put together people who can get the job done, regardless of their function." He terms it "swarming."

So far, only a few American producers—perhaps a half-percent—are swarming to embrace such drastic overhauls. They include Motorola, Hewlett-Packard, Deere, Caterpillar, and Carrier. But it may soon become a matter of necessity as competition heats up still more.

Tearing down internal walls could also have a spinoff benefit: People accustomed to working in a free-form environment should perform better in outside collaborations, too. The upshot: Japanese-style intra-company teamwork spiced with American superstar researchers and Yankee entrepreneurs. "The U.S. is extremely good at blending cooperation and individualism," says MIT's Dertouzos. "Look at professional sports." So with any luck, when Technology Superbowl 2000 rolls around, Team America may be in fitter form than ever.

4 VIEWPOINT

"The U.S. is gaining ground against global competitors, not losing it."

U.S. Manufacturing Is Rebounding

Alex Taylor III

Alex Taylor III is an associate editor with *Fortune*, a business newsmagazine. In the following viewpoint, he argues that U.S. manufacturers have improved quality control and productivity. He concludes that U.S. businesses have successfully responded to international competitors, and that the future of U.S. manufacturing is bright.

As you read, consider the following questions:

1. Why does Taylor consider the 1980s a transition period?
2. In which five areas have U.S. manufacturers improved, according to the author?
3. What must the U.S. do to maintain its competitiveness, according to Taylor?

American industry—a Gulliver in Lilliput, a feeble giant hamstrung by canny Asians and newly energized Europeans? There never was much truth to that idea, and these days it's downright absurd. The U.S. is gaining ground against global competitors, not losing it. The cheap dollar gets some of the credit, of course. But the Fortune 500 industrial companies—and some smaller manufacturers as well—have made long strides in productivity, management, quality, and cost control. They are blasting their way into new foreign markets and grabbing customers from overseas competitors. More than a few U.S. companies—notably in computers, pharmaceuticals, and telecommunications—are extending their worldwide leads. . . .

The Biggest Winners

The biggest winners from the 30% depreciation of the dollar since mid-1985 have been such worldclass exporters as airplane and computer makers, who have increased the demand for their sought-after products by cutting prices in foreign currencies up to 50%. Traditional homebodies such as food processors and toy manufacturers are discovering the allure of overseas markets. ConAgra is making a big push in Japan, where it is increasing shipments of seafood, frozen food, beef, and grain. Hasbro has found a worldwide market for its best-selling G.I. Joe.

For industrial companies of Fortune 500 heft, setting up factories abroad is often better than exporting. That way they get closer to overseas customers and simultaneously insulate themselves from currency swings. While the dollar was falling Americans were building smokestacks abroad, and now they are savoring the payoff.

Scott Paper, already up and running in France and Belgium, is adding paper machines in Belgium, Italy, and Spain, and raised European sales from $900 million in 1987 to over $1 billion in 1988. Europeans have customarily consumed less toilet paper and fewer paper napkins and hankies than Americans because those products were expensive and the quality was poor. Scott figures that consumption will rise substantially. . . .

Reynolds Metals, which was closing aluminum smelters in 1984, is adding fabricating machinery in Belgium, Brazil, Italy, Spain, and West Germany. Like Scott, Reynolds is trying to prime a nascent market. Western Europe consumes only one-twelfth as many aluminum beverage cans as the U.S. does.

Reconsidering Past Events

The comeback in American competitiveness is forcing experts to reconsider the events of the past 15 years. Economist A. Gary Shilling, who runs his own New York City consulting firm, now views most of the 1980s as a transition between the excess demand that erupted after World War II and the overcapacity that more recently inundated markets around the world. During the transition, many U.S. companies became temporarily exposed as the high-cost, low-quality producers. "We were naked as the proverbial jaybird," says Shilling. "It is a very tough road back, but we are correcting for not just years of mistakes, but decades."

A Window of Opportunity

We are in the early stages of a potential renaissance in American manufacturing, and the fundamental strengths of that sector are becoming evident again. The window of opportunity is open, and the extent of our success will depend on how long and how well we utilize the strengths of manufacturing.

Jerry J. Jasinowski, *USA Today*, January 1989.

In retrospect, the hard times U.S. manufacturers suffered in the 1970s and early 1980s may have been only the symptoms of a cyclical change, not a permanent reordering of the world economy. No one expects America to start making lots of T-shirts or radios again. But critics have tended to tar all manufacturers with the brush they used for automobiles, steel, machine tools, and semiconductors—the backbone of any modern industrial economy and thus the biggest weapons of international trade. Even in these once beleaguered businesses, an upturn is finally visible.

What gets overlooked are success stories like Timken's. The Japanese were driving the Canton, Ohio, maker of roller bearings to the wall in the early 1980s, so it redoubled efforts to make its products more competitive. Says President Joseph Toot: "Bad products or management weren't the problem, so it would have been foolish to go out and try something we had never done before." Timken cut prices 30% and increased quality enough to lengthen the guarantee on its truck axles from 100,000 miles to 500,000 miles. The company started selling to Japanese manufacturers in 1987 and expects to make big gains there.

Five Areas

Here's a closer look at five important areas where U.S. manufacturers are making big gains that are paying off in world competitiveness:

Productivity: In recent years, international comparisons made U.S. productivity appear worse than it was. As the second leg of the postwar economic boom roared along from 1960 to 1973, Western European countries and Japan posted annual productivity gains ranging from 6.6% to 10.3%. Because the U.S. had been running at full speed since the early 1950s, its annual increases of 2.9% looked puny by comparison. When worldwide recession took hold in the 1970s, the U.S.'s relative position continued to slip.

Yet the U.S. remains the world leader in per capita national output, with Germany and Japan lagging far behind. Each U.S. worker accounts for $33,000 in gross national product today vs. $24,000 in 1960, measured in constant dollars. "Productivity in most U.S. industries is still higher than in any other country in the world," says Gerald Godshaw, who heads long-term forecasting for Wharton Econometric Forecasting Associates (WEFA) in Bala Cynwyd, Pennsylvania. In the last half of the 1980s the U.S. has been coming on strong. U.S. manufacturing productivity grew at only one-quarter the Japanese rate from 1980 to 1982, but it rose 75% as fast in the years from 1983 to 1987. West German productivity increased only half as rapidly as Japan's in the same period. Says Janet L. Norwood, commissioner of labor statistics: "In the past 28 years, the comparative productivity of our factories has careened from problem to crisis to—possibly—a renewed position of leadership."

American manufacturers are making productivity gains in industries once regarded as mature, according to data compiled by WEFA. In lumber, for example, the U.S. limped along between 1978 and 1983 with annual increases of 1.5%, measured in 1982 dollars. Then productivity more than doubled, rising 3.6% on average in each of the next five years. In primary metals like steel and aluminum, annual productivity changes shifted from −2.8% to +6.5% over the same period.

Continuing Gains

Some forecasters predict that robust gains in productivity will continue for the next decade. Godshaw of WEFA looks for annual productivity increases averaging 4.4% in electrical machinery and 4.3% in textiles, for example. Overall, he expects durable-goods productivity to climb 3.6% a year through the 1990s.

Better workers help too. Though the idea defies conventional wisdom, Norwood insists that America's work force "is the most productive in history." More than one in four adult workers has a college degree, up from one in five a decade ago. Reports of a brain drain have been exaggerated. Employment in science and engineering has been growing at a healthy 6.3% annual clip for more than a decade. Scientists and engineers make up 2.8% of the U.S. labor force, compared with 2.5% in Japan.

The U.S.'s worldwide lead in computers gives a huge kick to productivity in the economy as a whole. By WEFA's calculations, productivity in that industry has shot ahead 14.7% annually, on average, since 1984. Despite strong international competition, American computer companies are striving to maintain their advantage. Compaq, the upstart maker of IBM-compatible personal computers, more than doubled its overseas sales to $800 million in 1988.

Management: U.S. manufacturers are also reaping the benefits of changes made at home—those painful reorganizations undertaken to rip apart top-heavy management and improve response time. Daniel Valentino, president of United Research, a Morristown, New Jersey, consultant to a number of large manufacturers, views the slump of the early 1980s as the consequence of progress along the learning curve as companies eliminated management by function and installed decentralized management by business unit. "What we did was take a whole set of functional managers and throw them up against the wall," he says. "The ones who adapted to a general management role are now helping us close the competitiveness gap."

Reasons for Optimism

It's been a long time coming, but American manufacturers finally have reasons to be optimistic. Profits are rising, and so are exports. . . . The quality of U.S. goods—so often deplored as fit only for the throwaway society that produced them—is improving. Says Dana Cound, chairman of the American Society for Quality Control, an international organization devoted to the quality-related sciences: "On virtually every front the quality of American products is better than it has ever been on an absolute scale."

Christopher Knowlton, *Fortune*, March 28, 1988.

That has clearly been the experience at Eastman Kodak. CEO [Chief Executive Officer] Colby Chandler figures the Yellow Father lost $3.5 billion in worldwide sales from 1981 to 1985 to competitors such as Fuji Photo Film. So he reorganized Kodak's entire $17-billion-a-year operation into 34 strategic business units. Managers who once perched atop a marketing or production pyramid took charge of a single unit and ran it worldwide. In 1988 almost every unit, from color film to copiers, gained market share. Kodak's exports leaped 23%, to $2.7 billion.

Better Quality

Quality: The goods Americans sell overseas are far better made than they used to be. Witness that longtime invalid, automobiles: Though both General Motors and Ford have large overseas operations, Detroit doubled its export sales in 1988. The Germans, who have a long-term love affair with the Jeep Cherokee wagon, are falling for Chrysler's minivan, which began arriving there in 1988. Consultants and academics now suggest that by the early 1990s, U.S. car plants really will be turning out vehicles that are nearly the equal of Japanese autos in fit, finish, and durability. European producers are making much smaller quality gains.

Some Americans are also making up lost ground against the Japanese in semiconductors. "The rising sun has hit a peak in the sky," proclaims T.J. Rodgers, the hyperaggressive CEO of Silicon Valley's Cypress Semiconductor. The key here is improving the yield of chips on the silicon wafers used to form them. In the past, U.S. chipmakers have gotten only 20% to 30% yields of usable static random access memory chips per wafer, compared with 80% to 90% for the Japanese. But Cypress now achieves a 70% to 80% success rate.

The Japanese have been eating Americans for lunch in the production of the common memory chips known as dynamic RAMs. Back in the mid-1980s, Japanese chipmakers generated revenue of at least $200,000 per employee, vs. $60,000 to $70,000 at Intel, a leading U.S. producer. But Intel has borrowed manufacturing techniques from the Japanese, doubling revenue per employee to $138,000—vs. $230,000 for the Japanese today. Along with Motorola and Texas Instruments, Intel is making important inroads in Japan's once impenetrable home market.

Specialty goods makers are also prospering. Penmaker A.T. Cross reluctantly launched a fountain pen in Europe in 1982 because many Europeans do not use ballpoints. To its surprise, Cross found that its quality reputation carried over to the nib pen as well. It was so successful that Cross brought it back to sell in the U.S. Cross has no such problems in the Far East. It is a leader in Singapore, where it has been selling ballpoints for more than 20 years.

Cutting Costs

Cost Control: Stung above all by Japanese encroachment on their traditional markets, U.S. manufacturers have counterattacked with a vengeance. In 1984 Henry Schacht, CEO of Cummins Engine, discovered that two key American truck builders, Navistar and Freightliner, were thinking about replacing his diesels with low-priced Japanese power plants. Schacht immediately slashed prices 30%. To get profits back, he cut production costs 20% by changing manufacturing techniques, buying castings and forgings abroad, and reducing factory floor space by one-quarter. The sinking dollar provided the other 10% by allowing him to restore part of the price cut and still undersell his competitors. By 1988 Cummins had recovered all its old truck engine profit margins, though it wound up losing money overall.

Outboard Marine also used deep price cuts to fend off a Japanese assault in Europe on its Evinrude and Johnson outboard motors. It laid off 2,000 people—25% of its nonproduction work force—so it could match prices offered by the likes of Honda and Yamaha. Margins suffered, but Outboard Marine repelled the invaders. Now the company, which also owns several boatmakers including Chris-Craft, has a new gambit: marketing boat-and-motor packages in Europe. The Japanese can't compete because they cannot afford to ship an 18-foot runabout 10,000 miles.

U.S. manufacturers are generally doing a better job keeping costs down than foreign competitors are. They are getting a better hold on labor rates. In the first eight years of the 1980s, hourly compensation for U.S. manufacturing workers grew on average only 5.7% a year, vs. 8% overseas, and because of productivity increases unit labor costs in the U.S. have been virtually flat since 1986.

Though they are starting to turn up again, labor costs should give the U.S. a sharper edge in the future. Management sage Peter Drucker argues that wage levels are becoming less relevant in world competition because their share of total production costs is shrinking. Drucker says the pay of U.S. hourly workers accounts for only 18% of costs at the average plant, not including the labor component in the raw materials used. That's down from 23% a few years ago. Going offshore usually carries hidden costs—a penalty of 7.5% for transportation, communications, and the like—so low-wage foreign producers are beginning to lose their edge.

Capital Investment: Measured by the ratio of investment to manufacturing employees, the U.S. outspent both Japan and Germany from 1980 through 1986. The investment-to-worker ratio reflects the speed with which companies are bringing new technology into manufacturing—a key ingredient in global success. The Federal Reserve Bank of New York predicts that investments already made will improve U.S. productivity for some time, since the lag between investment and more efficient output is often several years.

Heads-up investment can produce large dividends, as the U.S. steel industry has proved. The mini-mills that spent heavily on technologically advanced electrical furnaces are less capital-intensive and more productive than conventional integrated mills. Chaparral Steel operates America's most productive new mill, in Midlothian, Texas, and exports steel beams to Europe and Canada. It expects an official go-ahead to supply structural steel for Japanese public projects, which would make it the first company other than South Korea's Inchon Iron & Steel to be able to do so.

Take Off the Hair Shirt

As their critics are quick to point out, U.S. industries have some distance to travel. Asia's fast-rising Four Dragons—South Korea, Taiwan, Hong Kong, and Singapore—remain the world leaders in productivity improvement. Many technologists see an urgent need for greater industry-government cooperation to prevent a shortfall in research and development spending as well as a shortage of engineers and scientists. "We need a cohesive world view through which to filter and market our technology development," argues Thomas Vanderslice, CEO of Apollo Computer, a leading workstation maker. "Only a coordinated effort involving government, business, and academia can achieve it."

Whether Vanderslice is right or not—and lots of people would give him an argument—it is long past time to take off the hair shirt. U.S. industry has accelerated enormously in the past few years, and even if the dollar continues to creep upward, further payoffs are yet to come from other improvements already in the works. Maintaining competitive supremacy, however, is like speeding down an endless highway. The smart drivers keep their feet to the floor.

5 VIEWPOINT

"We need a strategy to innovate, produce, market and sell world class products in each and every industry."

The Government Should Help Corporations Develop Technology

Robert A. Mosbacher

Robert A. Mosbacher is Secretary of Commerce for the Bush Administration. The following viewpoint is taken from a speech to a gathering of business executives in Detroit. Mosbacher argues that leadership in high technology is important for ensuring future U.S. economic competitiveness and world leadership. He advocates government-business cooperation to encourage technology development, and describes ways that the government can assist U.S. corporations in maintaining America's strengths in technology.

As you read, consider the following questions:

1. Why is technology important to America's future, according to Mosbacher?
2. According to the author, who should take the lead in researching and developing technology?
3. What are the four main challenges facing the U.S. that Mosbacher describes?

From "America's Economic Security—Recapturing the Lead in the 1990s," a speech given to the Economic Club of Detroit, May 8, 1989, by Robert A. Mosbacher.

I am pleased to speak in your great industrial center about America's challenge to ensure this nation's economic security in the 1990s.

By way of introduction, let me say that I come here as one of you. I am a businessman, the only difference being I'm on furlough to do government work.

I've been in business 40 years of my life. I'm a wildcatter. I'm a competitor. I've met a payroll. Above all, I believe that economic liberty, free markets and industrious and inventive people are the keys to a prosperous and strong America. . . .

I believe government should be your partner, not your patron. But as partners, we must kindle a greater sense of urgency to solve this nation's problems.

America at the Crossroads

America is not in decline. However, America does stand at a crossroads. We have restored this country's ability to grow. Now we must act quickly and decisively to strengthen America's ability to compete in a dramatically changing world.

Looking across the oceans toward the horizon of the 1990s, one is struck by two profound changes in the relationships between nations of the world. Change number one is the rising importance of economic power in the equation of national security and world leadership. Change number two is the leading role of high technology in the sweepstakes of world competition, and the lightning speed with which technology transforms industries, enabling strong economies to create, capture or control markets of the future.

The Auto Industry Example

Certainly, I don't have to tell the leaders of the auto industry why total quality management and applying state of the art technology from advanced materials to electronics, is a must for production of top performance, world class cars. Foreign competition forced you to face a stark choice: adapt or die. The way you adapted your production to build new model cars can serve as a role model for other industries. Today, Detroit is an automotive center and a high-tech center. Your work in robotics and composite materials keeps you at the forefront of U.S. technology.

Fortunately, others are adapting, too. We see proof not just in industries like aerospace, telecommunications, biotechnology and medical products, where we lead, but also in selected company situations in industries such as apparels.

We are doing good things. My concern is that we are still not doing as much and as well as our competitors. Unless we do better, others will ride the waves of knowledge and technologies, and they, not we, could determine what America's future will be.

Consider a moment how the reality of economic power, driven

by high technology, is changing the course of history. Thirty years ago, Nikita Khrushchev came to America and boasted that socialism would bury the West. Many believed him. Well, the Soviets have discovered the heavy burdens of trying to impose their will with a first-rate military and a third-rate economy. Thus, the wrenching decisions called "perestroika."

I do not suggest that we can let down our guard. On the contrary, as we remain militarily strong, America must gird itself to meet new challenges to our security from political allies who are now also powerful economic rivals.

No Government Mechanism

We have lacked a technology policy that can address our declining competitiveness. We have recognized that wise macro-economic and regulatory policies and the strengthening of education in mathematics, science, and engineering are all fundamental to any technology policy, but we have been reluctant to embrace another key aspect of such a policy—the government role in helping secure the national technology base. This stems from the fear that such a role is tantamount to promulgation of an industrial policy.

Thus there is no basic governmental mechanism for supporting development of the nation's civil technology.

Robert M. White, *Issues in Science and Technology*, Spring 1989.

This nation's economic security rests on a strong industrial base oriented toward global demand for products and services of the future. Yet, our new rivals are moving to control industries we pioneered and capture critical markets for our future.

Our steel industry has struggled to survive and adapt. Yet, as we know, cars today use less steel. And weapons, such as bazookas, are no longer fired with steel-made triggers, but with keyboards directed by computer guidance systems.

High Stakes

What will happen if we cannot make the right system?

The stakes are awesome. If this nation surrenders to complacency, if we lose control of industries and the production of products vital to our defense and way of life, at stake is not just American jobs and prosperity, but America's freedom.

So, when the U.S. recorded its first high-tech trade deficit in 1986, that was a red flag of warning.

When nearly half of all U.S. patents awarded went to foreign inventors in 1987, that was one more red flag of warning.

Unquestionably, we command formidable strengths. We are blessed with gifted scientists, superb universities and strong traditions of entrepreneurship and innovation. We lead the world in new knowledge and new technologies. But we could lose the most important race for the future—the race to apply and commercialize new ideas and technology; the race to move ideas from designers' labs and design boards to the marketplace.

Foreign Competition

Technology can revolutionize industries in a few years, sometimes in a matter of months—as microelectronics did computers. But, if American business sacrifices research for short-term profits, the United States will end up trying to light the road to the future with lanterns, while our competitors are lighting it with lasers. The United States will permit profit sanctuaries and technology sanctuaries to flourish in industries of Japan, Korea, Taiwan and Germany.

My intention here is not to rebuke our competitors. In fact, I admire their accomplishments. We must continue to defend the Pacific and work for democracy together. And we'll have no cause for complaint in commercial relations, if we can compete on a level playing field. I am not here to condemn our competitors but to challenge America. If our allies in the struggle for democracy are now competitors in the struggle for economic security, then let us say to them: We stand shoulder to shoulder with you in the first struggle, but we will strive to be head and shoulders above you in the second.

The United States needs a strategy to compete in the world marketplace of the 1990s—and to win. We need a strategy to innovate, produce, market and sell world class products in each and every industry.

Here is what I believe our strategy for victory must be:

We can recapture the lead with an industry-led, business-government partnership to produce, in this country, consumer products of the future that drive American research and manufacturing. [Including] products such as HDTV [high-definition television], high-tech automobiles and smart homes and products from biotechnology and superconductors.

How can that strategy succeed? By summoning the American people to meet four great challenges for the 1990s:

- Strengthening our research base and workforce skills.
- Accelerating commercialization.
- Manufacturing superior, quality products, and
- Competing and winning new global markets.

Now, when I say an industry-led, business-government relationship, I mean that we in government will work to improve the conditions for risk-taking and research. We will contest restrictive trade barriers and help you locate and gain access to global markets.

But you in the American business community must lead the way and make the critical choices. We need your R&D [research & development]. We need your commitment to compete. We need your leadership to win.

Here is how I believe our partnership must work.

Mobilizing Capital

Our first challenge—strengthening our research and workforce skills—calls for a great national drive to mobilize to the fullest America's human and financial capital.

In Washington, the president will fight to lower the capital gains tax rate. Some resist, upset that he may help the wealthy.

They miss the central point: The real question is how much longer the U.S. grants Germany and Japan a unilateral advantage to lend more money, more cheaply, to finance their ideas and technologies, because they're competing to win, and we're not.

Lowering the capital gains tax creates jobs, reduces the cost of capital and makes business think long-term. We must lower the capital gains tax for all industries. And there is no better example of where this will be helpful than in HDTV and other high-tech industries.

Strengthen Research

We must do many things to stimulate more research. We must make the R&D tax credit permanent. We must create new partnerships to carry out basic public-private research in universities and in our national labs. And, we must consider reforming antitrust laws so that consortia such as Sematech and other innovative entities can pool research teams from small and large firms to take on the European and Japanese giants.

What Governments Can Do

Although democratic governments can seldom be effective in changing industrial practice directly, they can sometimes act both as a catalyst and as a resource to business. Thus we believe that federal and state agencies can play a role in fostering the more rapid and widespread diffusion of advanced automation technologies and in encouraging new cooperative relationships—among supplier firms, and between supplier firms and their business customers.

Maryellen R. Kelley and Harvey Brooks, *Issues in Science and Technology*, Spring 1989.

We also believe government procurement should be used as a tool to supply capital to help America compete. IBM just won a $3.6 billion award to redesign all our traffic controller computer systems. Now a part of that contract includes bids for work on the control station screens. Yet only Sony made a bid.

Why? Why shouldn't an American company, or consortium of companies, bid on that contract?

New vigilance is needed to safeguard technology and protect intellectual property rights. We're being robbed of $40-60 billion a year or more by foreign companies who infringe on our patents, copyrights, trademarks and semiconductor designs. We're working for an international agreement to protect intellectual property rights.

Also, foreign competitors often face lower product liability insurance premiums, because ours vary state to state. We support passage of a uniform federal law to solve this problem.

Improve Education

Finally, I believe society should begin to bestow greater honor and compensation on people who can apply knowledge to make things work.

Education's mission as described by Thomas Edison, "The seeing of things in the making," is of paramount importance. We need a graduation line that's on-line with the future: We need a bigger pool of electrical engineers and software engineers

Above all, we need a workforce of literate, skilled men and women who understand basic math and English, who can perform in a sophisticated, high-tech environment and also change and adapt.

More research is one side of the coin. Better directed, more purposeful research—research that leads to products made and sold is the other.

Commercializing our ideas is America's Achilles Heel, and accelerating commercialization is our second greatest challenge.

We can start by borrowing a page from our competitor's playbook. Their corporations, universities and governments rarely conduct research in a vacuum. They've developed a strong strategy and spirit of teamwork to push all their research toward developing and fulfilling their commercial objectives.

What's more, their company divisions do not work in separate specialized stages, but concurrently. In Japan and Germany, researchers, design engineers and manufacturing engineers all work together in cohesive teams beginning with the initial product concept phase.

Concurrent engineering hastens product development, and increases productivity and companies' ability to compete by permitting modifications and improvements at every stage of production.

It also permits "spin-ons"—the transferring of research knowledge from one division to any other divisions that can apply it to improve a product or to create a new one.

We are now seeing more examples of concurrent engineering in America. Ford Motors has a large effort underway to promote spin-ons in everything from autos to aerospace.

We must make it our goal to instill a similar sense of mission and teamwork throughout the United States:

• To improve government-university-private sector research cooperation;

• To bring better direction to the $65 billion a year in government-supported research where more thought can be given to serving America's commercial and competitive needs; and

• To streamline the regulatory process, so pharmaceutical companies do not have to wait 7 or 10 years and spend up to $150 million to move a new drug from a chemist's lab to the pharmacy.

The end product of strong research, inspired management and smart and dedicated workers is total quality manufacturing.

The Quality Challenge

Superior quality is America's third great challenge and our economic security can demand no less. The United States will not have it made, until *Made in the USA* stands for the best quality.

I will use my position as business's point man to honor examples of excellence with the Mac Baldrige National Quality Award. Quality must be the cornerstone of American enterprise. Nothing else we do to increase competitiveness will matter if our products are not first rate. Quality begins with personal effort.

Just as top quality must stand for what we sell, so free and fair trade must stand for the policies we pursue. Winning the battle to compete and sell in foreign markets is our fourth great challenge. I am a free trader, but free trade must be a two-way street. If it's not [a] two-way street, it's a dead-end street for America.

We have enough trade laws. What we need is vigorous enforcement of the laws on the books. And with that resolve by government, let us see the fierce determination by American companies to compete and win, and to start preparing now for exciting new opportunities—such as Europe 1992.

We have the ability. We have the people. We have the ideas. We have the dreams to make great things grow.

We Can Succeed

I refuse to believe the only country on earth to send men to the moon, cannot succeed in sending far more of our products to foreign markets—and cannot meet the other challenges to our economic security in the 1990's. We surely must. We surely can.

6 VIEWPOINT

"A nation's real technological assets are the capacities of its citizens to solve the complex problems of the future."

The Government Should Not Help Corporations Develop Technology

Robert B. Reich

Robert B. Reich is a professor of political economy at the John F. Kennedy School of Government at Harvard University in Cambridge, Massachusetts. A well-known economist, he has often written on industrial policy. In the following viewpoint, he argues that U.S. government efforts to foster technology development should focus on American workers rather than American corporations. He states that because many U.S. companies do much of their research and manufacturing in other countries, assisting these companies does little to strengthen technology in the U.S. Reich argues that America's technology base is helped more by foreign companies setting up factories in the U.S. than by U.S. companies manufacturing elsewhere.

As you read, consider the following questions:

1. Why does Reich consider the concept of "American" products to be obsolete?
2. What examples does Reich cite in which foreign corporations have improved U.S. technology development?

Robert B. Reich, "Members Only," *The New Republic*, June 26, 1989. Reprinted by permission of THE NEW REPUBLIC, © 1989, The New Republic, Inc.

The news out of Washington these days may leave some liberal Democrats wondering whether they've died and gone to industrial-policy heaven. A *Republican* administration has been insisting that we subsidize sunrise industries, guard American technologies from easy access by foreign companies, and force foreign countries to open their markets to American products. This unabashed display of economic nationalism—led by Special Trade Representative Carla Hills, Commerce Secretary Robert Mosbacher, and the Pentagon's [Defense] Advanced Research Project Agency (DARPA) director, Craig Fields—is reminiscent of Richard Nixon's historic overture to Peking: only a Republican administration could so brazenly do what Democrats advocated for so long—in this case, using the powers of government to rebuild the American industrial base.

Not so fast. In evaluating national policy, one of the most important questions is the one asked by Tonto after the Lone Ranger exclaimed, "We're surrounded!" To wit: "Who's *we* kimosabe?" When Hills, Mosbacher, and Fields use the pronoun "we"—as in "we are making progress opening their markets" (Hills) or "we must promote our future technologies" (Mosbacher)—they are referring to American corporations. Yet American corporations only tangentially embody "we" Americans.

The Case of Motorola

Consider the administration's demand that foreigners open their markets to "American" products. Hills now accuses Japan of excluding Motorola from the lucrative Tokyo market for cellular telephones, and hints darkly at retaliation. But where does Motorola design its cellular telephones? In Malaysia. Where does it make the ones it is trying to sell in Japan? In a factory in Kuala Lumpur. So who will benefit if Hills's tough talk opens the Tokyo market to Motorola? A handful of Americans who provide managerial, financial, and strategic services to Motorola's worldwide operations, and a much larger number of engineers and production workers in Southeast Asia.

Motorola's American shareholders will also benefit, of course, but most of them are passive investors in pension funds, insurance funds, or mutual funds that own Motorola shares for a few days or hours. If the price of Motorola's shares rises a few points because it can now sell its pagers in Tokyo, fine. But if Carla Hills fails, there will always be another company to bet on, somewhere else in the world; American investors now roam the globe in search of quick returns. Moreover, foreign investors have also gone global; Motorola's good fortune will no doubt make some Japanese stockholders wealthier as well.

The irony runs deeper. It so happens that thousands of Americans are now making cellular telephone equipment in the

United States for export. And some of the components they produce find their way into telephones sold in the Tokyo market. But the companies these Americans work for aren't of concern to Hills because they have Japanese names and receive financing and managerial services from Japan—even though more American labor is now being exported to Japan through them than would be exported through Motorola were all trade barriers removed.

"American" Products

This pattern is emerging for a wide range of goods and services: foreigners are working for us (in the sense that the labors of foreign engineers, fabricators, and production workers are being combined with American capital and management services); and we are working for them (vice versa). Sony now exports to Europe audiotapes and videotapes made by Americans in a factory in Dotham, Alabama, and audio recorders from another plant in Fort Lauderdale. Honda sends about 50,000 cars to Asia (including Japan) from its American factories. There's even a Japanese-owned rice mill in California whose output is converted into sake, then exported to Japan. At the same time, IBM employs thousands of people in its Japanese factories and laboratories; it is now Japan's major exporter of computers. General Electric is Singapore's largest private employer. And about a third of Taiwan's trade surplus with the United States is attributable to American-owned firms making things there and shipping them back here.

National vs. Corporate Competitiveness

In any consideration of international competitiveness, it seems to me that there must be an explicit recognition of the occasional divergence of the goals of *national* competitiveness and *corporate* competitiveness. For example, if a U.S. company develops new technologies that are used in a foreign manufacturing facility, the bulk of the output of which is then imported for final assembly and sale in the United States, the company may experience great benefit but this country increases its trade deficit. . . .

Within this context, what is meant by the phrase, "to reestablish U.S. industrial leadership"? If we use public policy tools to increase the number of useful innovations generated by U.S. industrial and academic research, what guarantee is there that they will be applied in this country?

Dennis Chamot, *Issues in Science and Technology*, Fall 1988.

The very idea of "American" products made by "American" firms is becoming obsolete. Lee Iacocca warns of the Japanese invasion of America, but American-made parts now constitute a smaller portion of the top models of the Big Three than they do of Honda's top-of-the-line cars. If the Commerce Department ever imposed a domestic-content rule for determining whether Japan was exceeding its yearly quota of cars exported to the United States, the Big Three would be in serious trouble.

A trade policy that focused on enhancing the value that American workers contribute to the world economy, rather than on raising the profitability of American-*owned* companies, would place highest priority on reducing foreign barriers to American labor, especially labor involving complex design, fabrication, and non-routine production (what I have referred to elsewhere as symbolic analysis). It would, for example, take aim at rules requiring that complex products or components sold in the country be made there—even if the rules permitted American firms to easily set up shop. Yet in general the administration's new get-tough trade policy has done just the opposite—focusing on barriers to the products of footloose "American" corporations.

Technologies of the Future

The same confusion mars the administration's new thrust into "technologies of the future," such as high-definition television (HDTV) and advanced semiconductors. Consider HDTV. Japanese firms have been developing it for almost 20 years; American firms have not. Now the Pentagon's DARPA is funneling some $30 million to firms wanting to develop it, and Mosbacher thinks more money may be needed, as well as special tax breaks and exemptions from antitrust laws. Both Sony and North American Phillips (a Dutch-owned company) want to be involved in these efforts, but Mosbacher says no; our industrial policy should be solely for American companies. "We need to be in the forefront of this emerging technology," he says.

But again, the question arises: What do you mean "we"? Even if Mosbacher and his friends at the Pentagon successfully launch America's version of HDTV, it's doubtful that many, if any, of the new televisions that emerge will be designed and manufactured in America. Zenith Electronics Corporation is the only remaining American-owned television manufacturer. And many of Zenith's TVs are designed and engineered in Japan; their innards come from Japan, South Korea, and Taiwan; and all are assembled in Mexico. In fact, the only television sets now made by Americans bear the labels—you guessed it—Sony and Phillips. *These* are the companies best positioned to get Americans involved in the HDTV business.

Or consider another target of the administration's industrial policy: those fingernail-sized silicon chips on which ever tinier electronic circuits are etched. Japanese firms now make most of the world's memory chips, a fact that worries Mosbacher and Pentagon officials no end. Intent on strengthening America's chipmaking abilities, the Bush administration is now providing $100 million a year to "Sematech," a consortium of American semiconductor companies that includes Texas Instruments, Motorola, AT&T, and eight others. There is talk of even more federal money for additional computer and chip consortia, along with targeted tax breaks, antitrust immunities, and other benefits.

Helping Working People

Since World War II, the United States has not had an explicit industrial policy to guide public investment in the economy. Instead, postwar industrial policy has been implicit but active, favoring military manufacturers and, more recently, financial services. With the continued erosion of high-wage jobs and the proliferation of low-wage employment, now is the time to advocate an industrial policy that promotes the standard of living of all working people.

John Miller and Ramon Castellblanch, *Dollars & Sense*, October 1988.

But even as Sematech gets under way, its members are going global. Texas Instruments is building a new $250 million semiconductor fabrication plant in Taiwan, which by 1991 will produce four-megabit memory chips and other integrated circuits. TI has also joined with Hitachi to design and produce a "superchip" that will store 16 million bits of data. Motorola has teamed up with Toshiba to research and produce a future generation of chips. Not to be outdone, AT&T has committed to building a state-of-the-art chip-making plant in Spain. So who will be making advanced chips in the United States? Japanese-owned NEC announced plans to build a $400 million facility in Rosedale, California, for making four-megabit memory chips and other advanced devices not yet in production anywhere.

The administration's industrial policy-makers apparently think of technologies as things that a nation's citizens "own," like gold mines, machines, or other tangibles. Thus, bolstering "our" technologies is equivalent to enlarging the assets of American-owned firms, wherever on the earth these firms happen to be designing and making their newfangled products. But leading-edge technologies don't exist in three-dimensional space; they exist in people's heads. Technologies are potential insights, born of cumulative experience. Today's high-tech gadgets will be obsolete in a few years or months. A nation's real technological assets are the capacities of its citizens to solve the complex problems of the future—which depend, in turn, on their experience in solving today's and yesterday's. Thus NEC's move to Rosedale may be of more lasting value to the nation than any operation that Texas Instruments, Motorola, or AT&T opens somewhere else; it will probably build the technological experience of American engineers, technicians, and manufacturing workers more than an AT&T plant in Spain will build the technological experience of any Americans who are indirectly involved in that project.

The point is that our standard of living (and that of citizens of every other advanced economy) depends increasingly on returns to intellectual capital, rather than to physical or financial capital. Money, plants, and equipment can go anywhere, along with their corporate logos; brains, however, tend to stay put, and to teach and learn from one another in the same geographic area.

Any complex work that involves decision-making and knowledge-building—the work of factory technicians using flexible manufacturing technologies, of design and production engineers, of research scientists—adds to the nation's stock of accumulated skills, insights, and experience. Our economic future, as well as our national security, is better served by developing a large corps of technologically sophisticated workers within the nation than by boosting the profitability of America's global corporations.

What Should Be Done

An obvious first step toward that goal is to devote resources more plentifully to education, ranging from kindergarten to postdoctoral work. A second step is for the administration to encourage Sony, Phillips, NEC, or any other global company to train Americans to design and make high-definition televisions, advanced semiconductors, complex parts for jet aircraft, and other exotica of the future. Invite them in; we need the training. By the same token, any firm joining a government-organized consortium and accepting a handout from Washington should be required to design its most complex gadgets in the United States—and to make them here as well. Why give subsidies to American high-tech firms if what's discovered within a national consortium is transferred to the company's global partners or its overseas researchers and developers, who then perfect it?

The Bush administration deserves credit for bringing industrial policy out of the closet. . . .

Their present challenge is to do it right, by not confusing the interests of American corporations with the interests of Americans. For starters, when confronted by the legions of business lobbyists now parading through the corridors of power with proposals for tax relief, antitrust immunities, and other subsidies they say are necessary to make their companies and industries competitive, Bush's industrial policy-makers should ask a simple question: How will it build America's work force? For Republicans especially, this may be a hard question to keep in mind.

a critical thinking activity

Understanding Words in Context

Readers occasionally come across words which they do not recognize. And frequently, because they do not know a word or words, they will not fully understand the passage being read. Obviously, the reader can look up an unfamiliar word in a dictionary. However, by carefully examining the word in the context in which it is used, the word's meaning can often be determined. A careful reader may find clues to the meaning of the word in surrounding words, ideas, and attitudes.

Below are excerpts from the viewpoints in this chapter. One word is printed in italics. Try to determine the meaning of each word by reading the excerpt. Under each excerpt you will find four definitions for the italicized word. Choose the one that is closest to your understanding of the word.

Finally, use a dictionary to see how well you have understood the words in context. It will be helpful to discuss with others the clues which helped you decide on each word's meaning.

1. The development of the *EMBRYONIC* but rapidly advancing Japanese defense industry suggests that the U.S. might in the future become militarily dependent on Japan.

   EMBRYONIC means:

   a) slow
   b) young
   c) complacent
   d) mature

2. Auto makers don't try to invent totally new forms of transportation every year. It was *INCREMENTAL* innovation that replaced manual transmissions with automatics and resulted in power steering and power brakes.

   INCREMENTAL means:

   a) sudden
   b) expensive
   c) gradual
   d) foreign

3. Much evidence suggests that Japan has achieved *PARITY* with or even superiority over the United States in many information technologies.

   PARITY means:

   a) success
   b) equality
   c) failure
   d) dependence

4. Even in the *BELEAGUERED* industries of steel and automobiles, after years of decline an upturn is finally visible.

   BELEAGUERED means:

   a) strong
   b) struggling
   c) important
   d) heavy

5. If this nation no longer cares about its productivity and surrenders to *COMPLACENCY,* we could lose control of industries vital to our defense and our way of life.

   COMPLACENCY means:

   a) immorality
   b) lack of concern
   c) capitalism
   d) the enemy

6. Japan, not wanting to depend on the U.S. for technology, protected and supported its high technology industries in response to American *HEGEMONY* in science and technology.

   HEGEMONY means:

   a) inferiority
   b) standards
   c) pride
   d) dominance

7. American corporations only in a very minor and *TANGENTIAL* way embody "we" Americans.

   TANGENTIAL means:

   a) steadfast
   b) close
   c) realistic
   d) incidental

8. Other countries have had access to U.S. technology, while protecting their own technology from U.S. researchers. This *ASYMMETRIC* relationship must end.

   ASYMMETRIC means:

   a) fair
   b) limited
   c) unequal
   d) negotiated

9. Today the *ASCENDANT* nations, those with booming economies, are masters not of land and material resources but of ideas and technologies.

   ASCENDANT means:

   a) dominant
   b) declining
   c) largest
   d) dependent

Periodical Bibliography

The following articles have been selected to supplement the diverse views presented in this chapter.

Norm Alster	"Sprechen Sie High Tech?" *Forbes*, April 17, 1989.
W. Michael Blumenthal	"The World Economy and Technological Change," *Foreign Affairs*, America and the World 1987/1988.
Everett M. Ehrlich	"Information Technology, Global Linkage, and U.S. Competitiveness," *Vital Speeches of the Day*, October 1, 1989.
Philip Elmer-DeWitt	"Battle for the Future," *Time*, January 16, 1989.
Louis Friedman and Tim Lynch	"Science as a National Priority," *USA Today*, September 1989.
Andrea Gabor	"The Graying of Silicon Valley," *U.S. News & World Report*, October 2, 1989.
Stuart Gannes	"The Good News About U.S. R&D," *Fortune*, February 1, 1988.
Ralph E. Gomory and Harold T. Shapiro	"A Dialogue on Competitiveness," *Issues in Science and Technology*, Summer 1988.
Jerry J. Jasinowski	"Revitalizing Our Economy: Manufacturing Is the Key," *USA Today*, January 1989.
John B. Judis	"The Problem with Letting Chips Fall Where They May," *In These Times*, September 14-20, 1988.
Janet Novack	"First You Borrow, Then You Innovate," *Forbes*, May 16, 1988.
Simon Ramo	"How to Revive U.S. High Tech," *Fortune*, May 9, 1988.
Robert B. Reich	"The Rise of Techno-Nationalism," *The Atlantic Monthly*, May 1987.
Barbara Rudolph	"Eyes on the Prize," *Time*, March 21, 1988.
Adam Smith	"Putting the Byte on Japan," *Esquire*, September 1988.
Robert M. White	"Toward a U.S. Technology Policy," *Issues in Science and Technology*, Spring 1989.

CHAPTER 4

How Can American Education Be Improved?

Chapter Preface

In 1987, E.D. Hirsch's book *Cultural Literacy* received national attention. Hirsch's thesis was that the American education system was failing to teach certain cultural facts to its students. Students had no concept of a basic historical chronology, either for the U.S. or the world, for example. They also had no understanding of basic philosophical and artistic accomplishments. In addition, students could not identify geographical areas and did not know the importance of certain dates. This was why, Hirsch concluded, American students did so poorly on tests of knowledge at which their Japanese and European counterparts excelled. Hirsch called for a standard national curriculum so that each American would become "culturally literate."

While Hirsch's views do not seem very inflammatory, they nevertheless rocked the education world. Teachers argued that Hirsch's ideas would impair educational freedom and emphasize rote memorization of facts rather than serious critical analysis. These critics see the problem with American education as a lack of funding and poor pay for teachers, not what is taught.

Hirsch's book points to a pervasive issue in American education: what to teach and how to teach it. While the authors in this chapter pursue a variety of ideas, they all share a desire to improve the education of America's youth.

"A second wave of reform must include restructuring."

Schools Must Be Restructured

Bill Clinton

Bill Clinton was elected governor of Arkansas in 1978 and is now serving his fourth term. He is also chairman of the National Governors' Conference and the Educational Commission for the States (ECS), which analyzes U.S. education. In the following viewpoint, he argues that schools must be restructured to allow more control by individual schools and more involvement by business and parents. In addition, Clinton believes schools must teach students problem-solving and critical thinking skills.

As you read, consider the following questions:

1. Why does the author believe it is important to improve America's schools?
2. Why must schools teach students higher-order thinking skills, according to the author?
3. What are America's future needs, according to Clinton?

Three major concerns have dominated discussions about educational reform. First, at a time of increasing international economic competition, the productivity of the U.S. economy and work force is declining. Second, demographic shifts are altering the characteristics of students at all levels of education. Increasing numbers of elementary and secondary school students are ethnic and racial minorities. Many come from homes where English is not the dominant language. Unacceptably high numbers of young people are growing up in poverty or in social conditions that weaken motivation, capacity to learn, concern for others, and public spiritedness. A growing percentage of college students are older people hoping to start a second career or learn new skills to meet changing job requirements. Third, skepticism is mounting about the capacity of traditional public and private institutions to respond to declining productivity and demographic change. . . .

A Second Wave of Reform

It is clear that a second wave of reform is needed: the concerns that touched off the first round have intensified, and strong barriers to change remain. The Carnegie Forum on Education and the Economy recently warned that the world economy is in the midst of a "profound transformation, one that demands a new understanding of the education standards necessary to create a high-wage work force that can compete in a global economy."

Because low-wage workers with very basic skills are available in many parts of the world, the United States cannot compete successfully in the long run in industries that depend on low-wage labor. The Japanese are already learning this lesson with respect to South Korea and other newly industrialized nations in the Pacific Basin. If the United States does not move toward a high-wage, high-technology, innovative economy, each succeeding generation will have to accept a standard of living lower than the one before. Four out of 10 Americans experienced a decline in real income between 1981 and 1986, a trend that cannot be allowed to continue in the future.

Making a high-wage, high-technology economy a reality will require a radically new and different educational system in which mathematics and science are central. Even those citizens who have no interest in being technical workers will have to understand complex technical and scientific issues to make public policy and judge its effects. Vigorous basic and applied scientific research require an informed public willing to invest large amounts of public and private capital.

Mathematics and science education must not simply become more widely available and technically enriched. They must also be embedded in a broader education about the ethical, moral, and social implications of technology. In some ways our technological

Reprinted with permission from *School Is Hell* by Matt Groening. Pantheon Books, a division of Random House, Inc., New York.

expertise already exceeds our capacity to deal with its moral implications. To create a new generation of scientists ill-prepared to make morally complex social decisions would not be in the best interest of the country.

The vision of a high-technology economy calls for a higher order of general literacy. It requires a more general diffusion of inquiry skills and more widespread sophistication in reasoning, analyzing, and interpreting information. This advanced economy will demand more creativity and more capacity to adapt to rapidly changing work demands and job structures. It will also require an education that creates a stronger sense of community and an assumption of greater responsibility for the public good on the part of far more citizens than in the past. The challenge to our current institutions and our current way of doing business could not be more profound.

The continuing problems of the U.S. educational system defy easy solution and make needed reforms difficult. For the past two decades, for example, there has been a disturbing trend in the achievement of American students. The proportion of students who can perform very basic literacy tasks in reading, writing, science, and mathematics has grown slowly but steadily. However, there have been steady declines in the proportion of students demonstrating higher literacy skills such as advanced writing, problem-solving, critical thinking, ethical discourse, analysis, synthesis, interpretation, and evaluation. The most recent reports from the National Assessment of Educational Progress make it clear that although almost all U.S. students easily meet the lower literacy standards of a generation ago, most do not meet today's higher standards and are unlikely to meet tomorrow's. Not only have fewer students been exhibiting higher literacy skills and habits, but researchers paint a gloomy picture of schools' capacities to turn the trend.

Teachers Talk Too Much

In his comprehensive study of schooling, *A Place Called School*, John Goodlad of the University of Washington finds that very few classrooms are conducive to teaching higher-order thinking skills. Teachers monopolize classroom discussion, out-talking entire classrooms of students by a ratio of 12 to 1. Extended discussion, writing and rewriting, debate, contextual learning, and all of the myriad ways in which students might develop more sophisticated information-processing skills are simply not present in many classrooms. Goodlad finds that those teachers who want to cultivate such skills in their students either do not know how or are constrained by the structural conditions of teaching and schooling.

Paramount among those conditions is the need to control large numbers of restless students in a small space. Other conditions conspire with this management problem to make it difficult for teachers to try innovative programs, spend more than a few minutes on any task, attend to individual needs that require writing, or reduce their dependence on the lecture. Teacher isolation reduces opportunities for collaboration, and teachers' many noneducational duties absorb time desperately needed for planning complex learning activities. A sprawling curriculum guarantees shallow coverage of a multitude of subjects but hampers in-depth understanding of any one of them. A synoptic grasp of how different subjects relate to each other—how mathematics relates to science, for instance, or how both relate to history—is out of the question.

Most troubling, Goodlad finds that to the extent that training in higher thinking skills appears anywhere, it appears in the courses reserved for the college-bound student. Students in general education, vocational education, or in low-track courses are instructed in the basics, very fundamentally defined. These students, disproportionately minorities and disadvantaged children, at risk in many social and educational ways, are being trained with a preindustrial model of literacy that will not serve them well in the years ahead. They are subjected to the drill, practice, and rote kinds of learning that do not lead to creativity or to any capacity to interpret, analyze, synthesize, or solve problems.

Because the structures of schooling often seem to prevent radical improvements in higher literacy skills, many leaders today use the word "restructuring" when they talk about changing the educational system. Clearly, a second wave of reform must include restructuring. But there is little agreement about what the term means. It has something to do with clarifying and simplifying the goals of education. It means that more students should be able to learn what today only a handful learn. It means changes in the system of instruction, better use of time, creating an atmosphere more conducive to learning, integrating technology more efficiently, and managing and leading schools more effectively. . . .

Paying More

If Americans really want quality education, they must be willing to pay for it. . . .

Teachers are still dramatically underpaid compared with other professions that require a college education. In 1987, the average starting salary for an accountant was $21,200, new computer specialists received $26,170, and engineers began at $28,500. The average starting salary for teachers was only $17,500.

Today's education system cannot begin to prepare students for the world they will enter on graduation from high school. By 2030, when the class of 2000 will still be working, they will have had to assimilate more inventions and more new information than have appeared in the last 150 years. By 2010, there will be hardly a job in the country that does not require skill in using powerful computers and telecommunications systems.

Marvin J. Cetron, *The Futurist*, November/December 1988.

Restructuring in many cases will mean decentralizing districts stifled by their own bureaucracy and "flattening" management structures. Power can shift from "downtown" to each individual school. Extremely large schools might be broken into schools within schools. Teachers can be given a far greater say in the running of the school, much as factory workers have in some industries here and abroad. Teachers' work itself can be restructured with creative uses of technology, freeing them to work more closely with students on projects of their own or collaborative design. The teacher as repository-of-facts is already doomed by information technology; new definitions of teaching must inevitably emerge. Classrooms need not have four walls and 35 seats lined up in rows. They can be anywhere, inside or outside, as long as learning is taking place.

These kinds of restructuring face formidable obstacles. Many communities lack direction and have no strong leadership. Communication throughout the educational system is poor. Many school officials presume that as long as their students' test scores hover around the national average, they are doing all they need to do. Many others know they need to do more but do not know how. Bureaucratic constraints often discourage creative alternatives and experimentation and burden teachers with paperwork. A powerful inertia grips the system; many within it have tired of state mandates and educational fads and have decided to "wait this one out" as they have waited out reforms in the past.

If attempts are made to change a complex system through outside pressure but without the support of people inside the system, not much will happen. Conversely, people inside will never change the system radically without the help of policymakers, community leaders, and others outside the system. The governors who have been most active in educational reform over the last 5 to 10 years know that the key to success in the second wave of reform is to get those inside and outside the system to work in tandem.

2 VIEWPOINT

"The biggest reason we ought not to follow the advice of the education profession is that its ideas about the goals of schooling are mostly wrong."

Restructuring Will Not Improve Schools

Chester E. Finn Jr.

Chester E. Finn Jr., who served as assistant secretary of education from 1985 to 1988, is professor of education and public policy at Vanderbilt University in Nashville and director of the Education Excellence Network. In the following viewpoint, Finn argues that current reform proposals, including restructuring of schools, are superficial. What is needed, he believes, is a reexamination of what is failing in our schools, setting clear-cut goals, and then making the necessary reforms.

As you read, consider the following questions:

1. Why does Finn believe it is a mistake to give more power to local schools?
2. What is wrong with teaching students higher-order thinking skills, according to the author?
3. Why does Finn believe it is wrong to depend on education professionals to initiate change?

Concern with the output of the education system has proved more durable than anyone expected, and some of the actions taken in its name have been imaginative, more than a few of them courageous. Such terms as "accountability" have gained currency. One state after another has enacted "comprehensive" education-reform legislation, adding to graduation requirements, installing a kindergarten level, shrinking the average class size, obliging teachers to take literacy exams, making students pass all manner of tests, rearranging the rules for teacher licensing, experimenting with "school site management," revamping administrative arrangements, and more.

Such changes cost money, and as a nation we have been paying generously. We have also been raising teacher salaries nearly everywhere. Though impoverished schools can be found here and there, and although occasionally a school levy is rejected, the average per-pupil expenditure in American public education in 1988 was about $4,800, some $1,500 higher than when [the national education study,] *A Nation at Risk* was released in 1983. Today we are spending roughly twice as much per student in real terms as in the mid-60's, and nearly three times the level of the mid-50's. . . .

Why are we not getting better results? Why have so many sincere efforts at reform yielded so little? It is not for lack of concern, not for lack of national self-reproach, and not for want of money. . . .

Our reform efforts to date have lacked any coherent sense of exactly what results we are seeking to achieve.

In education, as in any enterprise that strives to turn one thing into another, the normal way to begin is by describing as clearly as possible the product one proposes to create. With specifications in hand, it then becomes possible to design a system that will yield the desired result. If we are clear about the skills, knowledge, habits, and attitudes a young person should possess upon emerging from school into adulthood, practically everything else can be fitted into place: the detailed curriculum, the allocation of resources, the choice of textbooks, the requisites for teaching, the amount of time (which will surely vary) individuals must spend in order to progress through the subordinate levels that accumulate into the eventual result.

Tinkering with the System

A basic failing of education-reform efforts in recent years is that they have tried to work the other way around. We have tinkered endlessly with the production system—its resources, processes, organizational arrangements, and employees—without pausing to specify the product we want to emerge at the other end. The consequence has been a lot of wasted motion.

With goals, of course, must come standards and expectations, or the goals will never be achieved. Most young people learn pretty much what they are obliged to learn by parents and teachers—and in matters academic, not a great deal more. That is why educational norms are so important, especially for disadvantaged youngsters. And that is why uncommonly demanding teachers—like Jaime Escalante, recently portrayed in the movie *Stand and Deliver* and the book *Escalante: The Best Teacher in America*—succeed.

In the absence of clear goals, it has been easy to ignore the primordial finding both of educational research and of common sense: people tend to learn that which they study, and to learn it in rough proportion to the amount of time they spend at the task.

Obvious though this maxim sounds, we have not taken it to heart. A look at the transcripts of the high-school graduating class of 1987—the youngsters who entered high school in the autumn the nation was declared "at risk"—reveals that only 30 percent of them actually took four years of English and three years each of math, science, and social studies. And even this minimalist core was unevenly distributed, with more than half of Asian-American but fewer than a quarter of black and Hispanic youngsters toiling through it.

Young People's Ignorance

Effective education would require us to relinquish some cherished metaphysical beliefs about human nature in general and the human nature of young people in particular, as well as to violate some cherished vested interests. These beliefs so dominate our educational establishment, our media, our politicians, and even our parents that it seems almost blasphemous to challenge them.

Here is an example. If I were to ask a sample of American parents, "Do you wish the elementary schools to encourage creativity in your children"? The near-unanimous answer would be, "Yes, of course." But what do we mean, specifically, by "creativity"? No one can say. In practice, it ends up being equated with a "self-expression" that encourages the youngsters' "self-esteem." The result is a generation of young people whose ignorance and intellectual incompetence is matched only by their good opinion of themselves.

Irving Kristol, *The Wall Street Journal*, October 24, 1989.

We know perfectly well that learning takes time and perspiration, yet in our high schools important academic subjects—history, chemistry, foreign languages—are commonly studied for just a single year, while in other countries they are part of *every* year's curriculum. Moreover, our children have shorter school days and school years than their peers in most of the rest of the industrialized world; they spend far fewer hours doing homework; and big chunks of the typical American school day and class period are given over to nonacademic pursuits, ranging from assembly programs to the time spent passing out and collecting materials.

Education Will Not Improve

These failings are grave. Unchanged, they will keep us from making significant educational gains. Setting them right will be arduous, maybe harder than we have the stomach for. But they are not beyond our capacities to resolve. We can, if we choose, accept the fact that it is *our* children, and the school down the street, that are "at risk." We can become clear about what we desire the education system to produce, and settle upon a satisfactory minimum level of attainment. (Several states and a number of localities are already demonstrating what a core curriculum might look like, and so is the Thatcher government in England.) And we can become much more exacting about performance standards, and more generous with the amount of time and instruction devoted to meeting them.

It is no mystery what needs doing. It is, rather, a matter of the will to do it. But here we come smack up against [another] obstacle—the one now being rolled into place by the education profession itself.

It begins with the warning, trumpeted by professional educators and their advocates in every medium at their command, that "top-down" changes of the sort urged by commissions, designed by governors, and enacted by legislatures, *cannot* yield significant gains in student learning, and that such moves actually worsen matters by curbing the professional discretion of teachers and turning them into tightly controlled educational mechanics. Instead, we are instructed, the way to make progress is to "empower" teachers and principals to do pretty much as they see fit, school building by school building.

Accompanying these notions is—no real surprise—a demand for still more money for education. The additional outlays are to go mainly for higher salaries and for hiring more teachers, the latter proposal often justified by the desire to reduce class size, begin school at a younger age, and provide more "services," especially for "children at risk."

It is obvious why educators should warm to this set of suggestions—collectively termed the "second reform movement" by Albert Shanker, president of the American Federation of Teachers—and why they have already become the conventional wisdom within the profession, filling the journals, the annual conventions, many union contract negotiations, and myriad faculty meetings at colleges of education. . . . In any event, if the new

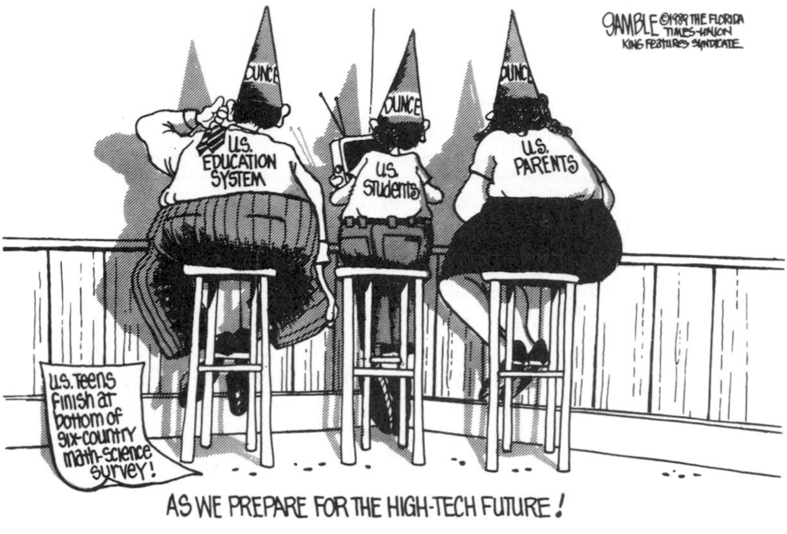

Ed Gamble. Reprinted with permission

agenda is followed, it will assuredly lead to greater public expenditures on education, endless palaver, and myriad reports and studies. It will also serve to enlarge the professional education industry. But will it do any good for students? Will they actually learn more? No one has the faintest idea, though worthwhile experiments are under way in such places as Miami, San Diego, and Rochester that may eventually shed some light on this question.

Certainly, there is much to be said in principle for cutting back the stultifying central-office bureaucracies of school systems, for recognizing the individual school as the essential unit of educational activity (and accountability), for encouraging schools to distinguish themselves from one another, and for allowing families to choose those that will best serve their children. In these respects, the "second reform movement" contains ideas that ought not to be dismissed. But we dare not romanticize the capacity of the average school, turned loose on its own, rapidly to bring about marked gains in the skills and knowledge of its students. Neither is it prudent to dash off in hot pursuit of an unproven strategy until we have corrected the mistakes in our present plan of attack.

But the biggest reason we ought not to follow the advice of the education profession is that its ideas about the goals of schooling are mostly wrong.

Simply put, the underlying problem we confront as we set about to produce more knowledgeable citizens is that few of our educators have much use for knowledge. The same is true of those who prepare them for classroom teaching, and, by and large, it is also true of the intellectual elites now propounding their own notions of how to fix the schools. *This* is the condition most menacing to the hopes and prospects of school reform.

American education is dominated by the conviction that it is not really important to know anything in particular. Facts are out. What is in is exemplified by this recent episode:

A fourth grader is assigned by the teacher to write a report about the Navaho. The teacher's instructions carefully set forth the aspects of Indian life that the students are to cover, such as dress, food, housing, rituals, and transportation.

The boy seeks assistance from his mother, who sensibly begins by asking what era the report is to describe. Spanning the entire history of the Navaho people over the millennia seems a bit much for the fourth grade; to the mother, it is plain that a report will differ enormously according to whether one is looking at the 15th century, the 19th century, or last month.

The boy does not know. The teacher has not said. So mother calls teacher to inquire about this elementary but—she thinks—fundamental feature of the class assignment. What historical period does the teacher have in mind?

The teacher, it emerges, not only has no answer, she does not think the question appropriate. The report, she says, is intended to be about Indians, not about any particular time period. "We teach the process method," she explains.

This is what E.D. Hirsch, the author of the best-selling *Cultural Literacy*, calls "educational formalism." According to this way of viewing the learning enterprise, it is not the knowledge entering one's head but the act of thinking that matters. So long as one can analyze, it is not important what is being analyzed. Knowing how to read is important, but what one reads is not. In general, it is not the role of educators to tell youngsters what they should know. It is their solemn obligation to help them "think critically."

Intellectual Skills

This emphasis on intellectual skills—"higher-order cognitive skills" is today's term of art—eases all sorts of pedagogical dilemmas. "Thinking critically" avoids the relativist's agony of having to designate "right" and "wrong" answers. It skirts those endless disputes about "canons" and about "what knowledge is of greatest value," the kind of thing that can tie up a faculty committee for months. It sidesteps the clash between supporters of a common culture and partisans of cultural pluralism (while awarding sure victory to the pluralists, since no common culture consists wholly of "reasoning skills"). It helps educators deal with the thorny issue of "values"—a term which, when used by the education establishment, signifies something one examines and at times "clarifies" rather than something one absorbs from elders, spiritual leaders, or teachers.

How to teach "higher-order cognitive skills" is the stuff of hundreds of education workshops and "in-service days" every month. Yet for all its trendiness, the notion is also of a piece with the long-prevailing philosophy of education schools and journals. This is the philosophy of progressive education, according to which the role of the teacher is not to dominate but to facilitate, and thinking creatively, being imaginative, and solving problems are preferable to following rules, internalizing traditions, and assimilating knowledge. . . .

Education and Politics

Contemporary politics enter the educational debate, often clad in progressive pedagogical garb. One might have supposed facts to be ideologically inert, elements that all might agree on even while battling furiously over explanations and interpretations. But that is not true of American education today. My colleague Diane Ravitch and I have often cited with concern the astonishing finding that only a third of the eleventh-grade students surveyed for our 1987 book *What Do Our Seventeen-Year-Olds Know?* could place the Civil War in the correct half-century. Yet here is how Professor Catherine Stimpson dismisses that concern: "We would be more literate if at least two-thirds of those kids could pin the tail of time more accurately on the donkey of war." And here is former [student radical] William Ayers—a professor of, needless to say, education—on our book:

> They are not interested in teaching as an activity that empowers the young to ask their own questions and seek their own answers. They are not concerned with teaching for self-determination, teaching for invention, teaching for transformation. They are not interested in teaching as a dialectical interplay of content and experience, past and present. . . .

In math education, among today's avant-garde the rage is for "problem solving," usually with the help of electronic calculators. "Drill and practice" are deemed archaic, and computation—those long rows of fractions to multiply and six-digit numbers to divide—is thought tiresome, hence dispensable. Nor is precision highly valued: getting the "right answer" is less important than devising a "creative" strategy for attacking the problem.

This is the view of the National Council of Teachers of Mathematics, which in March 1989 laid before the nation a whole new approach to math education. It is a view shared by the National Academy of Sciences, which has just published its own glossy tome entitled "Everybody Counts: A Report to the Nation on the Future of Mathematics Education." The panel that assembled it reads like a who's who of American education. Financial support came from four private foundations and five federal agencies. Here is a representative passage:

> Unfortunately, as children become socialized by school and society, they begin to view mathematics as a rigid system of externally dictated rules governed by standards of accuracy, speed, and memory. . . . A mathematics curriculum that emphasizes computation and rules is like a writing curriculum that emphasizes grammar and spelling: both put the cart before the horse. . . . Teachers . . . almost always present mathematics as an established doctrine to be learned just as it was taught. This "broadcast" metaphor for learning leads students to expect that mathematics is about right answers rather than about clear creative thinking. . . .

One wonders how many of Jaime Escalante's poor Hispanic students in East Los Angeles would pass Advanced Placement calculus if their teacher scorned "standards of accuracy, speed, and memory"—or how many middle-class adults could hope to balance their own checkbooks.

Science Education

As for science, millions of dollars are now being spent in a highly publicized effort by the American Assocation for the Advancement of Science (AAAS) and its allies to revamp the nation's entire educational approach to the subject. The plan differs in two large ways from customary approaches. In the words of the panel:

> One difference is that boundaries between traditional subject-matter categories are softened and connections are emphasized. . . .
>
> A second difference is that the amount of detail that students are expected to retain is considerably less than in traditional science, mathematics, and technology courses. Ideas and thinking skills are emphasized at the expense of specialized vocabulary and memorized procedures. . . .

And here are some of the classroom precepts for teachers as set forth in the AAAS report: "do not separate knowing from finding out"; "deemphasize the memorization of technical vocabulary"; "use a team approach"; "reward creativity"; "encourage a spirit of healthy questioning"; "avoid dogmatism"; "promote aesthetic responses"; "emphasize group learning"; "counteract learning anxieties.". . .

Nothing we have learned about education, past or present, at home or abroad, gives us any grounds for believing that the "process method," however elegantly refined, will ever produce people who know anything. This may seem a minor defect to educators, for whom specific knowledge is an unfashionable commodity. But it is also, finally, the reason why civilian control of education remains absolutely essential. We do not allow soldiers free rein with the "shooting method," doctors with the "surgery method," or bus drivers with the "honking method." Experts have their place. They also have their interests, and their severe limitations as shapers of policy. Left to follow their own norms, professional educators and their kindred organizations and think tanks will not just preserve the legacy of progressivism, they will enshrine the "process method" in larger, and emptier, cathedrals than ever before imagined.

Most Americans, when asked, say they want their children to know more than they do, and are appalled by the prospect that the next generation will know less. Yet so long as today's professional norms and beliefs hold sway, so long as they shape what actually occurs in the classroom, that is precisely the future that awaits our children. Changing the culture of any large enterprise is far more difficult than altering the specific policies by which it operates. But that is the central task confronting us—and also, one might add, confronting the man who would be our "education President."

3 VIEWPOINT

"The submediocre performance of American youngsters in science and math . . . should sound an urgent alarm."

Science Education Must Be a National Priority

Carl Sagan

Carl Sagan is an internationally known scientist, writer, speaker, and television personality. He is David Duncan Professor of Astronomy and Space Sciences, director of the Laboratory for Planetary Studies at Cornell University, and the author of many articles and books, including *Cosmos* and *Dragons of Eden*. In the following viewpoint, Sagan deplores the American public's lack of science knowledge. He argues that in order for America to remain competitive in technology and engineering, science education must become a national priority.

As you read, consider the following questions:

1. What point is the author making when he starts his viewpoint with the anecdote about the cab driver?
2. Why does Sagan think it is essential that everyone know more about science?
3. What are some of Sagan's recommendations for science education?

Carl Sagan, "Why We Need to Understand Science," *Parade*, September 10, 1989. Reprinted with permission from Parade, copyright © 1989.

As I got off the plane, he was waiting for me, holding up a sign with my name on it. I was on my way to a conference of scientists and TV broadcasters, and the organizers had kindly sent a driver.

"Do you mind if I ask you a question?" he said as we waited for my bag. "Isn't it confusing to have the same name as that science guy?"

It took me a moment to understand. Was he pulling my leg? "I *am* that science guy," I said. He smiled. "Sorry. That's my problem. I thought it was yours too." He put out his hand. "My name is William F. Buckley." (Well, his name wasn't *exactly* William F. Buckley, but he did have the name of a contentious TV interviewer, for which he doubtless took a lot of good-natured ribbing.)

As we settled into the car for the long drive, he told me he was glad I was "that science guy"—he had so many questions to ask about science. Would I mind? And so we got to talking. But not about science. He wanted to discuss UFOs, "channeling" (a way to hear what's on the minds of dead people—not much it turns out), crystals, astrology. . . . He introduced each subject with real enthusiasm, and each time I had to disappoint him: "The evidence is crummy," I kept saying. "There's a much simpler explanation." As we drove on through the rain, I could see him getting glummer. I was attacking not just pseudoscience but also a facet of his inner life.

Real Science Is Exciting

And yet there is so much in real science that's equally exciting, more mysterious, a greater intellectual challenge—as well as being a lot closer to the truth. Did he know about the molecular building blocks of life sitting out there in the cold, tenuous gas between the stars? Had he heard of the footprints of our ancestors found in 4-million-year-old volcanic ash? What about the raising of the Himalayas when India went crashing into Asia? Or how viruses subvert cells, or the radio search for extraterrestrial intelligence or the ancient civilization of Ebla? Mr. "Buckley"—well-spoken, intelligent, curious—had heard virtually nothing of modern science. He *wanted* to know about science. It's just that all the science got filtered out before it reached him. What the society permitted to trickle through was mainly pretense and confusion. And it had never taught him how to distinguish real science from the cheap imitation.

All over America there are smart, even gifted, people who have a built-in passion for science. But that passion is unrequited. A recent survey suggests that 94% of Americans are "scientifically illiterate."

We live in a society exquisitely dependent on science and technology, in which hardly anyone knows anything about science and technology. This is a clear prescription for disaster. It's dangerous and stupid for us to remain ignorant about global warming, say, or ozone depletion, toxic and radioactive wastes, acid rain. Jobs and wages depend on science and technology. If the United States can't manufacture, at high quality and low price, products people want to buy, then industries will drift out of the United States and transfer a little prosperity to another part of the world. Because of the low birthrate in the '60s and '70s, the National Science Foundation projects a shortage of nearly a million professional scientists and engineers by 2010. Where will they come from? What about fusion, supercomputers, abortion, massive reductions in strategic weapons, addiction, high-resolution TV, airline and airport safety, food additives, animal rights, superconductivity, Midgetman vs. rail-garrison MX missiles, going to Mars, finding cures for AIDS and cancer? How can we decide national policy if we don't understand the underlying issues?

Threatening America

By the year 2000, the U.S. will need between 450,000 and 750,000 more chemists, biologists, physicists and engineers than it is expected to produce.

The science deficit threatens America's prosperity and possibly even its national security. Economically, the nation will be unable to compete with rising technological giants like Japan, South Korea and West Germany.

Susan Tifft, *Newsweek*, September 11, 1989.

I know that science and technology are not just cornucopias pouring good deeds out into the world. Scientists not only conceived nuclear weapons; they also took political leaders by the lapels, arguing that *their* nation—whichever it happened to be—had to have one first. Then they arranged to manufacture 60,000 of them. Our technology has produced thalidomide, CFCs [chlorofluorocarbons], Agent Orange, nerve gas and industries so powerful they can ruin the climate of the planet. There's a *reason* people are nervous about science and technology.

And so the image of the mad scientist haunts our world—from Dr. Faust to Dr. Frankenstein to Dr. Strangelove to the white-coated loonies of Saturday morning children's TV. (All this doesn't inspire budding scientists.) But there's no way back. We can't just conclude that science puts too much power into the hands of morally feeble technologists or corrupt, power-crazed politicans and decide to get rid of it. Advances in medicine and agriculture have saved more lives than have been lost in all the wars in history. Advances in transportation, communication and entertainment have transformed the world. The sword of science is double-edged. Rather, its awesome power forces on all of us, including politicians, a new responsibility—more attention to the long-term consequences of technology, a global and transgenerational perspective, an incentive to avoid easy appeals to nationalism and chauvinism. Mistakes are becoming too expensive.

Science is much more than a body of knowledge. It is a way of thinking. This is central to its success. Science invites us to let the facts in, even when they don't conform to our preconceptions. It counsels us to carry alternative hypotheses in our heads and see which best match the facts. It urges on us a fine balance between no-holds-barred openness to new ideas, however heretical, and the most rigorous skeptical scrutiny of everything—new ideas *and* established wisdom. We need wide appreciation of this kind of thinking. It works. It's an essential tool for a democracy in an age of change. Our task is not just to train more scientists but also to deepen public understanding of science.

How Bad Is It? Very Bad

"It's Official," reads one newspaper headline: "We Stink in Science." Less than half of all Americans know that the Earth moves around the Sun and takes a year to do it—a fact established a few centuries ago. In tests of average 17-year-olds in many world regions, the U.S. ranked dead last in algebra. On identical tests, the U.S. kids averaged 43% and their Japanese counterparts 78%. In my book, 78% is pretty good—it corresponds to a C+, or maybe even a B− ; 43% is an F. In a chemistry test, students in only two of 13 nations did worse than the U.S. Compared to us, Britain, Singapore and Hong Kong were so high they were almost off-scale, and 25% of Canadian 18-year-olds knew just as much chemistry as a select 1% of American high school seniors (in their second chemistry course, and most of them in "advanced" programs). The best of 20 fifth-grade classrooms in Minneapolis was outpaced by every one of 20 classrooms in Sendai, Japan, and 19 out of 20 in Taipei, Taiwan. South Korean students were far ahead of American students in all aspects of mathematics and science, and 13-year-olds in British Columbia (in Western Canada) outpaced their U.S. counterparts across the boards (in some areas they did better than the Koreans). Of the U.S. kids, 22% say they dislike school; only 8% of the Koreans do. Yet two-thirds of the Americans, but only a quarter of the Koreans, say they are "good at mathematics."

Why We're Flunking

How do British Columbia, Japan, Britain and Korea manage so much better than we do?

During the Great Depression, teachers enjoyed job security, good salaries, respectability. Teaching was an admired profession, partly because learning was widely recognized as the road out of poverty.

Little of that is true today. And so science (and other) teaching is too often incompetently or uninspiringly done, its practitioners, astonishingly, having little or no training in their subjects—sometimes themselves unable to distinguish science from pseudoscience. Those who do have the training often get higher-paying jobs elsewhere.

We need more money for teachers' training and salaries, and for laboratories—so kids will get hands-on experience rather than just reading what's in the book. But all across America, school-bond issues on the ballot are regularly defeated. U.S. parents are much more satisfied with what their children are learning in science and math than are, say, Japanese and Taiwanese parents—whose children are doing so much better. No one suggests that property taxes be used to provide for the military budget, or for agriculture, or for cleaning up toxic wastes. Why just education? Why not support it from general taxes on the local and state levels? What about a special education tax for those industries with special needs for technically trained workers?

American kids don't do enough schoolwork. The average high school student spends 3.5 hours a week on homework. The total time devoted to studies, in and out of the classroom, is about 20 hours a week. Japanese *fifth*-graders average 33 hours a week.

But most American kids aren't stupid. Part of the reason they don't study hard is that they've received few tangible benefits when they do. Competency (that is, actually knowing the stuff)

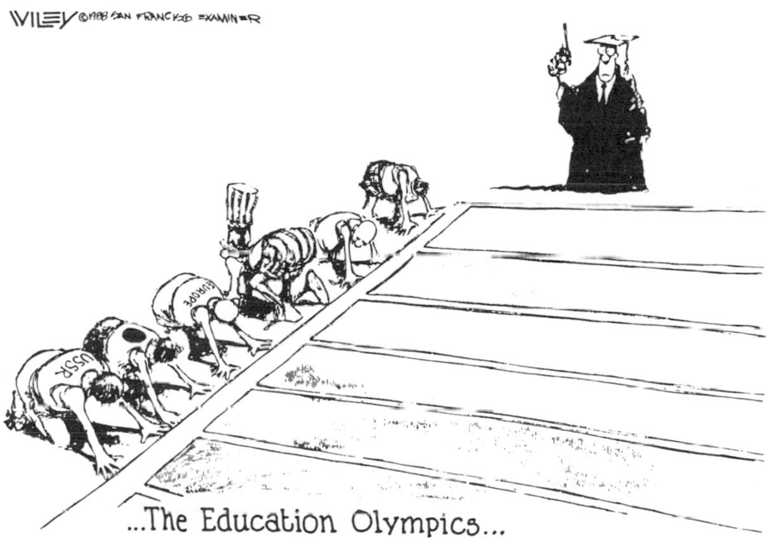

Wiley. Reprinted with permission of *The San Francisco Examiner.* © 1989 The San Francisco Examiner

in verbal skills, mathematics and science these days doesn't increase earnings for average young men in their first eight years out of high school—many of whom take service rather than industrial jobs. . . .

What We Can Do

Those in America with the most favorable view of science tend to be young, well-to-do, college-educated white males. But three-quarters of new American workers between now and 2001 will be women, nonwhites and immigrants. Discriminating against them isn't only unjust, it's also self-defeating. It deprives the American economy of desperately needed skilled workers.

Black and Hispanic students are doing better in standardized science tests now than in the late 1960s, but they're the only ones who are. The average math gap between white and black U.S. high school graduates is still huge—two to three grade levels; but the gap between white U.S. high school graduates and those in, say, Japan, Canada, Great Britain or Finland is more than *twice* as big. If you're poorly motivated and poorly educated, you won't know much—no mystery here. Suburban blacks with college-educated parents do just as well in college as suburban whites with college-educated parents. Enrolling a poor child in a Head Start program doubles his or her chances to be employed later in life; one who completes an Upward Bound program is four times as likely to get a college education. If we're serious, we know what to do.

What about college and university? There are obvious steps similar to what should be done in high schools: salaries for teachers that approach what they could get in industry; more scholarships, fellowships and laboratory equipment; laboratory science courses required of everyone to graduate; and special attention paid to those traditionally steered away from science. We should also provide the financial and moral encouragement for academic scientists to spend more time on public education—lectures, newspaper and magazine articles, TV appearances. This requires scientists to make themselves understandable and fun to listen to. To me, it seems strange that some scientists, who depend on public funding for their research, are reluctant to explain to the public what it is that they do. Fortunately, the number of scientists willing to speak to the public—and capably—has been increasing each year. But there are not yet nearly enough.

Virtually every newspaper in America has a daily astrology column. How many have a daily science column? When I was growing up, my father would bring home a daily paper and consume (often with great gusto) the baseball box scores. There they were, to me dry as dust, with obscure abbreviations (W, SS, SO, W-L, AB, RBI), but they spoke to him. Newspapers everywhere printed them. I figured maybe they weren't too hard for me. Eventually I too got caught up in the world of baseball statistics. (I know it helped me in learning decimals, and I still cringe a little when I hear that someone is "batting a thousand." But 1.000 is not 1,000. The lucky player is batting one.) . . .

Television as Teacher

By far the most effective means of raising interest in science is television. There's lots of pseudoscience on TV, a fair amount of medicine and technology, but hardly any science—especially on the three big commercial networks, whose executives think science programming means ratings declines and lost profits, and nothing else matters. Why in all America is there no TV drama that has as its hero someone devoted to figuring out how the Universe works?

Stirring projects in science and technology attract and inspire youngsters. The number of science Ph.D.s peaked around the time of the Apollo program and declined thereafter. This is an important potential side-effect of such projects as sending humans to Mars, or the Superconducting Supercollider to explore the fine structure of matter, or the program to map all human genes.

Life Better for All

Technology, developed and utilized by an enlightened citizenry, offers tremendous potential to improve virtually all material aspects of our lives. If as a nation we begin now to make the investments necessary to advance our technology, improve our educational system, and enhance the power of private enterprise, our children will be able to take advantage of advances in computers and communications, in microelectronics and the life sciences, and activities in space and under the ocean to make life here on earth better for all.

Lawrence P. Grayson, *The World & I*, November 1988.

Every now and then, I'm lucky enough to teach a class in kindergarten or the first grade. Many of these children are curious, intellectually vigorous, ask provocative and insightful questions and exhibit great enthusiasm for science. When I talk to high school students, I find something different. They memorize "facts." But, by and large, the joy of discovery, the life behind those facts, has gone out of them. They're worried about asking "dumb" questions; they're willing to accept inadequate answers; they don't pose follow-up questions; the room is awash with sidelong glances to judge, second-by-second, the approval of their peers. Something has happened between first and 12th grade, and it's not just puberty. I'd guess that it's partly peer pressure *not* to excel (except in sports); partly that the society teaches short-term gratification; partly the impression that science or math won't buy you a sports car; partly that so little is expected of students; and partly that there are so few role models for intelligent discussion of science and technology or for learning for its own sake.

But there's something else: Many adults are put off when youngsters pose scientific questions. Children ask why the Sun is yellow, or what a dream is, or how deep you can dig a hole, or when is the world's birthday or why we have toes. Too many teachers and parents answer with irritation or ridicule, or quickly move on to something else. Why adults should pretend to omniscience before a 5-year-old, I can't for the life of me understand. What's wrong with admitting that you don't know? Children soon recognize that somehow this kind of question annoys many adults. A few more experiences like this, and another child has been lost to science.

Don't Be Afraid to Say I Don't Know

There are many better responses. If we have an idea of the answer, we could try to explain. If we don't, we could go to the encyclopedia or the library. Or we might say to the child: "I don't know the answer. Maybe no one knows. Maybe when you grow up, you'll be the first to find out."

But mere encouragement isn't enough. We must also give children the tools to winnow the wheat from the chaff. I'm haunted by the vision of a generation of Americans unable to distinguish reality from fantasy, hopefully clutching their crystals for comfort, unequipped even to frame the right questions or to recognize the answers. I want us to rescue Mr. "Buckley" and the millions like him. I also want us to stop turning out leaden, incurious, unimaginative high school seniors. I think America needs, and deserves, a citizenry with minds wide awake and a basic understanding of how the world works.

Public understanding of science is more central to our national security than half a dozen strategic weapons systems. The submediocre performance of American youngsters in science and math, and the widespread adult ignorance and apathy about science and math, should sound an urgent alarm.

VIEWPOINT 4

"If educators insist on crying 'the sky is falling,' they had better be sure that it is."

Calls for Science Education Are Superficial

Morris H. Shamos

Morris H. Shamos is emeritus professor of physics at New York University and a past president of both the National Science Teachers Association and the New York Academy of Sciences. He now heads a consulting firm in the high technology field and is author of *The Myth of Scientific Literacy*. In the following viewpoint, Shamos argues that calls for more science education are not enough. Proponents cannot prove that proposals such as more money, more mandatory courses, and better facilities will improve general knowledge about science.

As you read, consider the following questions:

1. What was the "crisis" in science education, according to Shamos?
2. What does the author believe is wrong with simply encouraging minority students to major in science?
3. Does the author come to any conclusions about what science education can achieve? Why or why not?

Science education has just weathered a crisis—at least that is the impression given by those who declared its existence in the first place. . . .

The reasons given for the crisis? A dearth of qualified science teachers, a lack of interest among students for careers in science, and declining test scores—all of which threatened to produce shortages of scientists and engineers. Worse yet was the alarming possibility that unless all citizens became scientifically literate they would be unable to function properly in the workplace, or even as intelligent voters and consumers. Before long, it was feared, we might become a second-rate nation. . . .

The crisis quickly took on a life of its own as numerous non-scientific groups and legislators added their voices to the outcry. And it was not all lip service. A number of states and local communities, fearing the worst, took direct action by mandating more science and mathematics in their schools. Most increased salaries and incentives for teachers, a measure that must be counted as the single most productive response to the cry of "crisis." Science-oriented programs and activities outside the classroom were initiated in many communities and school systems. The news media began showing renewed interest in science and education. Several new science magazines aimed at the layperson were launched (some of which have since failed). There seemed to be no end to how far the snowball would roll.

Such was the genesis of the crisis. Suddenly, a few years later, the crisis was over. "What was a clamor in 1982 has diminished to a murmur in 1986," reported Ward Worthy in *Chemical and Engineering News.* The signs of crisis—the reports, the media attention, the political activity—had all tapered off.

Yet crises by their nature vanish only when the causes are removed or when solutions are in sight. As anyone in education fully appreciates, it is impossible to effect significant educational change overnight; hence if the responses in this case were mostly limited to reports and promises of action, what made the crisis disappear? The irresistible conclusion is that the crisis never really existed—it was mostly smoke, with perhaps a little fire behind it. . . .

Defining the Problems

The cry of "crisis" may have been false, but what has happened to these other issues—problems such as low student interest in science and poor scientific literacy? We don't hear as much about them now, because the science education community, perhaps reassured that someone in Washington cares about them after all, seems to have adopted a wait-and-see attitude. Nevertheless, there are some real problems, and a few years of commotion have done nothing to solve them. In fact, science education continues to face the same problems that surfaced 30 years ago when Sputnik was launched.

If the problems have not been solved with all the resources poured into them in the past—nearly a billion NSF [National Science Foundation] dollars for precollege activities alone since the mid-fifties, plus a larger sum expended under the Elementary and Secondary Education Act of 1965—is there any hope of solving them in the future? That depends upon the objectives. If we continue to state the problems of science education in vague, unsubstantiated terms, then our efforts are doomed.

To Change the Status Quo

Science teaching and testing tend to be divorced from present educational theory. Educators have argued convincingly for greater emphasis on higher-order thinking skills and for integration of hands-on and laboratory projects in the classroom. Yet current practice tends to emphasize results rather than processes, to rely heavily on memorization of facts rather than the understanding of concepts, and to incorporate few activities involving students in experimentation with a variety of materials and apparatus.

Until innovators are given sufficient opportunity to conduct further research on alternative assessments and instructional practices, we will not be able to put theory to the test.

Lynn B. Jenkins, *Issues in Science and Technology*, Spring 1989.

For example, those who believe we must encourage more students, especially minority students, to go into science and engineering have yet to show unambiguous evidence of an impending manpower shortage. Yet they blithely assume that jobs in these fields will be available for all who qualify. This is not the way our economy works. We have seen spot shortages of scientists and engineers in the past, and will continue to see them in the future, simply because the supply cannot be turned on and off as quickly as the demand. But the same is true of surpluses in the field, and we have seen times when engineers were pumping gas or driving cabs. It would be irresponsible of the educational community to train more scientists and engineers than the economy can absorb, just as it was irresponsible to warn of a manpower crisis without accurately quantifying the problem. What many fail to realize is that in the final analysis the scientific manpower pool is limited more by demand in the job market than by any shortcomings of the educational system.

Vaguer still is the problem of achieving widespread "scientific literacy" in our population. Educators have no idea how best to define such literacy, let alone achieve it. It is not at all obvious that improving precollege science education or requiring more science for all students will lead to scientific literacy. The real test, if such literacy is to contribute to society, is its staying power. Compulsory science courses, both precollege and college, may appear to be successful on the basis of test scores at the time. But do they turn the students into literate adults later on? The evidence here, however one chooses to define scientific literacy, is very discouraging indeed. The reason is that most students see no real need to understand science or math, and hence to make the necessary effort.

Roughly 10 percent of our high school freshmen express an interest in science as a career, with about half this group actually going on to become natural scientists, mathematicians, or engineers. The remaining 90 percent, so-called "general students," are the main target for efforts to achieve widespread scientific literacy. These students will have no contact with science—not directly, anyway—for the rest of their lives. How do we persuade this group to seek a sound understanding of science? Do we simply say, as we have so often said in the past, "It will make you a better citizen, one who will be better able to think critically and to exercise independent judgment on science-based issues, which are bound to increase in the future"? If we do, the student, looking about at contemporary society, could very well respond: "But will it make me a better lawyer, or businessperson, or historian?"

Logic favors the student in such a debate. First of all, we have no evidence that given the best possible curriculum, the best-prepared teachers, and increased science requirements (within reason), we can educate most children to become scientifically literate adults. Nor can we show that adults who are modestly literate in science will exercise better judgment on science-based issues. Many of these issues are simply too complex, even for scientists, as witness the "Star Wars" debate. Moreover, most science-based issues also have an emotional ingredient that distorts people's judgment regardless of how literate they may be in science. . . .

Will More Education Help?

Despite our efforts over the past half century to instill reasoning into students, we still find that when it conflicts with politics or religion, or with any other emotionally charged domain, reason is often the loser.

Of course, there is a more persuasive argument for scientific literacy than the claim that it improves one's judgment on science-based issues. Educators often argue these days that as we move toward a more technological economy, those who have a good understanding of science will find better opportunities in the workplace. This rings true. But so far the prescription suffers from

Rising to the technological challenge, American education makes science more exciting, more compelling, more fun!
AND HERE COMES TOMMY THE TEST TUBE ... HOP! HOP! HOP!
DANZIGER
The Christian Science Monitor

Danziger in The Christian Science Monitor © 1989 TCSPS

a lack of specificity. Students and teachers both ask: "What science or technology, and what degree of understanding, will satisfy this need?" Here the science education community, and scientists generally, have failed to reach any sort of agreement.

What of the students who are science bound? Are they well served by the educational system? With perhaps minor exceptions, the evidence (in terms of numbers and quality of professionals in the field) suggests that they are. Certainly, better facilities and better-trained teachers would provide such students with a richer experience, but for the most part these are highly motivated achievers who manage to overcome most of the obstacles they may find in their early education. In any event, improving the precollege education of science-bound students is obviously a far easier task than developing scientific literacy in all students.

We appear to have come full circle since the post-Sputnik days, when support for science education was abundant and educational experiments flourished. We also appear fated to repeat many of the mistakes that were made then. Science teachers take as a given that improving education in their subject will contribute to the national good. This may be true, but it will never be demonstrated as long as they continue to state the objectives of science education in terms that are lacking in reason or practicality or specifics.

Imperative at this point is a fundamental assessment of what science education can reasonably be expected to achieve. If literacy for all is to become a reasonable goal, the term must first be circumscribed as precisely as possible. One could then examine whether such literacy is best achieved through precollege and/or undergraduate college programs, or through adult (continuing) education programs, where its chance of long-term survival may be greater. Either way, realistic incentives will have to be found to make the target audience receptive to the concept.

Gauging Success

Science educators must also find better ways to gauge the success of their efforts. Test scores are useful only to a point. As a basis for comparing the science achievement of U.S. and foreign students—comparisons in which the U.S. students generally suffer—they are seriously misleading. One must take into account that students in other countries often have a greater incentive for academic performance. No other nation in the world enjoys the equivalent of universal higher education. We reap enormous social and economic benefits from this system, but part of the price we pay is an overall decrease in competitive spirit and student motivation, particularly in school science.

As indicators of future scientific literacy, moreover, test scores are virtually meaningless. New modes of measurement must be devised for predicting such long-range effects. In the end, the only reliable measure may turn out to be carefully designed studies that track individuals over time.

If there is a real concern about future manpower shortages, these must be quantified as to type and numbers. Where teacher shortages are claimed to exist, it should be acknowledged that the real issue is not just the number of teachers but the number of *qualified* teachers. It should also be shown how and to what extent such shortages affect both the science-bound and the general student. Finally, and most important, if the science education community sincerely believes that the future workplace will demand technical sophistication from most nonscientists—beyond the simple operation of computers—it must specify the type and level of sophistication needed, so that teachers as well as students know what is expected of them. Vague pronouncements in this regard do a great disservice to all concerned.

Unless the science education community begins to rigorously apply the test of reason to its pronouncements, its worst fears will be realized: The current round of support for improvements in science education will be no more successful than the last, and future support for its pet projects will dry up completely. In short, if educators insist on crying "the sky is falling," they had better be sure that it is.

5

VIEWPOINT

"Global education programs aim to foster in U.S. students greater understanding of other peoples and cultures."

Schools Should Teach Global Education

The Ad-Hoc Committee on Global Education

In 1986, the National Council of the Social Studies Board of Directors established an ad-hoc committee to examine the controversy over global education. The following viewpoint is an excerpt from their report. In it, the authors argue that global education must be used to improve students' knowledge of the world. American students' lack of global knowledge may seriously impede America's future in world finance and foreign policy, conclude the authors.

As you read, consider the following questions:

1. What is the purpose of global education, according to the authors?
2. What do the authors believe is wrong with current criticisms of global education?
3. What are the committee's recommendations for curricular materials for global education?

The Ad-Hoc Committee on Global Education of the National Council for the Social Studies, "Global Education: In Bounds or Out?" Reprinted from *Social Education*, April/May 1987, vol. 51, no. 4, pp. 242-249.

Global education has grown rapidly in the past two decades. As a "movement," it embraces a large variety of actors, institutions, and ideas. Global education's growth stems in part from increased national recognition of the importance of knowledge about other nations. The Southern Governors' Association report of November 1986 bemoans the "international illiteracy" of American youngsters, who know less about the world than their counterparts in other advanced industrial nations.

[Former] Secretary of Education William J. Bennett recognized this need in an address on "America, the World, and Our Schools" in which he affirmed, "We have global responsibilities, and international politics have a more pressing claim on our attention than ever before. We need to know—and pass on to our children—as much about the world as we possibly can."

Ignorance of other nations and cultures will not serve the United States well as it competes in an international economy and seeks to exercise leadership in a changing and interdependent system of states and alliances. The Southern Governors' Association report states, "The best jobs, largest markets, and greatest profits belong to those who understand the country with which they are doing business," and further, "Americans do not realize the effect our international ignorance has on our national security."

Debate Welcomed

Criticism of global education is by no means an infringement of academic freedom. Debate about global education is appropriate and desirable for clarifying its aims, identifying points of contention, and clearing up problems. . . . How might the debate proceed more fruitfully? What are the issues that give rise to concern or dissent?

Global education clearly promotes certain values, and there can be confusion and conflict about some of them. For example, does global education foster attitudes that are at odds with patriotism and national loyalty?

Many of the goals of global education, such as thinking, valuing diversity, seeing commonalities, and many of the processes and methods common in global education, Willard Kniep [an official of the Global Perspectives in Education program,] points out, are valuable, but not distinctive. From his analysis of curriculum materials and the literature, Kniep settles on the idea that what defines and characterizes global education is its substantive focus. The following four elements are basic and essential to a global education:

a. The study of human values: both the universal human values that transcend group identity and the diverse values that define group membership and contribute to our unique perspectives and worldviews

b. The study of global economic, political, ecological, and technical systems

c. The study of global issues and problems: peace and security, development, environment, and human rights

d. The study of global history

Tackling the Problems Facing Our Planet

We live in a world where people and nations are increasingly connected with one another economically, politically, technologically, and ecologically; therefore, today's young people also need a sense of global history, an awareness of common human aspirations, and the will and abilities to tackle the great problems facing not only our own nation but the entire planet.

The global education movement has responded to this need by attempting to influence the curriculum in elementary and secondary schools. It has focused on educating teachers and on changing their curriculums and classrooms. These strategies, often supported with funds from government or foundation sources, have helped teachers infuse global perspectives and concepts into existing programs.

Willard M. Kniep, *Educational Leadership*, September 1989.

One of the underlying assumptions of global education is that better understanding of the world and its people will bring us considerably closer to a better and more just world—one that is more stable and cooperative and less divided by conflict and hostility. It is hard to take exception to the desire for a better and more just world, but certain confusions can arise about how acquiring a "global perspective" is supposed to promote this outcome. Global educators sometimes fuse two very different ideas. We can see the potential problem in a rather vague statement from the Michigan Department of Education's *Guidelines for Global Education*:

> Global Education requires an understanding of the values and priorities of the many cultures of the world. . . . Global Education leads to the implementation and application of the global perspective in striving for just and peaceful solutions to world problems.

The second proposition in this quotation lends itself to more than one interpretation. On the first interpretation, it may be taken to suggest that better understanding of others itself promotes justice and peace. On the second interpretation, it may be taken to suggest that global education promotes taking up a certain point of view for judging international conflicts—namely, the "global" point of view. If this second interpretation means that, whenever there is a conflict between the United States and one or more other countries, a U.S. citizen should always support the resolution that is best for the world as a whole, it is obvious how global education, on this interpretation, would be controversial. It would teach a lesson that, on its face anyway, seems at odds with the special loyalties and commitments that characterize communities.

Patriotism and Education

Better understanding of the world is one thing. Refusing to give special weight to your country's welfare or to your own countrymen is quite another. If global education is thought to teach the latter, then it will be perceived as promoting attitudes that are at odds with patriotism and national loyalty.

Basic principles of morality and justice require that the interests of all humanity be taken into account, but these basic principles have to be implemented in a world of nations and communities, constituted of special loyalties and commitments. How our duties to our own are to be adjusted to our duties to humanity remains a persistent problem. There is as wide a range of answers among global educators as among the public at large. Nevertheless, unclear and confused statements of the aims of global education can fuel the perception that it aspires to inculcate a "one-worldism" that fails to give due place to national loyalties and special duties.

The concept of relativism, as it is used in much of the global education literature, can also be a source of confusion and misinterpretation. Global education programs aim to foster in U.S. students greater understanding of other peoples and cultures. Such understanding serves a distinctly moral goal: to promote tolerance and respect for peoples different from ourselves. Tolerance and respect have to be worked at because of our natural proclivity to measure the worth of others by their similarity to ourselves and our customs. There are two reasons in particular why it is morally valuable to cultivate a check on this proclivity and to encourage caution about passing judgment on others.

Ignorance and Arrogance

First, we are often very ignorant about the cultural and political institutions of other peoples, and judgments made in ignorance run great risks of being inaccurate and unfair. Comparing others unfavorably to ourselves often reflects no more than unthinking chauvinism and arrogance.

Second, students often fail to distinguish between fundamental values and their institutional forms. The same basic value can be given life in different societies through different customs and conventions. It is good, for example, to show respect to people and not give them needless insult. The specific conventions of politeness, however, through which this good is accomplished need not be the same everywhere and, indeed, differ from society to society.

Likewise, it is important that the helpless, ill, and weak be cared for; but different patterns of family life and social support may accomplish this care. Thus, although other peoples have different conventions from ours, they need not differ in their fundamental values. It is hasty and insensitive to depreciate another group because it does not share our conventions and customs.

Cultural Relativism

Global educators and global education materials sometimes speak of "cultural relativism." Generally this phrase is just a way of referring to the fact that cultures differ from one another in their beliefs and customs. Not infrequently, however, it gets confused, by both global educators and their critics, with "moral relativism." People sometimes try to support tolerance and respect by saying things like "their customs are what is right for them and our customs are what is right for us" and "all customs are equally valid." These propositions are often joined to the more explicit conclusion that judgments of moral right and wrong cannot be made across cultures (moral relativism).

Moral relativism is a confusing, or confused, way of supporting tolerance and respect. It is confusing if it is meant as just another way of recommending tolerance and respect. It is confused if it

HIYA DOON', SWEETHEART! I'M BUD BUDSON FROM AMERICAN THINGUMMIES, ELKHART, INDIANA. YOU LOOK LIKE YOU NEED A NEW THINGUMMY.
YA GET ME?
SAVVY?
CABEESH?
JEFF DANZIGER - STAFF

Danziger in The Christian Science Monitor © 1989 TCSPS

is meant as a philosophical thesis about the scope of moral judgment.

First of all, the philosophical thesis is a thesis *about* morality; but tolerance and respect are themselves moral values that have to be supported and defended from *within* morality. That is why it is confusing to intend by moral relativism to convey no more than a policy of being tolerant and respectful.

Second, the philosophical thesis taken literally undercuts support for tolerance and respect. Moral relativism tells us not to pass judgment on another society or culture. Suppose, however, that that society or culture is itself aggressively intolerant and disrespectful of others. If we refuse to condemn intolerance and disrespect in it, why do we have reason to condemn it in ourselves? How can we believe tolerance and respect are centrally important values without believing they are important for others too? Indifference to the intolerance of others cannot effectively motivate concern about tolerance in ourselves.

The chauvinist disparages all differences because he fails to see that basic moral values can be advanced in social forms not familiar to himself. The antidote to chauvinism is not an indiscriminate nonjudgmentalism. By refusing to pass judgment on any customs not his own, even when they badly serve or actually violate basic moral values, the relativist signals no confidence in the reasonableness of his own moral convictions, including convictions about tolerance and respect. This is not an effective way to recommend them to others.

The moral aims of global education—understanding, tolerance, and respect for others—are not promoted by moral relativism. To the extent that global education teachers equate "cultural relativism" with moral relativism, they disserve their own goals.

Some global education materials may contain language and strategies for teaching tolerance and respect that blur the difference between respectful judgment and abdicating judgment, or that confuse caution in judgment with lack of confidence in judgment, or that self-defeatingly seek to support a value (respect) by denying differences in values ("all values are equal"). Greater clarity about relativism and the aim of global education could forestall much of the criticism against global education and improve the moral understanding it seeks to promote. . . .

Higher-Order Thinking

By their very nature, the kinds of issues that students confront in global education programs compel the use of higher-order mental processes. This is especially true when the student is confronted with the choice of two competing goods—for example, patriotism vs. internationalism, local community needs vs. food for starving foreigners, protectionism for a domestic industry vs. free trade.

Grappling with such issues not only requires substantial factual knowledge but also forces the student to analyze, extrapolate, synthesize, and come to a defensible conclusion. Nor is this only an academic exercise. Students, even adolescents, do indeed make decisions that impinge on our global society. Do they save for the purchase of a foreign or domestic car? Do they contribute to their church world relief funds? Do they buy clothes made in the United States or elsewhere?

The absence of global education in the schools would eliminate one vital source for the development of critical thinking skills. It is apparent that the schools are preparing social surgeons who are performing daily operations on the body politic. It is beneficial to them, and to society as a whole, to have adequate skills for these operations. . . .

Conclusions and Recommendations

A. *Global education curricular programs must have scholarly integrity.*

A large body of knowledge is available in the disciplines of history, the social sciences, law, geography, international relations, the behavioral sciences, other related fields, and in the studies of serious journalism. Young people need to see that this body of knowledge is not fixed, but changes over time as inquiry leads to better conceptual formulations and theory. Young people also need to see the ways in which claims to knowledge are generated. The best knowledge we have comes from the fields of scholarship. Young people are entitled to make it their own.

Knowledge in global education must inevitably include various frames of reference and points of view. It must be balanced enough to represent achievements and failures, good and bad. An integral part of growing understanding will come from comparisons of past and present, one area with another, one culture with another, one proposed course of action with another. Moreover, what is chosen for one grade level or another must be sufficiently related to young people's experiences and development to allow for learning.

These requirements are likely to mean that several sorts of professionals must participate in the development of curricular programs: scholars with expertise in whatever fields are involved, specialists in curriculum development, and teachers skilled in proposing learning activities and in instruction.

B. *Global education can hardly avoid values.*

While young people are developing knowledge, they must also be developing their values. Younger children will learn them primarily through models, practices, and statements of others. Increasingly as they grow, young people need to learn understanding of and ways of careful thinking necessary for developing reasoned commitment to the core values of a democratic society. Global education, then, must pay attention to the development of values from simple awareness to critical judgment leading to mature understanding and commitment.

Consequently, global education curricular programs and instructional materials ought to help young people (1) develop, as their own, values consistent with the public welfare, (2) recognize that the particular expressions of basic values characterizing other countries and cultures, both present and past, may be different from our own, but may also enrich us, (3) evaluate the values of other countries and cultures without assuming that all values have equal merit, and (4) accept the necessity of accounting for different values in deciding upon policies and courses of action.

C. *Instructional materials and learning activities ought to allow for and even promote curricular organization.*

Most global education materials are intended to add a global perspective to ordinary curricular topics and to fit into regular curricula, although others are developed as units of study or even whole courses. Whatever the form, materials and learning activities should allow integration, fit into a stream of classroom activities, promote focus and direction, and, in the end, achievement. Global education materials ought not to be a mere collection of materials and activities, however appealing they may be, for use here or there as time or inclination may permit.

Curricular materials must avoid content that is more unsettling than young people can handle, but challenging what is familiar and common. They must offer over time several frames of reference and balance among several points of view.

6 VIEWPOINT

"Most of the professional global educators seem to have an expressly political purpose."

Global Education Is Politically Motivated

David Brock

Many states have adopted mandatory global education programs, but often the materials to teach the programs are prepared by private organizations and individuals. In the following viewpoint, David Brock takes issue with several current global education programs, claiming that the materials studied are too liberal and laced with ideology. Without objective information, Brock maintains, students are indoctrinated into the views of their liberal teachers and politically motivated organizations. Brock is a writer for *Insight* magazine.

As you read, consider the following questions:

1. Why does Brock believe global education cannot be objective?
2. What is wrong with the kinds of materials used in global education, according to the author?
3. Does Brock believe global education can be salvaged? Why or why not?

David Brock, "Selling Globaloney in the Schools," *The American Spectator*, December 1988. Reprinted with permission.

Ten-year-old school children in New York City are studying their candy bars. "What would happen," their teacher asks, "if there were a dock strike in Africa or big forest fires in Canada?" The answer: The manufacturers might not have enough chocolate to make the bar or enough paper for the wrapper. Thus the students see there is a world in their candy bars. Such exercises are by no means unique to the nation's cosmopolitan centers. In Prairie View, Illinois, students in a mathematics class learn about currency by examining not only American dollars but also Japanese yen and Mexican pesos.

The concept of international education is at least a decade old, having grown from the findings of a U.S. presidential commission in 1979 that found American students sorely lacking in foreign language skills and the ability to understand cultures other than their own. Throughout the current decade, the movement gathered steam as both federal and state education officials—citing such statistics as the fact that 40 percent of high school students cannot locate Japan on a world map—touted reforms to require more study of foreign languages, world history, and geography in the schools.

The Governors' Report

A practical impetus for such education was emphasized by a group of Southern governors in a 1986 report that called American students "internationally illiterate" and endorsed international studies as a way to bolster U.S. efforts to compete in the world economy. Most appeals like the governors' report proceeded from an essentially conservative premise, urging the reinstatement of curriculum requirements scotched in the 1960s movement for "educational democracy" that gave students more control over what they studied. This 1980s reform movement can be said to have been at least moderately successful: the U.S. Department of Education says that more than thirty states have mandated tougher foreign language requirements and fifteen have increased world history and geography courses in the last five years.

At the same time, a parallel and sometimes overlapping movement in education circles—often with radically different objectives—has also been gaining strength, under the rubric of "global education." The term does not refer to a course or courses, but rather to a new way of teaching existing courses. A study by the Commission on Global Education, underwritten by the Rockefeller Foundation, said that standard courses in schools, from history to geography to biology to physics, should be "infused with a global perspective." The Commission, chaired by former University of California president Clark Kerr, found that 1,300 schools already have a formal "global" component to their curriculums.

A report by the National Governors' Association found that

almost every state has recommended to local school districts some type of global education. For example, New York's Department of Education has urged principals to "integrate a global perspective" into their curriculums. California has initiated a statewide global education project, including funds for new curriculum materials and teacher training. According to the National Council on Foreign Language and International Relations, there are thirty-five so-called "magnet" high schools across the country that specialize in global education.

A Good Educator

Such controversial issues as nuclear weapons or U.S. involvement in Central America require teachers to skillfully negotiate strong feelings on many sides. Ronald Herring, public programs director for the Institute of International Studies at Stanford University, notes that while "no single librarian or teacher could ever command a full knowledge of all the arenas of controversy" involved in global affairs, "a good educator will make effective use of diverse points of view." Once again, it is important that educators not necessarily rely on materials that are most accessible but seek a broad range of sources.

John O'Neil, *Media & Methods*, March/April 1989.

The potential problem with all this was summed up simply by former Education Secretary William Bennett, in a response to the Kerr Commission report: "When I hear 'geography' and 'history,' I'm pleased. When I hear 'global perspectives,' I'm usually a little nervous."

A review of the governors' report shows that global education is indeed an elastic term: in addition to such offerings as world history and foreign languages, other global curriculums included current events classes, sister-school projects with foreign countries, international business courses, nuclear-war education or "peace" studies, and state-sponsored "international events." What all the courses have in common is that they "show the diversity of cultural patterns" in a world that is "a series of interrelated systems," the report said. A world history class would become "global," for example, by studying Africa in as much detail as Europe. A Spanish language class would include study of politics and culture in Spanish-speaking countries. In many globalized curriculums, Dick and Jane books become Juan and Maria books; world history becomes "galactic" history; and the Pledge of Allegiance is translated into a different language each day.

The educational establishment—groups like the National Education Association, the National Association of Elementary School

Principals, the American Association of School Administrators, the National School Boards Association, and the Parent-Teacher Association—has warmly embraced the concept of global education. But it has been pushed most strongly by private groups that generate global curriculum materials and market them to school districts and individual teachers.

One of these is Educators for Social Responsibility, a Cambridge-based group with 15,000 members nationwide and a $500,000 annual budget. "The global perspective brought into physics would be a discussion of nuclear war. In chemistry, it would be toxic waste," explains ESR's Shelley Berman. ESR has already succeeded in convincing such states as Oregon and cities like New York, Milwaukee, Pittsburgh, and Los Angeles to require that nuclear war be discussed as part of the public school curriculum; in a survey by New York University's Herbert London of every major school district in the country, all respondents claimed to have formal or informal courses on nuclear-weapons issues. ESR currently has contracts with school districts in New York, Boston, and Portland to develop "conflict resolution" curriculums. "Rather than debate, we aim to resolve global issues through dialogue and resolution," Berman says.

Anti-Nuclear Teachers

In some schools, no doubt, global education is the province of serious local educators out to combat ignorance and parochialism. But most of the professional global educators seem to have an expressly political purpose. ESR, for example, was founded in cooperation with its namesake, Physicians for Social Responsibility, which played a leading role in the nuclear freeze campaign of the early 1980s. ESR has distributed curriculum materials urging students to "break the law" to "ban the bomb." ESR's intent was to move the freeze campaign into America's classrooms, according to writer André Ryerson. In an essay in *Commentary* (June 1986) Ryerson dissected curricular guides and described efforts by the NEA, ESR, and the Union of Concerned Scientists to make their concept of peace education mandatory. Discussion of the atomic bombing of Hiroshima, for example, focuses on death and destruction without supplying any political or military context. And the peace curriculums usually fail to present a balanced view of the Soviet Union, teaching students that, as Ryerson wrote, "our difficulty with the Soviets is essentially a problem in our heads."

The literature of another group pushing global education, the Northwest Regional Educational Laboratory in Portland, Oregon, is even more explicit in its activist mission. The group says "serious global educators" are "change agents . . . that influence development of attitudes." The laboratory's materials for teachers discuss the "political socialization of young people" and suggest that "visibility lends credibility to a position regardless of what it is." Since global education is a "world view," a "highly nationalistic" person would not make a good global educator, the materials warn. . . .

The American Federation of Teachers, in a July 1987 report entitled "What Must Be Taught," called for teaching world history with an emphasis on Western civilization. The report criticized the global education approach for detracting from American students' "ability to understand the role and meaning of democracy in world history."

The AFT document served as the basis for the founding of a new group called the Alliance for Education in Global and International Studies (AEGIS), a consortium of education organizations, both national and local, concerned about the political tilt of the global curriculum. Among the group's professed goals is: "to strengthen our society's ability to pass on to our young an understanding of those traditions and values of our heritage which undergird our democracy and the principles and commitments that sustain it."

One of the prime movers behind AEGIS is Dr. Robert Pickus, president of the World Without War Council and an early backer of global education. "Initially [global education] was supposed to

Don Meredith. Reprinted with permission

emphasize foreign language and world history and ethics," Pickus says. "But it ends up being a threat to education, not education. A class on military history turns out to be an all-out attack on the American military without a mention of the Soviet Union. Current events classes are used to support Marxism-Leninism in the Third World. The courses designed to combat ethno-centrism leave students acentric, having no morals or values at all."

Cultural Relativism

Similar concerns were raised in Colorado by an analyst for the U.S. Department of Education, Gregg Cunningham, who examined the activities of the Center for Teaching International Relations (CTIR) at the University of Denver, which conducts teacher workshops, provides consulting services to public schools, and publishes global education materials. His scorching 1986 report found that CTIR "boldly proclaims its quest for a 'new world order' and dismisses those who resist the creation of this new age millennium as 'miseducators.'" The report highlighted the relativistic or value-neutral stance of the global curriculum, where political systems and cultural practices are not more or less virtuous, only different. CTIR's Teacher Resource Guide suggests teachers ask students: "Do we sometimes have a tendency to define our values and behaviors as 'right' or 'correct' and determine that others' values and behaviors are 'wrong' or 'weird'? Is any one person or culture 'right' or 'wrong'?"

On questions of international relations, the Cunningham report found the CTIR materials "profoundly dovish." In one exercise, students are instructed to see "the United States and the Soviet Union as rival street gangs." Later, it is suggested that students "don't need to understand the global political situation or the details of the arms race. . . ." They should just "give up blaming" and "find a Russian and get to know her or him." One exercise on nuclear conflict proposes students act out the following: "To fully impress the President of the United States with the magnitude of his intended action, he is not to be permitted to resort to nuclear defense until he has killed one of his own aides with a butcher knife so as to remove the missile firing codes from a capsule previously implanted in the aide's chest cavity."

As to CTIR's influence, the Cunningham report noted that some 500 teachers per year have completed CTIR programs over the past decade and that 6,000 copies of CTIR's curriculum had been sold. "CTIR has worked its programs into the course offerings of many school districts in the Western states," the report concluded.

Up to now, most global curriculums have [been] concerned [with] U.S.-Soviet relations, especially nuclear-weapons issues; critiques of the curriculums have focused on how these issues are treated as well. But with the Reagan Administration's embrace of détente with the Soviets, it was only natural that the political agenda of global education would begin to shift, taking up more contentious issues like Central America. Let's examine, in some detail, how this issue is approached in Minnesota's schools, where one of the nation's most comprehensive global education efforts is underway.

The Minnesota department of education, spurred on by a state-funded project called "Minnesota in the World and the World in Minnesota," declared in 1986 that between 1990 and the year 2000—the "Global Education Decade"—all of the public elementary and secondary schools in Minnesota should introduce a "global perspective" to the disciplines they teach. The move was endorsed by the state board of education and by Gov. Rudy Perpich, who called it a "chance to explore the world." . . .

Balancing Opposing Views

Some global education materials are, in fact, badly flawed, many experts concede. "It's more than an 'image' problem, it's a substance problem as well," says Andrew Smith of the American Forum: Global Perspectives in Education, a leading proponent of global education. Numerous advocacy groups, for example, make curriculum materials on controversial global issues available to schools, but educators should examine them closely to ensure that they present objective information.

John O'Neil, *Media & Methods*, March/April 1989.

Implementation of a global curriculum is left to individual school districts. "The state's role," says Roger Wangan, the director of international studies for the state department of education and Minnesota's global education guru, "is to help interpret what global education means." In anticipation of the global education decade, many Minnesota school districts have begun experimenting with the concept "in the last half dozen years," says Wangan. Many have also instituted the global approach in fulfilling a statewide high school requirement that all students take one year of "Contemporary World Studies" to graduate. "We've been focusing on current events, first the nuclear issue, then South Africa, now Central America. We haven't gotten to the Israeli-Palestinian issue yet," says Wangan. Though Wangan says the state strives for "balance" in such controversial matters, an examination of how the schools deal with Central America shows that Minnesota has fallen far short of that professed goal.

On Central American issues, Minnesota's educators have come to rely almost exclusively on a local left-wing organization called the Central America Resource Center (CARC). The activities of

CARC in Minnesota show how vulnerable the education world is to committed political cadres accomplishing their task through emotional manipulation, indoctrination, and exploitation of school children. The state's reliance on CARC not only debases educational standards, but also teaches students to accept the crudest falsifications of international issues at face value. . . .

In January 1986 CARC produced a directory of Central America "classroom resources" for grades K-12 in response to "teachers' repeatedly expressed needs for up-to-date, substantive resources for teaching about Central America." The 135-page book is advertised as "all you need to read to know about what's going on in Central America" and recommends books, articles, and audio-visual materials to help teachers present current information about the region.

Among the recommended documents are: "Back in Control: The CIA's Secret Propaganda Campaign Puts the Agency Exactly Where It Wants to Be," published by Common Cause; "Endgame: A Special Report on the [U.S.] Military Strategy in Central America," published by the North American Coalition on Latin America, as well as that organization's "The Real War," which "exposes U.S. war against the progressive movements in El Salvador and Guatemala"; "Guide to U.S. Military Aid and Strategy in Central America," a "listing of U.S. corporations supplying arms to Central America" published by National Action/Research on the Military-Industrial Complex. . . .

Of the 132 entries, the only material listed in the directory that does not follow the pro-Sandinista, Marxist-Leninist revolutionary line is something called "Special Reports, Gist, Current Policy and Horizons," a U.S. State Department document described as "giving the current administration line." But this document, Wangan says, "is not usable. The reading level is too high and it was all political. It didn't have the facts.". . .

A Leftist Newsletter

In addition to Wangan's office at Minnesota's department of education, teachers look to another organization for guidance on curriculum matters and in-service training: the University of Minnesota College of Education's Global Education Center. The center, run by Prof. John Cogan, exercises its influence mainly through the publication of a quarterly newsletter which goes out to every school principal in the state.

[The Winter 1987/1988] issue focused on Central America. The newsletter unabashedly endorsed the work of CARC, which was described as possessing "a wealth of materials for teachers K-12." It specifically recommended the CARC directory, as well as other "resources" including the North American Coalition on Latin America, a pro-Castro group; Vets for Life, composed of "vets opposed to the Reagan administration's policies toward Central America'' who ''share their Vietnam experiences through prose and poetry and relate it to the current Central American situation''; and the Traveler's Society, a local group founded by Mary Shepard, a CARC board member and a founder of Women Against Military Madness (WAMM). According to the group's literature, it organizes tours which ''take participants to societies in the midst of dramatic change,'' and ''helps them develop fresh approaches to . . . regional conflicts and personal biases.'' At the request of the state department of education, the Traveler's Society organized and conducted a January 1987 Minnesota teachers' tour of Central America which focused on curriculum development for the public schools.

The global center newsletter also endorses what is known as ''glocal'' education, ''thinking globally and acting locally.'' In this view, merely studying Central America is not enough. ''Issues are more than facts,'' the newsletter said. ''Students who understand that the lives of millions in Central America and in the U.S. are impacted by foreign policy decisions will hopefully want to influence these decisions and will care enough to insist that the government be accountable to the people.''

Politics of Central America

The main section of the state's newsletter recommends three specific Central American curriculum units, two of which are described as ''widely used high school curricula that foster critical thinking skills.'' One of these is called ''Identifying Unstated Assumptions: El Salvador,'' written by a Minnesota elementary school Spanish teacher. It describes a young man and an older woman in dialogue. ''Gee!'' the man says. ''I just read that human rights in El Salvador are so bad that we might have to stop giving aid to that government. Hmm . . . but then we have to stop the Communist threat. I guess human rights will have to wait.'' Then the woman responds, ''Wait a minute! You are assuming: that the U.S. aid to El Salvador is used to improve people's lives; that the rebels are all Communists; that human rights are not always worth supporting; that the war in El Salvador is an East/West conflict.'' The unit also includes background information from a Salvadoran ''union federation'' called FENASTRAS, another FMLN [Farabundo Marti National Liberation] front group. This document goes on to condemn Minnesota corporations like Pillsbury, Cargill, and 3M by name, denouncing them for making ''huge profits off the labor of workers in El Salvador.''

The second curriculum unit recommended by the College of Education's newsletter is called ''Indian Family Life,'' which is based, according to the preface, on CARC information. In the section on El Salvador, students read a play which depicts the trial of four American nuns charged with helping incite a "revolution of love" in the country. At the end of the trial, the curriculum instructions say, "The judge can either condemn the four women to death or say something like, 'This is a serious case. We need more discussion. Is there anyone in the audience who wishes to speak either for or against these women?'" So students have two choices: favoring revolution and opposing the nuns' execution or questioning revolution and coming down on the side of killing the nuns. A democratic outcome is never even considered.

"Amigos" is the title of a recommended curriculum unit aimed at elementary school students. It is the work of the Minnesota/Leon Project, which runs a sister-city program between Minneapolis-St. Paul and Leon, Nicaragua. Nancy Trechsel, one of the project directors, says she has sent dozens of students to Nicaragua in exchange programs where they "work on chlorination systems for the city of Leon." The link to global education, she says, is that "everyone in the world needs clean water." Of her political views of the Nicaraguan situation, Trechsel says, "We [the project] are on the side of the people. We accept the government in Nicaragua as the legitimate elected government.". . .

Truth?

At Como Park Senior High School in St. Paul, students learn about Central American politics in a Spanish language class taught by Miriam Peterson, who has invited CARC-affiliated speakers into the classroom. Peterson says she has encouraged students to participate in protests against U.S. policy in the region and to write letters to the U.S. Congress against contra aid. The students get credit for "being globally aware," Peterson says. When one student complained about the one-sided picture of the Central American conflict presented in class, he was told the other side would be allowed to speak only if the student himself could arrange for a speaker. As far as Peterson was concerned, she says, her class had already heard "the truth," the same truth now wafting through classrooms across Minnesota—and who knows where else.

7 VIEWPOINT

"If we wish to improve the educational performance of our schools, we must first improve the quality of life for our youth."

Social Ills Make School Reform Impossible

Dennis C. Rittenmeyer

Many critics in the school reform debate believe that structural reforms are needed, including changes in funding, teacher certification, and state control. In the following viewpoint, Dennis C. Rittenmeyer argues that such reforms will do little good because the schools are besieged by social problems that prevent structural reform. Social ills such as drugs, divorce, and abuse besiege our youth, and until society tries to improve children's lives, children will be unable to learn, he concludes. Rittenmeyer is executive dean at Purdue University Calumet in Indiana.

As you read, consider the following questions:

1. What changes has society experienced that make school reform difficult, according to Rittenmeyer?
2. Rittenmeyer argues that society expects too much from schools. Why?
3. Why is the author pessimistic about improving America's schools?

Dennis C. Rittenmeyer, "Social Problems and America's Youth: Why School Reform Won't Work." Reprinted with permission from *National Forum: The Phi Kappa Phi Journal*, Volume 57, Number 1 (Winter 1987), pp. 34-37.

The emphasis on strengthening the school curriculum and changing teacher certification standards (the two most popular reform efforts) seems to emanate from a belief that we can solve our educational problems by "fixing" the schools. Actions of state boards of education and state legislatures imply such repair work is necessary, but the question is, Will it improve educational performance?

Teachers and principals have long argued that little attention has been given to the social issues which affect students; they have complained repeatedly that it is impossible to improve educational performance without addressing the quality of life youth experience today. Nevertheless, very little attention has been focused on this aspect of school reform. Nearly every critic has chosen instead to chastise the schools and the teachers.

During the last few years, the decline in student academic performance has been painstakingly chronicled. Decline in student performance is alleged to be the result of a poor curriculum presided over by poor teachers. Analyses of this decline appear to have been conducted with little consideration given to other contributing factors. Critics have not only failed to consider the ways in which society is different than it was a generation ago but also ignored the increased responsibility imposed on schools to address the problems created by social change.

If education reform efforts are to be successful, we must first broaden our view of education problems and develop a deeper understanding of the changes society has experienced. Second, we must determine whether it is proper for schools to carry the burden of responsibility for social ills which, while evident in the classroom, are not the result of action or inaction by the schools. Third, if we determine that the schools are the best place to attempt to ameliorate such noneducation problems faced by our children, then we must be willing to provide the necessary resources for schools to be successful and not expect that they will accept this responsibility in addition to their education mission with no increase in resources. . . .

There are numerous social problems which impinge on our quality of life and that of our children, and our schools are being asked, and in some instances required, to address these problems as well.

Schools and Poverty

The debate on the causes and cures for poverty seems unending. While one group argues the number of persons in the United States living below the poverty level is higher than ever, another group argues that the poverty rate is down. (Poverty is defined as follows: in 1969 a nonfarm family of four was counted as a family in poverty if family income was less than $4,679. In 1984 that figure was $10,609.) Undeniably, the number of children living below the poverty level has increased dramatically. According to the United States Census, nearly thirteen million children are living in poverty, a 35 percent increase since 1969.

The poverty rate is highest for Black and Hispanic children. Census data again indicate that nearly 50 percent of all Black and 40 percent of all Hispanic children live at or below poverty level. Since urban schools typically have large minority populations, these schools have especially serious problems. Writing in *The Changing Face of Poverty*, Emanuel Tobier claims that in New York City, nearly 600,000 children live at or below the poverty level; the *Chicago Tribune* claims that in Chicago the number is nearly 250,000.

The direct impact on schools is evident in the school lunch statistics. According to data provided by the Department of Agriculture in 1983, 51.7 percent of all school lunches were served free or fee-reduced. Each day over eleven million lunches are consumed by students from families which have so little income as to qualify for a federal food subsidy. The United States Department of Agriculture reports that the rate of free or fee-reduced lunches has increased 400 percent since 1960, although the public school population increased by only 15 percent.

Figure 1: CHILDREN IN POVERTY

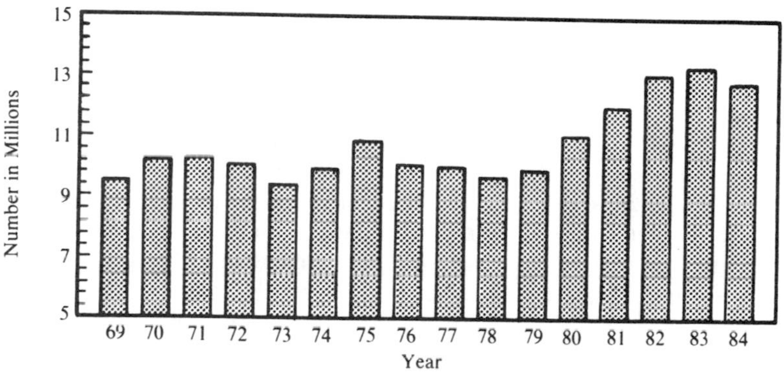

School-based breakfast and lunch programs are seldom criticized as an intrusion on the schools. As a group, educators are pleased to help feed children because they know a better diet develops sounder minds and bodies. Nevertheless, feeding students has now become the *responsibility* of the schools, a responsibility which has grown over the years and which few educators anticipated. "Lunch room duty," like "bus duty," has become a significant and burdensome responsibility for teachers.

The effects of divorce on children have been debated for years. While once a common lament, staying together "for the sake of the children" is a rationale rarely invoked to keep families together today. Although schools have not been asked to address the divorce problem specifically, they have no choice but to deal with the children affected by the breakup of a family. Twenty years ago this problem was of little consequence; today, it is one of the most critical problems facing our schools.

In 1983, according to the National Center for Health Statistics, 1.1 million children were affected by divorce. Between 1960 and 1983 the divorce rate doubled, but more important, the number of children affected by divorce increased by over 600,000 per year. Furthermore, the problems children have in coping with divorce are aggravated when coupled with minority status and/or poverty.

The school response to children who are experiencing divorce or who live in single-parent households is necessarily individualized. Teachers, counselors, and principals try to understand the feelings of the children and ready themselves to respond if needed. Since 50 to 75 percent of the children in some classrooms come from broken homes, teachers, the first line of intervention, are generally concerned enough to demand more information about their students and assistance in learning how they can help. In many school districts across the country, "Learning to Deal with Children from Broken Homes" is a highly sought in-service program.

Teenage Pregnancy

Sex education has been a hotly debated issue in the public schools for some time. The battle has never been whether children should receive information about sex, but rather who should provide such instruction: parents, churches, or schools. Behavioral scientists, social workers, and educators generally believe the best way to ensure that children receive some form of sex education is to incorporate it into the school curriculum, the same curriculum that we expect to cover English, math, social studies, and science. However, parents, religious leaders, and political leaders frequently object. Such action is seen as an unwarranted intrusion into family structure or religious beliefs. Thus, the issue continues to be debated, and each community responds in its own way—if at all. Unfortunately, while the debate rages, children continue to be sexually active at an ever-younger age.

Although birth control devices are easily obtained, the National Center for Health Statistics reports that in 1982 the birth rate among unmarried teenage girls in the United States climbed to 28.9 per 1000, an increase of nearly 90 percent since 1960. According to the Alan Guttmacher Institute, an independent research corporation based in New York, the United States now has higher

Figure 2: CHILDREN INVOLVED IN DIVORCE 1960-83

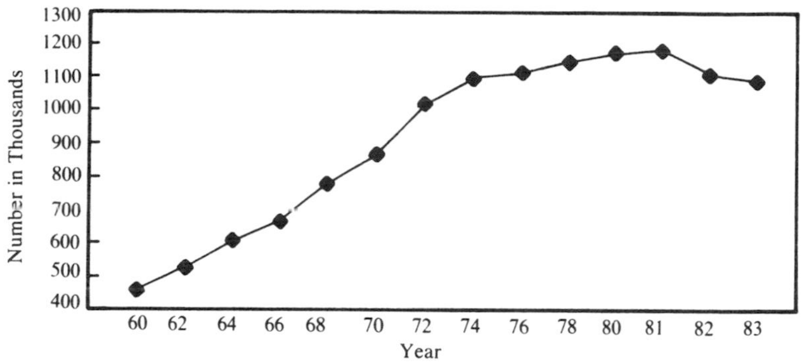

teenage pregnancy, birth, and abortion rates than most developed countries in the world. Furthermore, our teenage abortion rate is higher than the teenage pregnancy rate for most other countries. And, while the teenage pregnancy rate is higher for minorities and those living at or below the poverty level, the National Center for Health Statistics indicates that Caucasian females account for over 75 percent of all teenage abortions. Thus, according to many experts, the cycle of teenage motherhood and subsequent poverty among minorities continues.

The School's Dilemma

Schools are caught in a dilemma. Should they choose to address the sex education needs of their students, not only will they divert time away from the curriculum, but they may incur the harsh criticism of the community. If they don't address their students' needs, they fail to address an increasingly serious nonschool problem which accounts for more than 30 percent of the female dropouts in some schools.

One response, tried by over thirty schools and under consideration by many others, is the establishment of a health clinic on school grounds. Among other services, the clinic dispenses birth control devices, information, and counseling. Understandably, the creation of these clinics has generated a vigorous public debate on the appropriateness of such facilities. Despite the criticism, some school administrations believe the clinics are such an important contribution that even junior high schools are now being considered to house these facilities.

The truth about the use of drugs by students is elusive. Self-reported data are of dubious validity, but they do represent an important source of information on substance use and abuse. The National Center on Drug Abuse conducts many such studies; it indicates that although the use of alcohol and marijuana among high school seniors has decreased slightly since 1983, it remains at approximately 66 percent and 26 percent, respectively. More recently, a study conducted by the Division of Alcoholism and Alcohol Abuse in New York indicated that alcohol consumption among young people remains a serious problem. In that study, 10 percent of the teenagers surveyed admitted getting drunk at least once a week, and 11 percent admitted being "hooked" on alcohol. Twelve percent of the elementary school students surveyed admitted drinking at least once a week. According to James Leiber writing in *The Atlantic Monthly* (January 1986), marijuana has become the second largest cash crop in the United States, and because so much cocaine has entered the country, the price has fallen 40 percent in the last three years.

While the actual number of teenagers who are regular users and abusers of marijuana and cocaine may remain obscure, the effects of abuse are not. Every school in the country has had to deal with the drug problem. Responses differ, but the use of dogs, undercover narcotics agents, and searches of student lockers is now all too common. Moreover, the problem is not restricted to students or the schools. Leonard Buder, a *New York Times* writer, reports that there were 4,658 drug arrests in and around the New York City schools in 1983. Surprisingly, only 186 of those arrested were students.

The "Chemical People" program is the most recent and perhaps most publicized effort to address the substance-abuse problem. Not surprisingly, the site for virtually all "Chemical People" activities and programs is the schools. The schools are perceived by both those who sell drugs and those who would prevent their sale as the single most important point of access to young people. The activities of both groups intrude on the time available for learning.

Schools and Crime

According to the FBI's Uniform Crime Report of 1984, the violent crime rate in the United States had declined nearly 10 percent since its peak in 1980. While the decline is encouraging, the actual number of violent crimes remains alarmingly high. Furthermore, the 1.2 million violent crimes that were committed in 1984 represent nearly a 170 percent increase in the violent crime rate since 1965. More serious still is the fact that teenagers account for over 25 percent of all arrests for violent crimes. We should not expect our schools to be immune from this antisocial behavior, and they are not. A 1983 study of crime in the Boston city schools reported that three out of every ten high school students admitted carrying a weapon to school sometime during the school year, and 50 percent of the teachers reported being the victim of a crime on school property or at a school function.

Figure 3: CURRENT USERS HIGH SCHOOL SENIORS

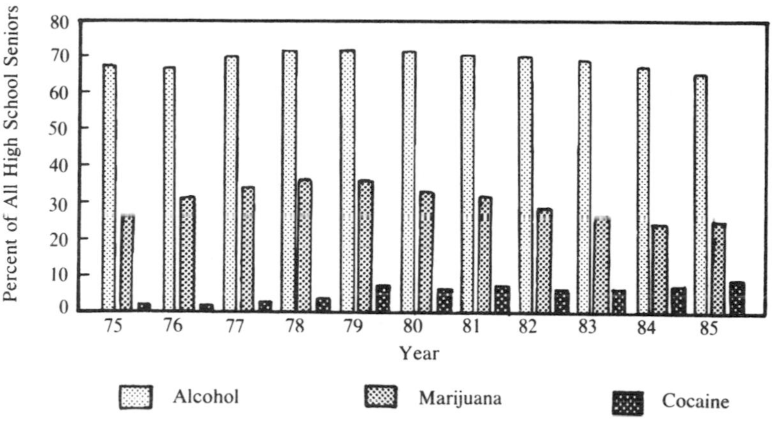

In 1985, Chicago took steps to address what it termed "youth gang violence." There were nearly one hundred gang-related murders in Chicago during the previous year; all victims were young people, and most were below the age of eighteen. Many had been on their way to or from school; so truancy and dropout, already problems in themselves, worsened. A similar situation exists in Detroit where the school response has been to install metal detectors at the entrance doors of some schools.

Teenage Suicide

Perhaps the most disturbing information of all concerns the rising teenage suicide rate. Between the years 1960 and 1982, the suicide rate for ages fifteen to nineteen increased by 140 percent according to the National Center for Health Statistics. Data from the National Center for Health Statistics also show that suicide is now the third leading killer of young people. Curiously, while many social problems affect minorities to a greater degree than Caucasians, the teenage suicide rate is highest for white males. The problem has become so serious that a national task force has been proposed. California has recently mandated suicide prevention programs in its schools; New York, New Jersey, Illinois, and Texas are considering similar actions. Many local communities in these and other states have already implemented broadly-based community action programs to address this serious and growing problem. Predictably, virtually every program includes the active participation of school personnel and the use of school facilities and time as part of the intervention strategy.

Everyone agrees the public schools in the United States have experienced a decline in educational effectiveness, and the recent emphasis on quality is needed. However, most critics of the public schools lack an understanding of the complex social service roles which have been imposed on those who teach our children. These critics ignore the fact that we have required our schools to become the largest and most comprehensive social service delivery system in the world. In *We the Teachers*, Terry Hernden, a former executive director of The National Education Association, asks:

> What is happening to our schools that we are obliged to run the largest juvenile delinquency program in town? To deliver the children to school and, once there, to feed them if they haven't been fed at home? To provide psychological counseling and otherwise do what society once held to be the responsibility of parents?

Our teachers should be capable and dedicated professionals, and our facilities and resources should be adequate for the educational tasks we wish to accomplish. However, we must understand that our schools can't do it all. Using the schools to achieve racial balance, eliminate poverty, fight drug abuse, prevent pregnancy, and reduce youth suicide is simply too much. Our teachers and principals should be required to address educational issues, not unmet social needs. Moreover, those who demand our schools' improvement would be well advised to pay significant attention to the social issues that have played such a critical role in the decline of our public education system. If we wish to improve the educational performance of our schools, we must first improve the quality of life for our youth. Only then can we fairly evaluate the degree to which our schools are fulfilling their educational objectives.

a critical thinking activity

Ranking Priorities in American Education

This activity will allow you to explore the values you consider important in making decisions about education. While your answers may differ from those of other readers, these disagreements reflect the complex considerations involved in establishing education priorities. In studying American education, you will discover that a variety of people—teachers, students, administrators, scientists, and business leaders, among others—have a stake in demanding an appropriate education system. Naturally, their priorities differ. Consider how the priorities of an inner city public school teacher might differ from those of the head of an American electronics manufacturing business. The teacher may be confronted with students who are poor and undernourished and who speak English as a second language. He may feel that the schools should try to improve social conditions for students through free lunch programs and access to libraries and other resources. In addition, this teacher might feel that for his students, learning to read and speak English is of primary importance. The company owner, on the other hand, may feel schools should emphasize science, math, and computer courses. Her business is becoming increasingly computerized, and she needs workers who can handle such machines and the information they generate.

The authors in this chapter offer different suggestions on what priorities guide American education. Some of these concerns as well as additional ones are listed in Part I below.

Part I

Step 1. On your own, rank the educational concerns listed below. Decide what you believe to be the most important priorities for American education, and be ready to defend your answers. Use the number 1 to designate the most important concern, the number 2 for the second most important concern, and so on.

______ increasing teachers' pay

______ teaching analytical skills

______ improving scores on standardized tests

______ encouraging memorization of facts and dates

______ learning more about other countries and languages

______ increasing the number of field trips

______ teaching ethics and morals

______ teaching students to read and write

______ increasing math and science education

______ lengthening school days and years

______ providing services to help students with pregnancy or drug abuse problems

______ providing vocational training

______ providing college preparation courses

Part II

Step 1. After each student has completed his or her individual ranking, the class should break into groups of four to six students. Students should compare their rankings with others in the group, giving reasons for their choices. Then the group should make a new list that reflects the concerns of the entire group.

Step 2. Compare your answers with other groups in a classwide discussion. Then discuss the following questions.

1. Did your individual priorities change after comparing your answers with others in your class?
2. Name some of the reasons your priorities differed from others in your group.
3. Would your priorities change if you were a student at a school in another part of the country? Would your priorities change if you were a teacher? How?

Periodical Bibliography

The following articles have been selected to supplement the diverse views presented in this chapter.

Melinda Beck — "A Nation at Risk," *Newsweek*, May 2, 1988.

Allan Bloom — "Too Much Tolerance," *New Perspectives Quarterly*, Winter 1988.

Ernest L. Boyer — "The Third Wave of School Reform," *Christianity Today*, September 22, 1989.

Ann Marie Radaskiewicz Butson — "Inside the Classroom," *Newsweek*, June 5, 1989.

Penny Colman — "Global Education: Teaching for an Interdependent World," *Media & Methods*, January/February 1989.

Educational Leadership — "Preparing Today's Students for Tomorrow's World," special issue, September 1989.

James Fallows — "Gradgrind's Heirs," *The Atlantic Monthly*, March 1987.

Chester E. Finn Jr. — "The Science of Bad Science," *The American Spectator*, August 1989.

Mary Hatwood Futrell — "Cooperation for Educational Excellence," *Vital Speeches of the Day*, December 1, 1986.

Paul Gagnon — "Why Study History?" *The Atlantic Monthly*, November 1988.

Jerome Harris and Eilene Petruzillo — "How to Save Our Schools," *American Legion Magazine*, February 1989.

E.D. Hirsch Jr. — "The Primal Scene of Education," *The American Spectator*, March 1989.

John E. Jacob — "Education: The Key to Economic Survival," *Vital Speeches of the Day*, February 1, 1986.

Jonathan Kozol — "The Dumbing of America," *Utne Reader*, December 1985/January 1986.

Thomas Lickona — "How Parents and Schools Can Work Together to Raise Moral Children," *Educational Leadership*, May 1988.

Lewis J. Lord	"The Brain Battle," *U.S. News & World Report*, January 19, 1987.
Merrill McLoughlin	"The Children's Hour," *U.S. News & World Report*, November 7, 1988.
Jaime O'Neill	"No Allusions in the Classroom," *Newsweek*, September 23, 1985.
Robert B. Reich	"Teaching to Win in the New Economy," *Technology Review*, August/September 1988.
Richard Rorty	"The Opening of American Minds," *Harper's Magazine*, July 1989.
Kevin Ryan	"Moral Education in the Life of the School," *Educational Leadership*, May 1988.
Eleanor Smith	"The New Moral Classroom," *Psychology Today*, May 1989.
Society	"Targeting Education for the 1990s," special issue, May/June 1989.
Carolyn J. Sweers	"Teaching Students to Examine Their Lives," *Educational Leadership*, May 1988.
Susan Tifft	"How to Tackle School Reform," *Time*, August 14, 1989.
Susan Tifft	"Who's Teaching Our Children?" *Time*, November 14, 1988.
Lawrence A. Uzzell	"Education Reform Fails the Test," *The Wall Street Journal*, May 10, 1989.
Stephen W. White	"Whither Education Reform?" *The Humanist*, May/June 1987.
The World & I	"Secondary Education and Values," special issue, March 1988.

CHAPTER 5

What Lies Ahead For America?

Chapter Preface

Economic analysts Pat Choate and J.K. Linger argue that America's prime resource is "neither its great stock of money, plant, equipment, and technology nor its abundant natural resources and rich cropland. Rather, it is the knowledge, skills, wisdom, enthusiasm, and versatility of the American people." Choate and Linger argue that America's human resources, its people, are the key to building its future.

Other observers foresee problems with America's people, however. Some, such as author Ben J. Wattenberg, predict that America might not have enough people because of a future population decline. Former Colorado governor Richard D. Lamm worries that growing numbers of Americans—especially minorities and immigrants—are becoming increasingly poor, uneducated, and alienated from the rest of American society.

What lies ahead for America? The following viewpoints examine this question.

1 VIEWPOINT

"America will be in serious trouble if it becomes an ordinary country, with people stuck in customary, class-bound roles in life."

America Is Still the Land of Endless Possibilities

James Fallows

James Fallows is Washington editor of *The Atlantic Monthly*, and author of *National Defense*, a book on America's military. From 1986 until 1989 he lived in and reported from Japan and Malaysia. The following viewpoint is excerpted from his book *More Like Us: Making America Great Again*. Fallows argues that America is a unique society because it enables people to pursue their ambitions and has fewer racial and social barriers than most other nations have. Fallows argues that the cultural traits of opportunity and openness are essential to America's future.

As you read, consider the following questions:

1. In what respects is America an abnormal society, according to the author?
2. What does Fallows maintain is the essence of capitalism?
3. What factors will determine America's future success, according to Fallows?

The purpose of this [viewpoint] is to remind Americans of how unusual our national culture is, and of why it is important that we not become a "normal" society.

Growing up, Americans hear that theirs is the strongest country, the freest and most fortunate, the most open to new ideas and change. We also hear that it is the world's most violent society, the most spoiled and pampered, the least sensitive to other cultures and their values. The real significance of such messages, whether complimentary or belittling, rarely sinks in. America is a large country, and most of its people never leave. Its popular culture has spilled over into nearly every part of the world. Americans can buy blue jeans in Thailand, watch *The CBS Evening News* in Korea, find *USA Today* almost anywhere they go. At first glance, Tokyo, Singapore, and Frankfurt may look like cities in the United States. It is not surprising, then, that many Americans should half consciously assume that America represents a universal culture, that other countries are steadily becoming more like it, that its peculiarities cannot matter very much. The world is full of potential Americans, since people can come from any other society and be accepted here. Therefore the world may seem to be full of potential Americas too.

An Erroneous Assumption

The assumption is erroneous: the United States is not an ordinary society. The differences between America and other cultures run deep and matter profoundly. They are differences of kind, not just of degree. Of course people are essentially the same anywhere on earth, but cultures are not. America is unusual because of its fundamental idea of how a society holds itself together. American society is not made of people who all happened to be living in a certain region or who have some mystic tribal tie. It's made of people who came or were brought here from somewhere else. This is perfectly obvious, but some of the consequences of the fact are not, and they affect our dealings with the rest of the world every day.

In the spring of 1988, after the right-wing candidate Jean Le Pen, running on an anti-immigrant platform, did surprisingly well in the French presidential election, a column in *The New York Times* was headlined RACISM STILL RUNS THROUGH EUROPE—LE PEN SHOWS IT. The truth is that racism runs through nearly all of the world, usually much more strongly than in the United States. We often give it some other name—tribalism or ethnic tension or, for Marxists, "the national question"—when Tamils and Sinhalese attack one another or when Indonesians slaughter Chinese, but the essence is the same. One of the things that make America most unusual is its assumption that race should not matter, that a society can be built of individuals with no particular historic or racial bond to link them together. This is a noble belief: it makes America better than most other societies. But it also means that America's strengths and weaknesses are highly unusual. Canada and Australia are the only countries that are remotely comparable.

Not Knowing Our Place

Japan is strong because each person knows his place. America is strong when people do *not* know their proper places and are free to invent new roles for themselves. Therefore, if Americans lose their sense of possibility and instead believe that they belong in predictable, limited roles, the United States will have lost what makes it special. It will have a harder time prevailing in economic and military competition, and it will no longer offer the freedom to start over that people have always come to America to find.

James Fallows, *More Like Us,* 1989.

Depending on their founding principles, different societies can use different incentives to make themselves go—to hold people together and make them rise to their best. Japan and, to a lesser degree, Korea seem to rely on an embattled sense of the national family standing united against the world. China, too large and varied to be a single family, seems driven mainly by the effort and honor of its hundreds of millions of component families. Germany, France, and England each has its national spirit. And America has a peculiar national genius of its own. The force that motivates the country is a vision of people always in motion, able to make something different of themselves, ready for second chances until the day they die.

This vision starts with the act of immigration—choosing to become an American—and continues through the choices and changes that make American life so different from Japanese or Italian life. People go away to college; they come back home; they go west to California to get a new start; they move east to Manhattan to try to make the big time; they move to Vermont or to a farm town to get close to the soil. They break away from their parents' religions or values or class; they rediscover their ethnicity three or four generations after their immigrant ancestors arrived. They go to night school; they have nose jobs; they change their names.

Other people don't do these things, not as much or as often or as gleefully. In most Asian societies, an unmarried woman will live with her parents until she is well into her thirties, unless she wants to give the wrong impression about her family and herself. It is hard to imagine a Belgian exclaiming, "Today is the first day of the rest of my life!" America's peculiar genius is responsible for some of the bad in America but also for most of the good. This country is the world's demonstration of how people behave when the usual limits are removed.

Any country will have trouble if its guiding idea is damaged or changed. Japan would lose its way if people across the nation did not feel a family connection to each other. China has suffered in the twenty years since the cultural revolution tried to uproot its old family values. And America will be in serious trouble if it becomes an ordinary country, with people stuck in customary, class-bound roles in life. Other countries have tools—tradition, ethnic solidarity—to help them get by in those circumstances. We do not. Therefore it's no small matter if America's belief in possibility and starting over is endangered. . . .

America's Culture

America's culture is America's greatest potential strength. Something about American values has enabled ordinary people, assembled haphazardly from around the world, to build the largest, richest, and freest economy in history, and to do so mainly through voluntary actions rather than state direction. The essence of our approach, the true American genius, is a talent for *dis*order.

Japan gets the most out of ordinary people by *organizing* them to adapt and succeed. America, by getting out of their way so that they can adjust individually, *allows* them to succeed. It is not that Japan has no individualists and America no organizations, but the thrusts of the two societies are different. Japan has distorted its economy and depressed its living standard in order to keep its job structure and social values as steady as possible. At the government's direction, the entire economy has tried to flex almost as one, in response to the ever-changing world. The country often seems like a family that becomes more tightly bound together when it must withstand war, emigration, or some other upheaval.

America's strength is the opposite: it opens its doors and brings the world's disorder in. It tolerates social change that would tear most other societies apart. This openness encourages Americans to adapt as individuals rather than as a group.

Few other societies could endure the unsettled conditions that have always typified America. Modern Japan would be shattered by the threat of substantial immigration. Few other Western societies have seen women's roles change as dramatically as in the United States. Western European countries generally have trouble finding new jobs for displaced workers or attracting them to new places when the jobs shift. In 1980, one American family out of thirty moved to a different state. Only one of about ninety families in England and one of eighty in West Germany made similar moves.

America not only can tolerate these disruptions, it needs them.

Ceaseless internal change is good for America. It causes America to bring out the best voluntary efforts of its ordinary people by offering them the constant prospect of changing their fortunes, their identities, their roles in life. Americans are most likely to try hard, adapt, and succeed when they believe that they can improve their luck, that the rules of competition are more or less fair, and that if they take a risk and fail, they won't be totally destroyed. Although these conditions have never been entirely met—the competition has never been completely fair; some people have been permanently stuck; many have been ruined when they took a chance—they have been closer to realization in the United States than anywhere else. They are America's counterparts to Japan's sense of duty and racial solidarity in that they give ordinary people a reason to make their best efforts voluntarily. America's radius of trust is expanded not by racial unity but by the belief that everyone is playing by the same set of rules. Indeed, in a country cobbled together from so many races and religions, the belief in playing by similar rules is the source of such "community" as we can have.

The Chance to Try

What attracts immigrants to America is the essential characteristic of American culture: the chance to try. There is a combination of two things that are important: culture and space. The culture allows you to try to be somebody—to find yourself, your place, your status. And there is space not only in a geographical sense, but in the sense of opportunity, of social mobility.

Ryzsard Kapuscinski, *New Perspectives Quarterly*, Summer 1988.

America's talent for disorder allows it to get surprising results from average people by putting them in situations where old rules and limits don't apply. That's the meaning of immigration, of the frontier, of leaving the farm for the big city, of going to college or night school to make a new start. No other society has managed disorder so well in the past; none of our competitors needs to keep promoting disorder, by endlessly rotating establishments, as much as we do. . . .

For better and for worse, this has always been a changeable, self-defining, let's-start-over culture, in which people with talent, energy, or luck believed they could invent their own lives. Not everybody has wanted to start over or invent a new role; the Amish, for example, seem content as they are. Many American blacks, descendants of the country's only involuntary immigrants, for years were not allowed to get a new start. Still, if antitraditionalism is only part of American culture, it is a very important part, which clearly distinguishes America from most other countries and has been responsible for much of our economic and political strength. On the whole, America's history is not the story of Amish-style traditionalism. It is the story of people who try to bend tradition to suit their immediate needs. The various forms of American mobility—social, occupational, geographic—have been connected with and have reinforced one another.

Geographic Movement

In the early 1970s, Vance Packard wrote a book, called *A Nation of Strangers*, about the many ways in which America injured itself because people moved so often. They didn't get to know their neighbors; they didn't have a stake in their towns; they couldn't sink any roots. Mona Simpson made the same point far more lyrically in her recent novel *Anywhere But Here*. One character in the novel was a hopeless dreamer who could never face reality or see things through to the end. While the rest of the family remained rooted in the Midwest, it was she who moved to California and kept switching houses, jobs, friends, and lives.

No doubt America pays a higher price for constant movement than, say, France or China does. But this has always been the case—Americans have moved, both socially and geographically, much more easily than other people—and it's not all bad. . . .

Almost every chapter of American history is a saga of people moving from place to place geographically and from level to level socially. The flow of immigrants from overseas is only the most obvious illustration. The other great theme in this saga is the continuing migration from the American farm. Before the Civil War, three times as many people worked on the farm as in the city. Fifty years later, twice as many people worked in cities as on farms. After World War II there was another huge exodus. At the beginning of the 1940s, farmers made up one fourth of the work force; at the beginning of the 1980s, only about one fortieth. During the 1970s and early 1980s, Texas surged to become the third most populous state, overtaking Pennsylvania and Illinois. But even during those decades of very rapid growth, most counties in the state lost rather than gained population as people moved to cities from farms.

In most cases, people moved because business was changing. They could no longer make a living where they were, or they were drawn by the hope of better opportunities somewhere else.

Behind this continual motion lies the hard truth about capitalism that is summed up in Joseph Schumpeter's famous phrase "creative destruction." "Capitalism" usually calls up images of big machines or powerful financiers or perhaps of class war, but what capitalism really means is change. Its essence is that nothing stands still. In the thousand years before the beginnings of eighteenth-century capitalism, Europe was feudal and its economy relatively static, built around guilds and traditional occupations. Industries remained concentrated in certain regions; jobs were passed down from father to son. Suddenly, with the coming of industrial capitalism, predictability vanished. Businesses started and then failed; products were invented, grew popular, became obsolete; people trained for one career at the age of eighteen and ended up doing something else at forty-five.

More Wealth, More Jobs, More Leisure

In the long run, all these shifts, changes, and adjustments bring more wealth, more jobs, and more leisure to more people. That, at least, has been the record of industrial capitalism until now, especially in America. For each blacksmith shed that disappears, some auto body repair shop opens up. The process is not, of course, that neat or symmetrical, but over time it works. Max Geldens, of the management consulting firm McKinsey and Company, has pointed out that in the three centuries since the beginning of the Industrial Revolution, two thirds of the jobs existing at the beginning of each century have been "destroyed" during that century—but three times as many people have been at work by the century's end. Despite all its problems of competitiveness and debt, the United States in the late 1980s employed a higher proportion of its population than ever before. (The official unemployment rate is higher than in the mid 1960s, but the work force itself represents a larger share of the population, mainly because more women are included.) . . .

Outside observers from more settled societies—most European visitors except Tocqueville; domestic travelers from Boston or Philadelphia who've been touring the frontier—have usually been alarmed by the self-made and mobile aspect of American society. . . .

During Houston's boom, Gregory Curtis, of *Texas Monthly*, recounted a one-sided conversation he'd held with the English poet Stephen Spender, who was spending a term teaching at Rice, in Houston. Spender was taken aback by the rawness and incivility of Houston, as well as by its total lack of tradition. As Curtis recalled the encounter, it perfectly illustrated the contrast between American and European cultures:

> I launched into a fairly standard [that is, classically American] defense of Houston. It was a city of constant change. A building that held a filling station one day could hold a flower shop the following day and restaurant the next. Thus Houston was being created and re-created before your eyes. Houston had hustle and vigor and grit. Houston welcomed everyone into its great chaos. . . . It was exciting to see what happens when people live in a place where few of the old rules apply, the bonds are let loose, and life is lived with the accelerator to the floor.

I let myself get carried away, so it wasn't until I neared the end of my speech that I looked up at his face, only to see quite clearly that there was no hope of carrying the day. Everything that I said was good about Houston was exactly what he thought was bad.

By Stephen Spender's standards, apparently, a disorderly, mobile society was a failure, not a success. Many other cultures are built on the same view: that the social costs of complete fluidity outweigh the economic benefits. . . .

Forces of Disorder

But in America, unlike Europe and China and Japan, the forces of disorder have usually won. When I was at graduate school in England, my English classmates talked about the jobs they would "get" with banks and firms and the civil service. Soon afterward, when I was living in Texas, my friends talked about the jobs they would make for themselves. That difference—creating slots rather than merely filling them—is the mark of America at its most adaptable ideal. . . .

America is strongest when it is most open and optimistic. This sounds like a platitude, but it has important practical effects. When ordinary people believe they have a fair chance, they usually do their best, and the whole country benefits from their efforts. The interests of individual Americans are well matched to the society's collective good. But if Americans think they are trapped, cheated, stuck, or doomed, most of them do not try. . . .

Anything that convinces Americans that they have been denied a fair chance weakens the country and exposes it to the many divisive forces built into a big, disorderly, untraditional, multiracial society.

To make America as productive, happy, and decent as it can be, we need to remove the barriers that keep people from imagining and making new places for themselves.

2 VIEWPOINT

"The task of realizing the American Dream has been in effect stalled."

America Is No Longer the Land of Endless Possibilities

Oxford Analytica, Inc.

Oxford Analytica, Inc., is a research and consulting firm that includes over three hundred faculty members of Oxford University in England and other leading universities around the world. In the following viewpoint, the authors question the idea that America is a socially unique country of unlimited economic opportunity. They argue that in the past, rapid economic growth and subsequent rising living standards created an image of America as a land of endless possibilities. But this image is no longer valid, they write, as America's economic growth stagnates and Americans' living standards decline.

As you read, consider the following questions:

1. Why do the authors make "American exceptionalism" a central focus of their study?
2. What evidence do the authors uncover to support their assertion that the American Dream is fading?
3. Why is a sense of vision important for America, according to the authors?

This [viewpoint will] focus on one central issue of America's future, namely, what is commonly called "American exceptionalism": the belief that within the family of nations, America is somehow exceptional, that it has a unique capacity to fulfill human aspirations—in a word, that the American Dream may not be just a dream, it may be a reality.

In analyzing the idea of American exceptionalism, we address these questions: Will the United States in the future continue (as those who subscribe to the exceptionalist view believe it will) to build a society with goals and values quite different in kind from those of even superficially similar countries? Or will American society come more to resemble other developed industrial democracies? Does the old promise still hold, in spite of social and political fragmentation and all the complex cross-pressures of technology and economic development, that "the best is yet to come"? Or are these trends working to weaken the common moral cement that enables the economic, social and political systems to cohere to powerful effect? In sum, is the claim that America is exceptional valid? . . .

The American Dream

How will current trends enhance or tarnish an image which enriches and haunts American life—the American Dream?

Part of the potency of the American Dream is, among other things, that it is an all-embracing belief. The idea also contains clear religious, economic and social elements, each of which can be separately analyzed. Our interest here is in the social elements. Thus, whatever else it has implied, the American Dream has meant the promise of continuing material advance and therefore of social opportunities for all citizens, regardless of class, race or creed. It has offered the prospect not only of steadily rising living standards, as all benefit from national economic progress, but also of distinctive individual success for those who show talent, enterprise and strength of will.

Belief in the American Dream—that progress indeed happens and that "the best is yet to come"—is also basic to the claim of American exceptionalism. For it supports the view that *America is set apart from other modern industrial societies, and especially from those of Europe, in being free from the threat of major class divisions and conflicts, and hence of the growth of political movements that are fundamentally hostile to the prevailing economic and social order.*

Because of the characteristic dynamism and expansiveness of the American economy—so the argument runs—even people in the poorest groups and strata realize that they stand to gain more from sharing in the general material advance than from even the most radical redistribution. The perceived "openness" of American society has thus given countless people powerful encouragement to seek to improve their relative position in society as individuals—that is, through their own personal achievements, rather than through claims based on race or class or forms of collective action.

We are therefore asking: What are the grounds for sustaining a belief in the American Dream at the present time? Or, more specifically,

- What has been happening to the living standards of Americans, both in general and in particular sections of the population?
- What has been happening to personal opportunities for economic and social mobility?

The best single guide to living standards is income. In 1969, the US Department of Health, Education and Welfare, in a document aimed at charting the nation's "social progress," could state: "The most obvious fact about American income is that it is the highest in the world and rising rapidly. In terms of gross national product per capita—or any other measure of the average availability of goods and services—the United States far outranks its nearest competitors."

Stagnating Living Standards

It seems clear that there has been a marked slowdown in the growth of incomes and that incomes have been distributed less equally—both at the individual level, as earnings from labor, and as total family incomes. These unfavorable shifts have followed a period of unprecedented favorable movement toward both faster growth and greater equality. . . .

The population at large has clearly somewhat cushioned the effect of this income growth slowdown. People have tried to maintain their consumption by borrowing more; but this strategy has limits—and long-term costs. Families have reduced the number of children they have, and so their resources need not be spread so thinly; but this strategy has limits as well. Although these behavioral changes have postponed the effect of the income growth slowdown, there is no question that reduced income growth over time would impose a constraint on living standards.

Joseph J. Minarik, *Challenge to Leadership*, 1988.

Today, however, what is "most obvious" is the extent to which the situation of 1969 has changed. It is not simply that the American lead in GNP per capita has been reduced. In the course of the last decade or so *the US has actually been overtaken by no fewer than six Northern European countries*—Switzerland, Denmark, West Germany, Belgium, Norway and Sweden—not to mention the "special case" of Kuwait. It is, of course, still possible to argue that, because of generally lower living costs, *real* living standards in the US remain above those of other nations. But whether or not this is so, there can be no question that *during the 1970s the deterioration in the performance of the American economy became manifest in income levels.*

Figure 1 gives some indication of what this has meant for American families. For twenty years or so, following World War II, median family income increased in real terms almost without interruption. But in 1969 this upward trend was checked and has not since been securely resumed. To some extent this flattening of the income curve reflects changes in family composition: for example, with a rising divorce rate, more families will be headed by low-income females, and as a result of a decline in family size some increase in average income per family member has actually been maintained. But the overall conclusion is plain: *most Americans over the last decade have faced a sharp slowing down, if not a virtual cessation, of growth in incomes. This represents a significant break with their previous experience and especially with the expectations encouraged by the unprecedented prosperity of the 1960s. . . .*

Figure 2 shows the proportion of the population with incomes below the official poverty level, from 1960 to the end of the 1970s. What is chiefly notable about the curve depicted is how closely it reflects that of Figure 1. *At exactly the same point at which family incomes ceased their steady rise, the proportion of population officially classified as poor ceased to decline.* It is evident, then, that during the hard times of the 1970s and likewise in the subsequent period of "recovery," no significant redistribution of income in favor of the poor has occurred. . . .

This finding is not in itself very surprising. But it creates difficulties for the argument that, after three decades or more of continuous increase in incomes, a period of leveling off, and now deterioration, may be viewed with some equanimity. It also highlights the fact that *over this period the task of realizing the American Dream has been in effect stalled. . . .*

Mobility

Another important factor in the American Dream is mobility. A concern with mobility runs through American social commentary from the early years of the twentieth century. Debate flares up intermittently over the openness of Amerian society—which, it is generally supposed, has always distinguished it from the older, more closed, "class-bound" societies of Europe. Is this openness being maintained or is it in decline? . . .

The idea of America as a "land of opportunity" still has a good deal of evidence for it. However, there are three less obvious points that also need to be made. . . .

First, while social mobility is obviously extensive in America,

FIGURE 1
Median Family Income, 1950-1984 in constant (1978) dollars

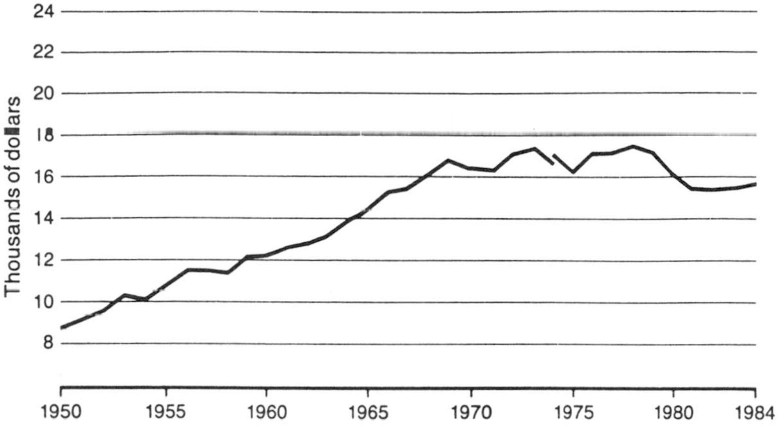

Source: Bureau of the Census, 1986.

FIGURE 2
Percentage of Total Population Below Official Poverty Level, 1960-1984

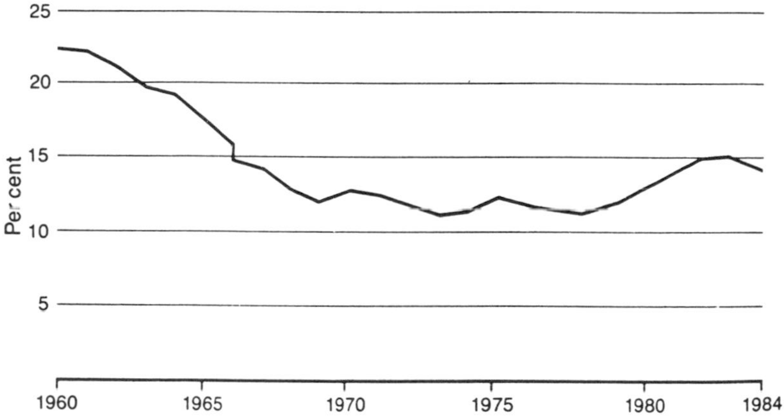

Source: Bureau of the Census, 1986.

it *does not seem to be substantially more so than in other industrial societies.* Contrary to what has been widely assumed, no strong claims can be made for American exceptionalism in this regard. America seems distinctive chiefly in the degree to which, among all sections of the population, there is a *belief* in the essential openness of society—derived perhaps more from history than from present-day reality.

Second, what appear as high rates of mobility can still coexist with quite wide inequalities in *relative* chances of class mobility. Thus, for example, the chances that the son of an upper white-collar father will be found in an upper white-collar position are over two and a half times greater than the chances of the son of a lower blue-collar father. For movement into a lower blue-collar position, more or less the reverse odds would apply.

Differences of Class

Last, and more important, recent American research shows clearly that over the last few decades—perhaps ever since the beginning of this century—relative class chances have changed rather little, at least insofar as inter-generational mobility is concerned. While this is strong evidence against the claim that America is becoming a *less* open society than it once was, there are at the same time other, less congenial implications. . . .

In sum, neither side in the great debate on social mobility can be fully vindicated at the moment. There is no reason to believe that America's openness to mobility has been diminished. On the other hand, to suppose that America is, and always has been, considerably more open than other industrial societies must be regarded as dubious. *The extensive opportunities for upward social movement that have certainly existed must be attributed not to some exceptional degree of equality of opportunity prevailing within American society, but to the relatively rapid growth and rate of structural transformation of the American economy.* . . .

All this points to two major conclusions. First, the continued realization of the American Dream, which is essential to American exceptionalism, assumes at the very least a healthy and prosperous American economy. So far as one component of the Dream is concerned—rising living standards all round, generation after generation—this is largely a truism. But, somewhat less obviously, sustained economic growth and structural transformation may also be seen as crucial to the other component of the Dream—genuine *opportunity* for people to raise themselves by their own efforts, whether by climbing out of poverty or by rising into upper-class well-being.

The American Dream may ultimately be a myth for many—but the kind of myth by which people and nations live. For long periods, including certainly the post-war decades, the promises of the American Dream have been sustained to a remarkable degree. But if the *extended* boom has now passed, to be succeeded by a period of less well-sustained growth, the chances of realizing the Dream are fading too. This, in turn, raises a far deeper question: Does American exceptionalism derive primarily from certain persistently distinctive features of American national character and culture, or is it merely inherent in, and contingent upon, the extent to which Americans are, in David Potter's memorable phrase, a "people of plenty"?

A second conclusion is that if the traditional "ways ahead" for Americans are now found to be increasingly constricted in a situation of virtual economic uncertainty or stagnation, in which merely holding one's own is a prime objective, new attitudes and modes of action may be expected to emerge. The American Dream's emphasis on the individual has in fact always been at odds with the well-recognized propensity of Americans to band together in order to protect and further common interests; and this in economic life particularly. The possibility of a significant change in this direction is clear.

The actual forms which *increased collective action* might take are difficult to anticipate, except that we can safely say they will be very varied. Old forms, such as trade unions, professional associations (acting more and more in a "union" role) and producer lobbies, may well take on new life. Some new forms—for example, highly orchestrated single-issue campaigns or, again, what has been termed "collective bargaining by riot"—are already in evidence. There is even the possibility that reaction to economic deprivation would assume an increasingly violent character. . . .

A Period of Testing

The claim to exceptionalism will no longer be able to rely on exceptional abundance or resourcefulness. The United States will remain wealthy and technologically advanced, but demographic trends, structural change and—paradoxically—technological change itself, both at home and abroad, will demonstrate that America can no longer take its leading position for granted.

Economic growth, however high, will not be able to relieve the ensuing social strains. Demographic trends will cause problems that cannot be "fixed" by mere technocratic solutions, and which a Europeanized, diffused society is unlikely to be able to handle very well. Faith in technology and precarious conservatism will see pragmatic personal effort and manipulation as the irresistible ways out. Perhaps more crucial, the underlying values here will promote individual desires above group sanction. More to the point, approaches based on these values are unlikely to be able to cope with the social tasks that will remain to be undertaken.

If gains in productivity bring greater wealth only to the owners of technology, at the price of laying off manual workers; if a newly stratified society polarizes chances of mobility and narrows life chances in general; if the clever, the expensively educated and the inheritors of capital flourish while others have perceptibly reduced opportunities, then faith in the American Dream—and the claim to exceptionalism—will clearly begin to waver.

Interestingly, it is the underlying belief in the Dream that is being tested here, and with it the notions of justice, equity and ultimately national purpose. This means equity beyond equal opportunity—it means a society where every person has a place and another chance, regardless of his or her position in the marketplace. Americans in the recent past have largely accepted a set of priorities that downgraded these concerns and gave a higher place to economic enterprise, personal fulfillment and competition. But that was not, and is not, the whole story where fundamental American traditions and beliefs are concerned. An underlying desire for equity and fair play, the willingness to put the social health of the wider community ahead of immediate self-interest—these, too, are traditional American values. . . .

What vision of itself will America adopt for the decade ahead? The search for an answer reveals a paradox at the heart of the American system of values. . . .

A Culture of Compromise

While many Americans want the society to seek the rewards of traditional morality and values, they do not want to pay for those rewards personally by pursuing traditional patterns of work, family life, sexual behavior, religious devotion, and so on. They want what they believe are the benefits of the good old ways, while at the same time they want to keep their new-won freedoms.

What seems to be emerging is a culture of compromise. As the suburb, the prevailing American way of life, is a compromise between city and country, so what we are seeing is a "suburbanization" of values. The philosophy is pragmatic; the style eschews conviction; the criterion is, does it work for me? . . .

The indications are disturbing, therefore, that the *dominant vision* of the next decade will most likely be one of strident individualism lacking in the idealism or moral conviction necessary to do more than muddle through. The irony of "harder times" is that pragmatism and manipulation in the pursuit of material self-interest become fashionable just when circumstances call for idealism, equity and cooperation. Moreover, this conflict is reflected in the competing values at the heart of America, and it brings to the fore the matter of choice. . . .

The beliefs and values on which the American Dream was built played a central part in generating the economic and political dynamism and the social integration of America at its best. In the world of the future, where America can no longer count on solutions in the form of exceptional resources, people or institutions, those beliefs and values will be needed more than ever. A genuine search for their core could lead Americans to a rediscovery of the purpose and vision that have always inspired the American nation.

3 VIEWPOINT

"The Birth Dearth hurts us in every conceivable geopolitical way: militarily, economically, politically, and culturally."

Population Decline Threatens America's Future

Ben J. Wattenberg

In the following viewpoint, Ben J. Wattenberg argues that U.S. citizens are not having enough children to keep the U.S. population from declining. He forecasts that the coming population decline will harm America's economy and world leadership. Wattenberg is a senior fellow at the American Enterprise Institute, a Washington, D.C. think tank. He writes a syndicated column and has authored several books, including *The Birth Dearth*, from which this viewpoint is excerpted.

As you read, consider the following questions:

1. What are the economic ramifications of population decline, according to Wattenberg?
2. According to the author, how might Social Security be affected by an aging society?
3. Why does Wattenberg worry about the population decline of the U.S. relative to the Third World?

Most of this [viewpoint] is a speculation and a provocation. It is mostly about the future, but it is based on facts of the past and present.

Of course, no one ever knows how the future will turn out, but the facts discussed here are not only quite remarkable but also seem to me to have an extraordinary amount of predictive power. I believe that these facts are so potent, and so different from what has come before, that they can frame the shape of much of what is yet to come. In doing so, they lay out the terrain of the playing field upon which we can act to mold—and try to change—our destiny. . . .

A Birth Dearth

What is happening is this: For about a decade and a half now the peoples in the nations of the free, modern, industrial world—that includes us in the U.S.—*have not borne enough children to reproduce themselves over an extended period of time.*

We had a Baby Boom.

Now there is a Birth Dearth.

And hardly anyone is paying much attention, certainly not in the U.S. After all, in the first generation of such a "baby bust," there is only a shortfall of babies, not of adults. And even some of that is smoothed out if the baby bust happens to follow a baby boom, as has happened here. This is so because there are so many potential parents around from the previous boom that even if they each have very small families, it can still add up to quite a few children (although a smaller number than in the boom years).

But as we enter the *second* generation of the Birth Dearth, which is just about upon us, the shortfall is not just in babies, but in young adults as well. The earlier "missing" babies become "missing" producers and consumers, soldiers and sailors, mothers and fathers. And then, assuming only that fertility rates remain at their current level, the *next* generation of babies—the small families of these smaller number of maturing Birth Dearth babies—starts shrinking. That, too, will likely be with us within a few years. And all this family size change, of course, reflects itself sooner or later in actual population numbers. The nations affected by the Birth Dearth move inexorably from high growth rates, to low growth rates, to no-growth rates, to negative growth rates that are already apparent in some of the West European nations.

My own view is that this remarkable development, this Birth Dearth, will hurt us in the United States, and it will hurt people and nations around the Western, modern world. This may prove to be so in a dramatic and absolute sense where we experience noticeable harm, in either a personal, economic, geopolitical or social sense. But I believe it will almost surely be so in the sense that even if things seem all right, we would have been much better off if the Birth Dearth were not proceeding in this way at this time.

I believe the Birth Dearth will, in the near future, begin to cause turbulence at every level of our economy, from the counters of fast-food restaurants to major corporate board rooms. Modern capitalism has always been rooted in the economic fact of vigorously expanding domestic markets. That phase is ending. . . .

I believe, too, the Birth Dearth will leave in its wake tens of millions of unhappy adults who, through no real choice of their own, will end up with no children at all, or fewer children than they really wanted—or many fewer grandchildren than they had hoped for.

Much as I abhor the thought, I believe it is possible that, because of the changing ethnic and racial balances that come along with the Birth Dearth, we may face some increased divisiveness and turmoil in America, which could have been avoided had the Birth Dearth not visited us now.

I believe further—perhaps most importantly—that the Birth Dearth may well turn out to be of great harm to the broadest value we treasure; it will make it difficult to promote and defend liberty in the Western nations and in the rest of a modernizing world.

The Danger of Population Decline

Modern Western economics based on the two-earner norm structurally discourage the birth of children.

If the United States stood splendidly apart from the rest of the world, this economic fact of life might be acceptable: our numbers would decline, slowly at first, then with accelerated speed; our society would rapidly age, yet there would probably be sufficient reserve wealth in the nation to see us all comfortably through to our graves; last one turn out the lights, please.

Yet we do not stand apart from the world. Over the long run, our ability to maintain the industrial base essential to our national security depends on relatively large numbers. Nations of 225 million people can afford to build Triton submarines and aircraft carriers. Nations of 25 million cannot.

Allan C. Carlson, *The Human Life Review*, Spring 1987.

I do not mean to sound apocalyptic, but the demographic forces now in motion may just yield a world—one in which we or our children will live—where the U.S. will no longer be "the most important country in the world." It could be a world where the alliance of Western nations will no longer shape either the political agenda, the culture, or the direction of the global community. This, I believe, could not only harm Americans and our Western allies. It would also harm all the other nations and peoples of the world, certainly in the poor areas of the globe, and quite possibly even among the Soviets and the Soviet bloc.

We have lived through an era of free-falling fertility in the modern democratic world. The key question it yields may well be this: *Over time, will Western values prevail?*

It is true that almost since the advent of the free, Western, "modern" world—and that dates back several centuries—its future has been questioned. It has been asked: Could the free, and capitalist, countries continue to prosper in the face of internal economic contradictions? Were these free nations with democratic politics made of stern enough stuff to stand up to external threats from totalitarian states? Would they doom themselves to death by pollution or death by environmental degradation?

We've managed. Those who have predicted Western demise have been wrong so far.

So far. We do not know the future. But if the dim outlines of the world we see through the lens of demography are any measure of what's to come, it may well be a world we don't like. We may face a situation where our birthright, our legacy, and our prosperity are diluted, and diluted, and diluted, perhaps even to a point where they gradually cease to be very relevant. . . .

A Look at the Past

To sense what may happen to capitalism and capitalist countries, we should start by looking backward. Everyone knows about the demographic poetry that has shaped American history. It is rooted in a tale of a near-virgin continent with a population of less than a million people (Indians) in the early 1600s. By the time of our first census in 1790, there were about *four million* ex-Europeans and ex-Africans living mostly on a sliver of land on the East Coast.

A century later, in 1890, the U.S. population was almost *65 million*. The 1990 Census is expected to record about a *quarter of a billion Americans*. By almost any reckoning, American demographic history must be counted as one of the great population explosions. . . .

Let us put a little recent American flesh on these numbers.

What did it mean in practice in America? Well, for one, there was always plenty of fresh demand for more housing. Accordingly, if an individual or a company was in the business of building or selling residences—from slums to penthouses—in Connecticut or California—there was almost always a demand for more residences.

If a person grew or sold or processed food or fiber—grain or granola, cotton or silk—there was almost always a demand for more food or fiber. If a company built or sold cars—Model Ts or El Dorados—there was almost always a demand for more cars.

If a company designed, manufactured, distributed, or sold word processors or personal computers—IBMs or Apples—there was almost always a demand for more of them. If a company sold fast food—Wendy's or Taco Bell—there were almost always more people to buy the burgers or the burritos. More. Always more. . . .

The End of Growth

That scenario is ending. The Western World—our world—is already moving from a situation of fast growth to slow growth. A no-growth circumstance is already in the deck. There will be actual declines in most Western nations unless there are important changes in fertility levels fairly soon. This scenario is quite apparent for Europe. It is also apparent for the U.S. although the timing is somewhat slower due to our large postwar Baby Boom and continuing immigration. Heroes in the business community will surely be harder to find. In America, a given city or state or region may continue to grow robustly, but as a nation growth is ending. . . .

So: a new modern Western world with less growth, a U.S. with less growth, and—in the not too distant future—the likelihood of fewer people, first in the West generally, and then probably the U.S. too. This should provide plenty of food for thought for businessmen looking ahead; for young people who one day will be not-so-young, in businesses that face shrinking markets; for middle-aged people who will soon be older and wondering where their federal Social Security pension money will come from; for people who may one day sell a house and not find a buyer at a reasonable price. In short, it is food for thought for almost everyone.

U.S. POPULATION 1987 TO 2100

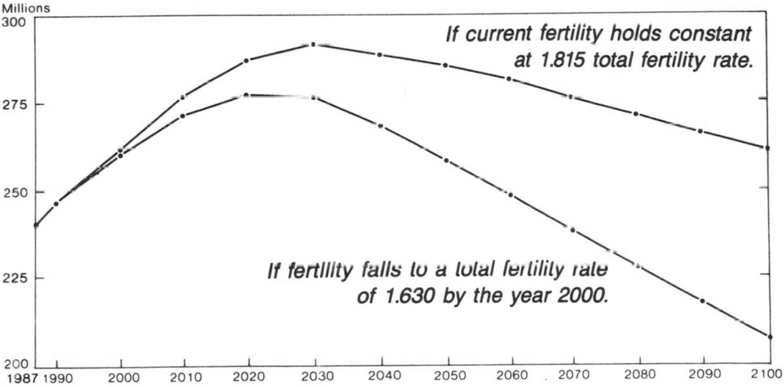

Source: Special World Bank Projection

What does the Birth Dearth yield from an economic perspective? Essentially, two intertwined problems: shrinking domestic markets and an older population. These, in turn, yield still other problems. Put together, all these problems don't typically occur at a precise moment, that is, at the instant population growth ceases, or at the instant population starts shrinking. The harmful economic effects of the Birth Dearth do not constitute an *event*. Rather they make up a process, almost ready to begin: low growth, no growth, shrinkage.

First on the agenda is: What if domestic markets shrink? Is it really so terrible? Some economists say probably not. It's true, you produce fewer widgets because there are fewer people to buy them. However, the optimistic economists say, there are also eventually fewer people needed to produce them. So, while total sales or total profits may decline, sales and profits *per worker* may not decline at all, and that's what counts—productivity. In fact, these economists say productivity may even go up. The optimists continue: A Birth Dearth yields fewer young workers. There is then more bidding for their services. Youth unemployment goes down. Wages go up. More capital is invested to buy equipment to replace the higher cost of labor. The newer equipment yields higher productivity per worker. We all get wealthier and everyone lives happily ever after.

That is a nice scenario; there is likely some truth to it. There are also gaping holes in the argument.

Who will buy those goods so efficiently produced?

As mentioned, a Birth Dearth not only provides fewer workers, it provides fewer buyers. And a Birth Dearth also sets up a sharply changing age distribution of the population, and sets that changed distribution in oddly staggered patterns. Some of these age patterns, along with some of the stark and discombobulating effects they provide, will be coming at us in the very near future. . . .

An Aging Population

So much for shrinking markets and the turmoil they can cause. We come now directly to a second and related facet of the economic implications of the Birth Dearth: the graying of a population. It has been mentioned here earlier in a noneconomic sense and in relation to shrinking markets. But it creates problems in other ways. . . .

The eminent French demographer Alfred Sauvy described the Birth Dearth circumstance some years ago most pungently: "A society of old people, living in old houses, ruminating about old ideas."

The logic of the situation is simple. A society where each succeeding generation of babies is smaller in number than the preceding generation—which is what happens sooner or later in a below-replacement fertility situation—is an aging society.

What are the economic consequences of an aging population? Sauvy might have expanded his remark about a society growing ever more elderly: "Old people, living in old houses, ruminating about old ideas"—to which he could have added *"and waging political warfare with younger people about who pay[s] the bills for old people's pensions."*

Social Security

There is a popular conception among Americans that our federal Social Security pensions are paid for by our very own contributions that have been put into an earmarked fund that is just waiting for us when we reach retirement age. Wrong. That is not how government pay-as-you-go social security programs typically work.

Let this be understood clearly: *Typically, we don't put money into the Social Security program for our own pensions. We put in babies.*

Thus, as a rule, most of *our* money doesn't pay for *our* own pension with *our* dollars. It pays for our *parents'* pensions and our *grandparents'* pensions. But who will pay for our pensions if we don't have children, or more precisely if we as a population have ever-fewer children?

That is the right question to ask, particularly if you are a Baby Boomer adult, age 22-42 in 1987, looking at small Birth Dearth-size cohorts coming up behind you.

Unfortunately, nice answers are in short supply in the modern world of the Birth Dearth. The coming years mean this: In 1985, there were 145 million people of working age in the United States to pay Social Security taxes for 29 million elderly. That's a ratio of *five* producers for *one* retiree. But in 2035, as the Baby Boomers retire and the Baby Busters fill the labor force, the ratio will be only *two-and-a-half* producers to *one* retiree. . . .

What to do? Sooner or later . . . Social Security "goes broke" unless something changes. The obvious answers are all unpleasant. Benefits can be cut for the elderly. (That's not very popular among the elderly.) Or taxes can be raised for workers. (That's not very popular among workers.) How would you like to run for office on a raise-taxes, cut-benefits platform? . . .

There is yet more to the economic problem. It's not just about age distribution, lack of markets, and dependency ratios. Another factor is tightly intertwined: spirit.

Unprovable as it may be, I believe we must face the idea that societies that keep getting older and smaller, older and smaller, older and smaller—will become dispirited. It was not an ever-older and ever-smaller population that yielded the dynamism that has become associated with American life. "Manifest destiny" was not the cry of a no-growth continent of old people. Our most recent spasm of dynamism is surely associated in part with the maturing of the 80 million Baby Boom babies—young, energetic, creative, and on the make. We have never been a society of old people in old houses fondling old ideas. . . .

Predictions

So then, this much we know:

• There is a Birth Dearth in our Western world. Birth rates have been well below replacement, for almost a generation in some places; there is no sign yet of reversal; many demographers believe rates are still headed down.

• There is moderate growth in the nations of the Soviet bloc.

• There is and will be rapid population growth in the Third World.

• We know with some certainty that the Birth Dearth will create economic change and turbulence in the Western world. With less surety, it is posited here that such economic change will harm us.

Question: Would the United States be a world power, the "leader of the free world," if our current population were still 4 million people, as it was in 1790? Or 62 million as it was in 1890? We shall come to an answer: No. . . .

I believe the geopolitical and geocultural situation will cause more long-range harm than the economic situation. I also believe it with more surety because both the data and the logic of the geopolitical case seem to me more powerful than the economic case. . . .

Let us say that the modern era began with the end of World War II in 1945. The years since have been a period of Western dominance. I would argue that it has been the most progressive epoch in human history. The Western nations themselves are the most prosperous, most technologically advanced, most productive, and most free collection of peoples ever assembled. For more than four decades in alliance—despite perpetual bickering—they have guaranteed a big-power peace.

The less-developed world has also prospered. Often under Western sponsorship there has been an explosion of independent nation-states, often modeled, at least in principle, on Western concepts. Although tragic poverty still exists, the Third World has benefited from Western medicine, science, and trade.

Even the Communist world has prospered from our advance. They have shared our life-enhancing technology. They have joined in the benefits of reduced big-power violence.

What has caused this remarkable moment?

I believe the fruits of Western culture and ideals, emanating from modern Western nations, have shaped the progressive nature of the world at this time. The specific content of that culture, the precise nature of those ideals, are hard to define. But they clearly involve political freedom. They involve intellectual freedom. They just as surely involve technological innovation. They involve commercial interchange.

The leader in this cause has been the U.S. It is no wonder that during this time American (or English, if you insist) has become the world's dominant language.

Is all this threatened? I fear so.

This international flowering began at a time when the West constituted almost *one-quarter* of the world's people. Today, about *one-seventh* of the world is Western. That may not be a critical difference.

But look at the trend, in twenty-five year bites, and remember that much of it is already pretty well locked into concrete by prior fertility patterns:

Fraction of Total World Population in Western Community

1950	22%
1985	15%
2010	13%
2035	8%
2060	7%
2085	5%

What happens when the West is less than 10 percent of the world? Less than 5 percent? . . .

A Long-Distance Race

Under such circumstances, will Western values remain strong and influential around the globe? Or will they wilt, barely noticeably from year to year, victim of an erosion in a political and cultural economy of scale? Will it turn out that, after several centuries of turbulent regnancy, topped by a half-or-so-century of making it work peacefully and progressively, we Westerners and we Americans will slowly begin to fall behind, or drop out, of the long-distance race? . . .

As it happens, if it happens, what will it mean? It is unlikely that the U.S. will be farmed by the power of water-buffalo. Will we worship cows? We will not. Will we willingly abandon democracy? We will not.

All that seems unreal. But it is equally unreal to suggest that our values will remain untouched as our numbers go down, and down, and down, if our economic and military power go down, and down, and down. It will be difficult for tiny minorities, growing weaker (we Westerners) to set the tone or values of the world. . . .

In short, the Birth Dearth hurts us in every conceivable geopolitical way: militarily, economically, politically, and culturally.

VIEWPOINT 4

"The population of the United States is not shrinking."

Population Decline Does Not Threaten America's Future

Roger L. Conner

Roger L. Conner is an immigration scholar at the Brookings Institution, a Washington, D.C. think tank. In the following viewpoint, he argues that long-term predictions of population growth are unreliable, and that even if population decline occurs, it is not necessarily bad for the U.S. He concludes that the U.S. population cannot continue to grow indefinitely, and that eventually America must prepare for a time when population growth stops.

As you read, consider the following questions:

1. Why are long-range population predictions so unreliable, according to Conner?
2. How does Conner respond to arguments that a slowdown in population growth would harm the U.S. economy?
3. Why does the author believe that population growth cannot continue indefinitely?

Roger L. Conner, "Answering the Demo-Doomsayers," *The Brookings Review*, Fall 1989. Reprinted with permission.

A small but influential band of futurists have been wringing their hands in public about U.S. population trends. Made up primarily of writers, led by Ben Wattenberg, and economists, Julian Simon and Clark Reynolds among others, this group foresees an imminent—and threatening—decline in the size of the U.S. population. "There is a no-growth future ahead," Wattenberg warned in a column, "leading to a demographic deficit" that portends larger "budget deficits and future Social Security shortfalls," not to mention a collapse in America's "geopolitical and cultural influence." . . .

The demo-doom rhetoric is more fear than fact. Though new to American ears, it dates back to the 1870s, when French intellectuals called low birth rates "race suicide" and proclaimed *Finis Galliae.* By the 1930s demographers throughout the Western world had taken up the alarm, gloomily proclaiming that Western societies would soon disappear. Before policymakers buy the latest iteration of this demo-doom scenario, they would do well to consider five myths that frequently cloud clear thinking on population and America's future.

Population Decline?

Myth 1: The United States faces imminent population decline unless we increase immigration or births.

Actually, the population of the United States is not shrinking; it is growing faster than any of the world's other developed countries. The National Center for Health Statistics reports 3.9 million births and 2.2 million deaths in 1988. Accepting the Census Bureau's very conservative estimate of 600,000 annual net immigrants (legal *and* illegal), the population is expanding by 2.3 million people a year.

Although the demo-doomsayers make it seem that decline is around the corner, when pressed they concede that what really concerns them is the size of the population 30 years and more from now. According to Wattenberg, under the "most likely" scenario the population will grow from its current level of 248 million to 300 million about 2020. It will stabilize at that level until 2050 and then return to 260 million or so by 2080. It is to avert the adverse consequences they associate with this scenario that moves the demo-doomsayers to insist that policymakers act now.

Even if government leaders were to assume that population stabilization or gradual decline would be bad, patience is called for. Long-range demographic projections have historically been off by huge margins. In 1944, for example, the Ben Wattenberg of his day, Dr. Frank Notestein, predicted that the combined population of the United States and Canada would be only 176 million in 1980 and called for government policies to promote larger families to avert a dismal future. Fortunately policymakers did not heed his warnings. Notestein was only off by 70 million or so. It is error of this magnitude, repeated over and over again, that makes trained demographers leery of treating long-range projections as certainties on which current policy should be based.

Harvard's Dr. Nathan Keyfitz, one of the grand old men of American demography, recently compared past population projections with what actually happened. He found that "relatively short term forecasts, say up to ten to twenty years, do tell us something, but beyond a quarter century or so we simply do not know what the population will be."

Unfounded Fears

It turns out that fears of an American birth dearth are largely unfounded. More babies were born in the United States in 1988 than in any year since the end of the baby boom. And the Census Bureau projects that even if American women continue to reproduce at their present modest rate, the population won't start to decline for over half a century.

David E. Bloom and Neil G. Bennett, *The New Republic*, June 19, 1989.

Keyfitz argues that demographers are no better today than in the past at predicting the key variable in the population equation: how many children women will choose to have. Tiny errors in fertility assumptions are compounded over time, producing massive errors in projections that run beyond a decade or so. "We know virtually nothing about the population fifty years from now," Keyfitz concludes. "We could not risk better than two to one odds on any range narrower than 285 million to 380 million for the year 2030.". . .

It follows that if the U.S. population does not decline as the demo-doomsayers expect, the consequences they worry about are unlikely to occur either. Let us assume for the sake of argument, however, that their population forecasts are correct and go on to examine whether the anticipated consequences are as adverse as they fear.

Social Security

Myth 2: Immigration is needed to help "solve the Social Security problem."

In one essay, Wattenberg predicted a shortfall in the Social Security fund if population growth stops after 2020. Increased immigration is the best solution, he argued, because the immigrants will be paying taxes "when the baby-boomers start retiring."

This is the wrong "solution" to the wrong "problem." Thanks to recent increases in tax rates, the Social Security trust fund is generating an annual surplus of $55 billion, which will grow to $150 billion a year by 1994 and continue for the foreseeable future.

What about 2020 and beyond? A Brookings study, *Can America Afford to Grow Old?*, argues persuasively that even if the demodoom demographic projections turn out to be correct, fears that the retirement of the baby-boom generation will bankrupt the system are overblown. With only modest increases in productivity, the study found, Social Security revenues and benefits will be in balance, without increasing tax rates, well beyond the middle of the next century.

To put it another way, if the workers of the future are more productive and, perforce, more highly paid, they can comfortably generate the revenues needed to support an increasing number of retirees. Future productivity, in turn, will depend on increasing savings, decreasing government deficits, improving labor-management relations, and a host of other factors. There is no evidence that increased immigration will help resolve these central problems. Indeed, immigration has been at historic highs during the past 15 years, a period during which productivity growth has slumped and government deficits expanded.

Henry Aaron, co-author of the Brookings study, puts this all in perspective: "My wife and I do not decide on whether to adopt a child based on the possibility that my income will grow so slowly that I will need support from my children when I grow old. Rather I try to save enough so that I will accumulate enough to live on. That is my advice for funding future Social Security obligations. Then I can decide about whether to adopt a child for the important reason—do I want a larger family?"

The immigration "solution," in fact, could worsen any long-term problem with financing the system. Adults who immigrate today will retire while the baby boomers are still alive and drawing Social Security. How many more immigrants will be needed to finance their retirement? . . .

Economic Shortages?

Myth 3: A slowdown in population growth will harm the economy by creating a "customer shortage."

The demo-doomsayers are also concerned that a slowdown in the rate of growth of the population will mean slackening in consumer demand, a "customer shortage." Here, they make the fundamental error of equating numbers with purchasing power. Switzerland, with a population of 6.2 million, and Norway, with 4.9 million people, are better markets than Nigeria, even though its population is 111.9 million.

They also make much of the anticipated rise in the median age of the population, which is now 33. It is true that a more mature population will buy a different mix of products; 40-years-olds will listen to more '60s releases and less hard rock. A more mature work force will also have proportionately fewer 20-year-olds and more experienced 45-year-olds in prime working years, with fewer dependent children as well as more dependent aged.

It is pessimistic in the extreme to fear that American companies cannot adjust to such changes in the marketplace. The median age rose more than twice as fast in the last 20 years as it will in the next 20, even accepting the worst demo-doom scenario. What does it matter to the economy if Johnson & Johnson features adults instead of babies in its commercials for shampoo and powder?

Numbers Not Decisive

Diminishing numbers do not forebode either military decline or cultural decay.

More individuals increase a nation's military strength, but population size is just one factor of many. Switzerland, whose population has never substantially exceeded 6 million, has escaped the ravages of many European wars for the last thousand years. Contrary to popular belief, not all of Switzerland is buried deep in the Alps, impregnable to military attack. Basel, Zurich, and Geneva are quite accessible through fairly flat terrain. The security of the Swiss must be attributed to their military preparedness, their unflagging national pride, and their tradition of neutrality.

Israel and Vietnam are similar examples—they have defended themselves against vastly more populous enemies. In all three cases (Switzerland, Israel, Vietnam) the decisive factors have been morale and love of country. The West will not perish as long as it does not lose these virtues.

Tyler Cowen, *Reason*, February 1988.

There is a special irony when such fears emanate from scholars associated with the Heritage Foundation (Simon) and the American Enterprise Institute (Wattenberg) and from *Forbes* magazine. These are the same places from which objections to government regulation are routinely issued on the grounds that the market can adapt, even when it comes to events—like international competition or leveraged buyouts—that hit with greater force and less warning than demographic changes.

Environmental Concerns

Myth 4: Population growth has no significant impact on pollution, natural resources, or the quality of life.

For years ecologists have been preaching that a larger population would put dangerous pressure on natural resources. Demo-doom convert Malcolm S. Forbes, Jr., called for legal immigration of 1.5 million a year to avoid a slowdown in population growth. Forbes complained that "we have been overly influenced by nonsensical notions that more people mean more pollution." After all, he said, "man invents technology that can reduce pollution overall."

Forbes and his colleagues seem to have something approaching a mystical faith in the power of technology to bail us out of any environmental problems that arise from the increase in human numbers. A look at Los Angeles might begin to shake that faith. Despite the best pollution controls technology provides, the air in the Los Angeles region violates the Clean Air act's health standards more than 100 days a year. That is because reductions in the pollutants each car emits have been overwhelmed by the increased numbers of people driving.

The Environmental Protection Agency has concluded that the only way to provide safe air to the people in Los Angeles is to restrict people's right to drive and to invest heavily in mass transit and vehicles powered by alternative fuels. Contemplating such costs, most Los Angelenos probably agree with humorist Andy Rooney. "I haven't noticed that bigger is better anywhere but in basketball," Rooney recently admonished the demo-doomsayers. "Our little town has doubled since we moved here 35 years ago, and I still like it, but it isn't twice as good since it got twice as big, I can tell you."

Overcrowding and unrelenting traffic congestion are only the tip of the iceberg. Irreversible ecological changes brought on by the needs of an expanding population are far more serious. The exhaustion of groundwater supplies, destruction of agricultural land, erosion of topsoil, loss of wilderness and natural areas, filled-in wetlands, and diminished wildlife habitat are only part of the list. There are also costs that cannot be measured in dollars, as when regular, intimate contact with untamed nature is an experience reserved increasingly for the well-to-do.

Serious people see these losses as trade-offs to be weighed against other social values that immigration unarguably provides. The demo-doomsayers simply dismiss them as unworthy of concern.

No Labor Shortage

Myth 5. A decline in the population coupled with the aging of the population means a labor shortage that will harm the economy unless immigration is increased.

There is no evidence of a general labor shortage in the United States today. More than six million workers are unemployed. As economist Robert Kuttner points out, this official figure takes no account of more than six million workers who are discouraged from seeking jobs, more than five million who are involuntarily working part-time, and more than one million who hold temporary jobs.

To be sure, there are spot shortages, particularly in areas with exceptionally high housing costs and in certain specialized skill categories, but immigration is a very blunt tool for meeting such needs. The majority of immigrants admitted to fill specific jobs go to work elsewhere within a short time, according to a study funded by the Labor Department. Some apparently exaggerate their qualifications and cannot do the job for which they were selected; some move to other jobs or locations. Talented immigrants obviously contribute to the country and to the economy just as talented natives do. But we should not expect to solve specific labor shortages through immigration unless we are willing to shackle immigrants to the bench or reinstate indentured servitude.

The demo-doomsayers are content to make a broader point. They argue that, skills aside, unless immigration is increased, the labor market as a whole will continue to tighten over the next few years.

So what if it does tighten further? The market will respond. The real question is what the pattern of adjustment will look like. Who will win, and who will lose? Some employers will be forced to offer higher wages and improved working conditions, especially in those sectors where immigrants cluster. Other employers will change their attitude toward workers they now disdain because of age, sex, disability, or race. Managers and entrepreneurs will have an incentive to use this more expensive labor force more productively. Some of the sweatshops will move to Mexico or Jamaica, taking the jobs to the people instead of bringing the people to the jobs.

Who Benefits?

It is this dynamic capacity for adjustment that explains why past predictions of labor shortages have not come to pass. It also explains why some employers are so enthusiastic about the demo-doom argument: population growth from increased immigration offers relief from market processes that would otherwise raise wages and working conditions.

To rephrase the earlier question, will a tighter labor market and consequent relative rise in the incomes of workers—especially the lower-skilled who compete with immigrants—be a good or bad policy outcome? Where you stand often depends on where you sit. Jay F. Rochlin, the director of the President's Committee on Employment of People with Disabilities, is cheered by the prospect of a tighter labor market. "Demographics have given us a 20-year window of opportunity" for "millions of Americans with disabilities," he observes. Low-skilled workers would benefit, not only from higher wages but also from the improved schools, churches, and public services they could support. Immigrants who have been here only a short time would benefit most, as they compete most directly with newcomers. A tighter labor market would dismay business owners who have benefited from lower wages or cheaper immigrant labor in the past, though entrepreneurs in sectors or regions without access to this labor supply would see it differently. . . .

In summary, it would be a mistake to change immigration policy now on the basis of a projection that the U.S. population will stabilize between 2020 and 2050, then decline very slightly over the next 30 years. Even if such projections turn out to be right, there is no reason for alarm.

Population Cannot Grow Indefinitely

It is, after all, a biological and physical fact that the population of the earth cannot grow indefinitely. By logical inference, every country in the world must ultimately pass through the transition that so frightens the demo-doomsayers—from growth to stabilization, with fluctuations thereafter. How ironic if the United States, which has spent the post-World War II era preaching the virtues of reduced population growth to the developing world, should react in panic at the prospect of stabilizing its own.

5 VIEWPOINT

"I would worry more about the future of America if the large immigrant and young minority populations were not here."

Immigrants and Minorities Will Revitalize America

Henry Cisneros

Henry Cisneros was mayor of San Antonio, Texas, from 1981 to 1989, and during that time was one of America's most prominent Hispanic politicians. In the following viewpoint, he argues that the rapidly growing number of immigrants and minorities can strengthen and enrich America. Cisneros argues that instead of restricting immigration, the U.S. should educate its minorities and expand its economy to provide jobs for them.

As you read, consider the following questions:

1. How will the minority population change by the year 2000, according to Cisneros?
2. What fact about immigrants do many people overlook, according to the author?
3. What economic trends worry Cisneros?

Henry Cisneros, "The Demography of a Dream," *New Perspectives Quarterly*, Summer 1988. Reprinted with permission of the Center for the Study of Democratic Institutions.

America is not declining. It is changing.

In the year 2000, 46% of the population of California will be Hispanic, Asian and black. In San Francisco County that figure will be 65%, mostly Asian. In Los Angeles, "minorities," mostly Hispanic, will account for 60% of the population. Even in traditional white, conservative bastions like Orange County, 40% of the population will be Hispanic and Asian. In San Diego, 40% of the population will be non-white, mostly Hispanic.

The most stunning statistic of all: 92% of Californians will live in counties where the "minority" population is more than 30%—a dimension that truly changes the complexion of a community, politically and culturally.

Similar demographic changes are taking place in most central cities and metropolitan areas across this nation: Baltimore, Philadelphia, Chicago, Miami, Atlanta, San Antonio, Denver, Dallas, Houston, New York. These changes will, in time, alter not only the state of California as a whole, but also the other major anchor states of American political and economic life: New York, Illinois, Florida and Texas.

A Source of Renewal

These demographic changes, largely the result of immigration, don't worry me. They may be the very source of the renewal of this country.

I would worry more about the future of America if the large immigrant and young minority populations were not here, and all we had was a classic, northern-hemispheric, advanced industrial nation with an aging white population and a birth dearth.

I would worry more about a nation with too few workers saddled with immense health-care and income-security costs for the aged. I would worry more about a country that had little future orientation because the heaviest voting bloc in the country—elderly whites—felt they already had their best day.

These things would worry me a great deal more than to see young Asians populating the West Coast and commanding the valedictory positions in high schools and colleges. Or young Hispanics with a strong faith in family values and the basic American ethic of hard work, and saving for the future.

Many people fail to see that the immigrants who come to America today, whether Asian or Hispanic, are predisposed to the American way of life. Immigrants come to America from other nations because they are dissatisfied with where they have lived. Those coming from Mexico, for example, have no inclination to go back because they have seen the fallacies and failures of other systems—economically, politically and in terms of personal freedom and upward mobility. Therefore, the commitment they are making to the United States is total.

That dedication brings with it the same kind of raw energy and talent that has characterized previous waves of immigration to America. These immigrants place a great premium on values that relate to the future. They have faith in the future—the most precious resource any nation can have.

A New Southwest Culture

Over time, the immigrants that settle here are fostering an important evolution in American culture. Traditional ethnic values are being matched to the new economy and American rationalism.

What we find in the Hispanic community is the melding of a certain "heart" to American rationalism. By "heart" I mean an affection for the extended family, compassionate values and a sense of sharing that is very deeply rooted in the Catholic tradition, a tradition that is almost synonymous with the Hispanic culture.

Those Catholic values are a useful leavening against the rootless, strictly rationalistic dimensions of American life. On the other hand, American life and education provide an Hispanic, for example, with a strong sense of discipline, management of time, respect for deadlines, mastery over routine and a results-orientation.

A New Pacific Civilization

It may be that the Euro-centered American nation is declining as it gives way to a new Pacific civilization that will include, but not be limited to, America. Historically speaking, America may not decline, but instead fuse with the Pacific culture to create a kind of vast Pacific collage, a mix of Hispanic and Asian cultures linked through the most modern communication technologies.

Ryzsard Kapuscinski, *New Perspectives Quarterly*, Summer 1988.

Contrary to the belief that this collision of values and principles is going to create cultural tension and confusion, in reality it produces a person who is a very complete human being. It produces a human being whose ability to cope with the essence of life—human trauma, pain, sharing and compassion—is matched with the imperative to succeed.

In some sense, what we are seeing in the Southwest is the development of a new culture.

I suspect the same kind of fusion is taking place within the Asian community, where Confucian values of the extended family and group loyalty are a leavening influence on the rootless rationalism which comes from the Protestant foundation of American society.

The identification of the model of a new culture in which people have sorted these things out is very useful for American society. Out of this cultural tension, I believe, comes a richness, even a higher order of human development.

By the year 2000, the dominant characteristic of this nation will be its ethnic heterogeneity. Hispanics will serve in the Senate. Blacks will serve as governors. An Asian will serve as president of Stanford University. Prestigious institutions like the Bohemian Grove will be composed of Hispanics, Asians and blacks. First Interstate Bank will be run by a woman. . . .

By the year 2000, I see an American economy that manages, during the 1990s, to restore some of its basic industries. While the future economy will ride on the advantages of technology and research, it will be a diversified economy that stresses everything from tourism to urban redevelopment, from construction to retailing and financial services.

By the year 2000, America's share of Gross World Product will decline to a lower percentage, but we will still be the single most important force in the global economy. We will have an intertwined and productive relationship with Japan, and a Europe that will, by then, have been integrated for nearly a decade. The Soviet Union and Eastern Europe will also be sizable trading partners of the US due to Gorbachev's reforms, which will be in their 15th year by the turn of the century. Korea, Taiwan, Thailand, Singapore, Hong Kong and China, Indonesia and Malaysia will be active trading partners with America. Brazil will arrive as a world-class economic challenger to the advanced nations.

In short, America won't be a nation in decline, but a trading state interlinked in a consensus-oriented world economy. I say consensus because we will all learn the Japanese way in time. It is the only effective mechanism for organizing affairs in the globally intertwined economic and financial setting of a world with plural centers of power.

Worrying Obstacles

America's demographic trends do worry me a great deal, however, if we fail to educate America's rising population groups and if we fail to produce a growth economy.

A couple of years ago, then Japanese Prime Minister Nakasone said that America would never be able to compete with the Japanese head-on in the next century because of its large population of blacks and Hispanics. He was properly criticized for that remark.

But had Nakasone altered the statement slightly he would have been correct. Had he said America will not be able to compete because it is failing to educate its large population of blacks and Hispanics, and as a result, America will have a large part of its population that is illiterate and underproductive—a permanent underclass—Nakasone would have been correct. Had he said that no nation can carry 10 or 15 or 20 million people in an underclass and still remain competitive, he would have been correct.

This question transcends civil rights, Christian compassion and national ideals. The growth of a permanent underclass has reached the dimensions of an American survival issue. How does America compete in the world? How does America penetrate technological barriers? How does America keep civil order? How does America develop its middle-class? How does America maintain its centrist political values? How do we do any of these things if we fail to bring our large and growing minority populations into the economic mainstream?

A Great Source of Strength

Immigrants are one of the great sources of strength in this country. Over a fifth of our engineers are foreign-born engineers. Look at the enormous positive role Asians have played—the 1989 class at Harvard is 14% Asian-American. These are the sources of strength which make us so very different from both the Soviet Union and the Japanese—the sources that will keep us on top.

Joseph Nye, *New Perspectives Quarterly*, Summer 1988.

This nation must realize there is a real potential explosion between growing minority populations and the traditional aging white population that has an increasing tendency to say, "We're going to vote against bond issues, and property taxes and capital expenditures because our children have already finished school. We have no interest in the future." That's a real political risk on the horizon.

Need for Economic Growth

My concerns with economic growth have to do with the changing pattern of the distribution of income in this country. In 1985, the top 20% of Americans earned 43% of the national income, the largest percentage earned by that group since World War II. The bottom 20% earned only 4.7% of the national income, the smallest percentage in 25 years.

That suggests to me a new polarization along income lines that is a result, primarily, of a transformation in the American economy. We've lost millions of jobs paying $12 and $13 an hour and replaced them with millions paying $5 and $6 an hour. We've shipped millions of jobs offshore and continue to lose our basic industries. . . .

This trend must not be allowed to develop further. A prosperous economy, whether national, regional or urban, is an essential precondition for creating a sense of upward mobility. It is the precondition for any social justice program. A job is clearly more effective than any poverty program.

To the extent that investment in education and economic growth is hampered by massive deficits, by a whopping trade deficit and by the loss of basic industry, much of what we must do to harness the new economy to meet both our demographic challenges and global competition is severely restricted. A recommitment to growth and education is vital to this nation's future. . . .

Need for Innovation

In my view, American society is becoming so culturally diverse that the center can no longer be held together by the older structures of elites with their school ties and cocktail parties. New and innovative structures of governance and goal-setting need to evolve.

There are precedents. I'm reminded of the brown bag lunches held between the black community and the business community in Atlanta during the 1960s. The phrase "a city too busy to hate" came from that experience.

In Minneapolis, the business community committed itself to annual contributions for social programs—the so-called "5% Club"—which William Ouchi cited in *The M Form Society* as the best example of consensus decision making in any American city.

These kinds of new structures of goal-setting and consensus building are models for future forms of governance in America.

The US still has immense resources. It has a unique capability to draw on the energies of its people through the free-market system. The US still calls forth the loyalties and patriotic spirit of its people. With a commitment to harness the new economy for our rising population groups, and leadership that believes in inclusiveness and consensus, this nation will prosper materially and enrich itself culturally.

6 VIEWPOINT

"America has become more segregated, more divided."

Immigrants and Minorities Will Divide America

Richard D. Lamm

Richard D. Lamm is a former governor of Colorado and currently directs the Center for Public Policy and Contemporary Issues at the University of Denver. The following viewpoint is taken from his 1985 book *Megatraumas: America at the Year 2000*. In this book, Lamm creates several futuristic scenarios written in the form of reports to the president. The following viewpoint, excerpted from one of these hypothetical reports, describes a deep division between racial and ethnic groups. Lamm predicts that uncontrolled immigration and large population growth of minorities threaten America's future development and will lead to massive social unrest.

As you read, consider the following questions:

1. What could happen in the next ten years, according to Lamm?
2. What things does the author believe Hispanics will demand?
3. Why does Lamm predict that American cities will turn into "social time bombs"?

The Unmelted Pot:
Report of the U.S. Civil Rights Commission
January 2000

America has had an almost mystical belief in its national ideals. It has been one of our strengths. America's image of itself was positive and optimistic, which was a dynamic of its success. America as a young and vigorous nation could solve any problem, meet any demand, execute every challenge. We absorbed an incredible number of people of diverse cultures and developed a heterogeneous but unified culture of our own.

This commission has always advocated an integrated America. We believe in racial equality and social justice. Our dream, expressed more than thirty years ago, was of an America that lived up to its promise of "equal justice under the law."

It is thus with heavy hearts and a profound sense of loss that we find that in the last ten years America has become more segregated, more divided, more Balkanized than it was thirty years ago. New racial and cultural conflicts abound, and America has not only failed to achieve equality but has reversed earlier progress. A new Jim Crow has developed in America.

We find that the southwestern United States has become a Hispanic Quebec, filled with tensions and conflict unimaginable twenty years ago. America thought it could avoid the problems that plagued other nations filled with diverse people. It worked up to a point—but it is no longer working.

Seldom has a nation had to absorb as many people as the United States has over the last twenty-five years. Even before the revolutions in South and Central America and Mexico, the United States was absorbing large numbers of Hispanics. There were so many that integration did not operate and demands for separate linguistic and cultural treatment soon developed.

Violent Conflict

Conflict was minor at first and the early provocation was clearly not caused by Hispanics. Illegal aliens were victimized and the Ku Klux Klan took it upon itself to "enforce" new immigration laws. Violence flared in many parts of the United States. Hispanics charge "cultural genocide," while Anglos charge that bilingual education is "de-Americanizing" our nation. It is a dialogue between the blind and the deaf.

Yet the revolutions south of our border made our border unmanageable. The numbers were too large and the desperation was too great. The sanctuary movement in U.S. churches grew dramatically. Soon the distinction between legal citizen and illegal alien blurred. Blacks felt that illegal immigrants were preventing their economic advancement; conflict arose between those two groups and soon became violent.

White and black citizens, fearing economic dislocation and the rising cost of providing social services, demanded a national identification card, and the ensuing legislative battle opened wounds that still fester. Hispanic groups, understandably, felt persecuted and organized their now-famous march on Washington at which Senator Henry Cisneros made his eloquent plea for "brown power."

A Hispanic Nation?

By the late 1980s, the Hispanic demand for the establishment of "Aztlan," a new nation, was asserted. It was argued that the United States "illegally" took the Southwest from Mexico with the 1848 Treaty of Guadalupe Hidalgo, and Mexico and Hispanic militants demanded it back. The simultaneous bombing of the immigration offices of New Mexico, Arizona, and California accented this demand. The People's Republic of Mexico pushed to "renegotiate" the treaty and for return of "Mexican property stolen from its people." Bilingual, bicultural education became less a transitional program than a demand for "cultural equality." The biggest civil rights issue today isn't the question of integration but the demand for segregation and return of land deemed "stolen."

Limited Options

If we refuse to control immigration, our options are severely limited. The least unattractive solution would be to implement the federal principle on a state and regional level, recognizing Hispanics and Orientals, in states where they form a majority, as the dominant group—much as the French are given special status in Quebec. . . . Descendants of the old settlers that fought and won the land from Mexico will be quite rightly indignant with what many Mexicans are already calling the Reconquest, and we shall probably have far more trouble than Canada in adjusting to a multicultural situation. Perhaps after a century or two we can evolve into a safely neutered society of consumers—like Switzerland. It is just as likely to be a bloodbath.

Thomas Fleming, *Chronicles*, March 1989.

Even the Congressional Hispanic Caucus has been pushed to the extreme. Their position on Aztlan was recently amended to say: "The U.S. government created by force an artificial boundary through the middle of Mexico in 1848 and it is arrogance to declare that those who cross this forced border are 'illegal aliens' in their own land."

We find that it is impossible to ascribe the blame for these tensions to any one event or group. Long before the assassination of the Mexican ambassador to the United States and the Los Angeles barrio riots, the breach had become irreconcilable. The United States now, tragically, has its own Quebec.

Thus we find that in America in the year 2000:

1. Our economy has not created and is not creating enough new jobs for our own citizens, let alone additional immigrants. Illegal aliens have become a large, resentful, and dangerous underclass of unskilled and untrained workers who cannot find employment.

2. We have lost control, not only over our border, but also over the size and nature of our work force, our nation's population size and policy, our linguistic heritage, and our foreign policy.

3. Not being able to control our own borders, we have been unable to control the inflow of political terrorists, foreign agents, and everyday criminals that other countries, following Castro's example, dump on us.

4. Our energy and natural resource shortages, severe since the 1970s, have been increased and aggravated by both legal and illegal immigration.

5. Our social cohesion and political unity have been severely disrupted. Our foreign policy is now held hostage to recently arrived aliens, militantly demanding influence.

The New Segregation

The falling birthrates have been largely a Caucasian middle-class phenomenon. The birthrate of minorities has stayed even, which means that the percentage of minorities in our society is increasing. By the late 1990s, minorities of all ages accounted for 25 percent of our population—but more than 30 percent of the younger age groups.

Legal and illegal immigration is dramatically changing the face of our cities. In New York City in the 1970s, for example, the overall population declined by 10.4 percent, but the Asian population grew by 250 percent. Los Angeles now has a 60 percent Hispanic population, with 20 percent of its total population estimated to be illegal immigrants. In many parts of the United States we have lost our social and linguistic cohesion.

Meanwhile, "white flight" has unbalanced the demography of our cities. Detroit has lost 50 percent of its white population; New York City, 30 percent; Boston, 25 percent.

These figures have dramatically affected urban schools. Public schools in twenty-three of the twenty-five largest cities in the United States now have predominantly minority enrollments. The change has been fast-paced and considerable. In these school systems in 1950, one student in ten came from a minority group; by 1960 it was one in three; in 1970 it was one in two. By 1980, seven urban students out of ten were children of minorities, and by 1990 the Joint Center for Political Studies found that nine out of ten students in big-city districts were members of a minority

Ed Gamble. Reprinted with permission

group. In forty years the racial make-up of these urban schools has been completely reversed.

In some areas, the change has been even more startling. Los Angeles's Hispanic enrollment was 20 percent in 1968, and it had grown to 49 percent by 1982. It is now 70 percent. Similar changes took place in Dade County, Florida, and in Chicago the proportion of Hispanic students is now 20 percent, with Hispanic students replacing whites as the second-largest group of students after blacks.

Minorities made up 10 percent of the public school population in 1950, but they now make up 45 percent in many states.

A Divided America

Our cities have become more segregated than any area of American life—more so than in the most racist days of Jim Crow. We have a divided America, characterized by minority cities surrounded by largely white suburbs, by poverty surrounded by wealth, by the unemployed surrounded by the employed, by despair surrounded by hope. We have the dream of desegregation replaced by the reality that America has not integrated but is experiencing, at best, an armed and uneasy truce between the races. This is a prescription for disaster. Our metropolitan areas are social time bombs, powder kegs sitting in the sun.

VIEWPOINT

7

"The extension of the democratic idea is, far from a fearsome trend, the essence and the raison d'être of America itself."

American Democracy Will Spread Worldwide

Gregory A. Fossedal

The destruction of the Berlin wall in East Germany, the student protests in China, and the economic and social reforms in the Soviet Union have led some to conclude that democracy is defeating communism. Many commentators attribute this defeat to the "shining example" of the democratic history of the United States. In the following viewpoint, excerpted from his book, *The Democratic Revolution*, Gregory A. Fossedal agrees with this assessment. He believes that America can greatly influence the trend toward democracy and play a significant role in the world by doing so. Fossedal is John M. Olin media fellow at the Hoover Institution, a conservative think tank in Stanford, California.

As you read, consider the following questions:

1. What can America hope to accomplish by promoting democracy, according to Fossedal?
2. Why does the author believe that either communism or democracy must perish?
3. What evidence does Fossedal give for his belief that the U.S. can achieve its goal? Do you agree?

"All men," our Declaration of Independence proclaims, "are created equal." Obviously this doesn't mean they are equal in the spurious sense of having the same color hair, the same size nose, or even the same merits and abilities. Yet they have been endowed, Jefferson and the Continental Congress declared, with certain rights fundamental to a just state and a just society. Because men are created with these equal rights, for example, no man or institution may justly rule over another without his enlightened consent. Abraham Lincoln argued: "As I would not be a slave, so I would not be a master. This expresses my idea of democracy. Whatever differs from this, to the extent it differs, is no democracy." Now, it is possible to build arguments for democracy without admitting to any of these universal rights. Democracy is efficient and productive. People like it better than other systems. But democracy is only a process. The goal, as our framers put it, is to secure the rights of mankind. . . .

Promoting Democracy and Freedom

In promoting democracy, America will promote the fundamental rights of mankind, those rights having been found to be unrealizable absent certain practical arrangements. It is important to note, however, that these rights—as Jefferson wrote in the Declaration—are prior to and higher than democracy itself, or any other form of government. That, as Lincoln observed, is the Declaration's great and radical principle. The rights of mankind are not good or just because they promote democracy, or any other form of government; rather, democracy exists to promote and protect those rights, and as soon as it ceases to do so, it ceases to act in accordance with the principles of just government, of natural law. To do this, however, democracy as defined would have to become undemocratic. . . .

Given that most people, in America and abroad, will agree with me that men have fundamental rights which it is the business of governments to promote—even the Soviet and South African constitutions say as much—my message on U.S. diplomacy is aimed at those who believe this. If the rights of man are the purpose of our government at home—"the animating and distinctive spirit which lies behind the laws and institutions" of America, as political scientist Charles Kesler has put it—then it follows that the rights of man exist. And if a "right" to self-government is to have any meaning, it must mean the rights of all men and women everywhere and in all times and conditions. Whatever is peculiar to some is no right at all. Whatever is a "right" is universal. And what is universal certainly applies to American foreign policy. . . .

The history of America is the history of the gradual realization of that Jeffersonian ideal. It gave life to all of America's greatest achievements: the forming of the Constitution and subsequent drafting of the Bill of Rights; the abolition of slavery; the extension of the franchise; the protection and gradual expansion of civil rights. Prudence has guided its application, making progress seem unduly slow. Hence the founders, rightly or wrongly, compromised with slavery; and even Abraham Lincoln stopped short of recommending its immediate abolition. Yet Lincoln persistently reminded Americans that a nation half-free, half-slave, could not long endure, and left no doubt that an America true to its own principles must abolish it.

A Democratic Revolution

The day of communist revolutions is over. There are no more colonial powers controlling the Third World. It is time now for the West to take the initiative and make a different kind of revolution—a revolution not *against* communism, but *for* democracy.

Doan Van Toai, *The World & I*, February 1988.

That same realism tells us that a world half-democratic, half-totalitarian, is a world that must change in one direction or the other. Communism, eventually, must either perish or rule the globe. It is possible to envision a world with one government; or a world composed of nation-states, all democratic; or a world of nation-states, all communist; or a world in which some new systems have swept these alternatives from the globe. It is not plausible to posit a world forever suspended on one side or the other of a vast Iron Curtain. Either the democracies will take the democratic idea to its conclusion or we will fail. Either America will help secure the rights of man for all, everywhere, or America itself, as a free and democratic state, will perish.

Let us be specific; let us say the great unsayable. "Everywhere" includes the Soviet Union. To say that we must help achieve democracy in Russia is not to say that we must achieve it by war; it is assumed, on the contrary, that such a war would likely bring the end of democracy as well. Nor must we complete our task in a fortnight. To say that our goal must be a democratic world does not mean we must achieve it in the next year, the next decade, or the next generation.

Indeed, History and Reality, though often called to the stand by self-proclaimed pragmatists, have stubbornly refused to testify against democracy, and the general tide of history points not toward Russian despotism but toward freedom. George Kennan, the noted scholar of Russian history, writes:

> When the Revolution [of 1917] occurred, Russia already was, and had been for some three or four decades, in a process of quite rapid evolution . . . in the direction of the modern liberal

> state. The development of a firm judicial system was far advanced; a beginning had been made toward the development of local government; public opinion was a force to be reckoned with. While the long-term trend of Russian society was interrupted by the Revolution and its consequences, I can see no reason to doubt that it still represents the direction in which, in the long run, Russia must move.

Can America actually assist in such a vast undertaking—the conversion of Russia and other great empires to the principles of our own declaration? We can and, indeed, already have made great progress. That we have done so almost unconsciously, by a kind of benign and invisible hand—even as the leaders of the free nations proclaim over and over again that such grand tasks are beyond our scope—only gives evidence of the power of the idea and the achievability of the goal. Imagine how effective we will be when the goal is proclaimed and the means orchestrated to the end. "France," wrote Charles de Gaulle, "is only her true self" when engaged in some great enterprise, for "France is not France without greatness." What is true and obvious of that great republic is truer and more obvious of America, perhaps the first nation since the New Ilium to be founded on an idea.

It is true, as historians as diverse as Paul Johnson and Paul Kennedy have noted, that America can no longer achieve great things merely by the mindless application of overwhelming resources. In fact . . . we never did. Our enterprises have been large and they have been great; but they were great not because they were large but because they were wise.

A Smarter Policy

It is ironic to hear so many leaders speak in terms of American limits. America cannot be "the world's policeman," they say. She has neither right nor might to "impose our system." Few would disagree. If so, however, it would seem all the more urgent to debate the means by which our (admittedly finite) power can be used more efficaciously; to determine how our foreign policy can be smaller, but smarter. Instead, the chanting of platitudes about limits seems to be an end in itself, a pretext, frankly, for inaction. Our leaders too often seem more concerned with talking about what cannot be done than with what we may still accomplish.

It is obvious, for example, that America's economy, as a share of the world economy, may well shrink. With it, in all likelihood, will shrink the preponderance of American arms—if not relative to the Soviet Union, then certainly relative to such countries as Japan and West Germany, whose rearmament it should be our design to promote. Yet in this sense, it may be a measure of our success if the U.S. role does shrink—provided the "decline" is a reflection not of stagnation here but of even more rapid growth in the surging democracies of Asia, Latin America, and Africa, and

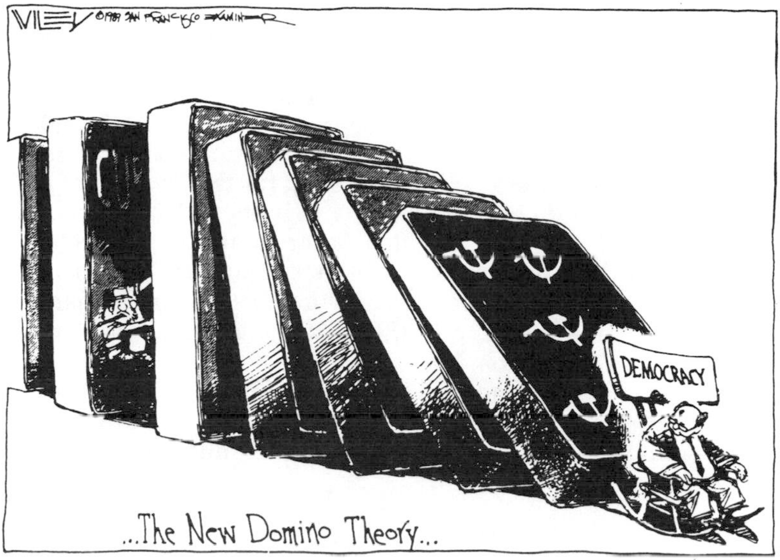

Wiley. Reprinted with permission of *The San Francisco Examiner.* © 1989 The San Francisco Examiner

of a recrudescent pride on the part of Europeans in the heritage of civilization they have shared with the world. What we cannot do alone, we can do in concert with a growing orchestra of proud and prosperous democracies. In this sense, the decline of American material hegemony should be a primary goal of American foreign policy.

"We cannot," said a writer in the London *Economist* of Britain's growing dependence on America in 1941, "resent this historical development. We may rather feel proud that the cycle of dependence, enmity, and independence is coming full circle." What was true for Britain in the middle of the twentieth century is true for America in the twenty-first. It is only by the extension of the democratic idea, after all, that our sisters of the world will become great nations. And the extension of the democratic idea is, far from a fearsome trend, the essence and the raison d'être of America itself.

If there was an American Century—as Henry Luce both urged and prophesied in his essay of that title—it is, in the narrow and ethnocentric sense, already over. Yet to reread his urgent essay almost fifty years later is to realize that Luce had something much bigger in mind. In a way, his label did not do justice to his idea. For the age of American dominance did not begin in the 1940s; it was nearing its end. What did begin, as Luce in some passages intimated, was something grander and nobler still: a Democratic Century. As America remains the most revered and daunting of the democracies, and will for some time, this may seem like a caviling distinction. Yet in its nuance, it is as important as the difference between self-interest and charity; between pride and humility. And truly, it is the promotion of a thing much broader than mere Americanism the author of "The American Century" had in mind: "a love of freedom, a feeling for the equality of opportunity, a tradition of self-reliance and independence and also of cooperation." It is fair to say that America has been especially blessed with these; it is wrong to think of the ideas themselves as peculiarly American, for as ideas, they are as old as man.

The Democratic Century, in this sense, is not an assertion of fact, or even a prediction, but a possibility. . . . It was half-born after the war, when America helped rebuild half a continent ill-fed, ill-housed, and more important, somewhat ill-led, threatened by a communist empire that had swallowed much of the world and still seemed unsated.

The Democratic Century

The Democratic Century is still, in its essence, waiting to be completed. Too often, our leaders have feared or rejected such grand notions. Yet the soul of the Democratic Century is the soul of our nation. Reviving, or, more precisely, rediscovering that spirit, then, is a vital task for America. For as Luce wrote:

> Other nations can survive simply because they have endured so long. . . . But this nation, conceived in adventure and dedicated to the progress of man—this nation cannot truly endure unless there courses strongly through its veins from Maine to California the blood of purpose and enterprise and high resolve. . . .
>
> Ours cannot come out of the vision of any one man. It must be the vision of many. It must be a sharing with all peoples our Bill of Rights, our Declaration, our Constitution. . . . It must be an internationalism of the people, by the people, and for the people. . . .
>
> For the moment, it may be enough to be the sanctuary of these ideals. But not for long. It now becomes our time to be the powerhouse from which the ideals spread throughout the world.

A half-century after Luce penned those words, America still stands at the head of the democratic revolution. This is not to say that America is morally or culturally superior. On the contrary, the democratic idea is a gift we happened to receive; a sign of our fortune, not our intrinsic merit. It is better because it is better, not because it is ours.

What is ours, nevertheless, is a unique responsibility. Some Americans will shrink from this challenge. But the American spirit will welcome it.

8 VIEWPOINT

"Not a single fully Communist country . . . has come on its own to democracy."

Communism Will Not Allow Democracy to Spread Worldwide

Jean-François Revel

While events such as Mikhail Gorbachev's economic and political reforms have led many commentators to predict the end of communism and the beginning of a "democratic century," others are pessimistic. In the following viewpoint, Jean-François Revel argues that foretelling the death of communism is premature. While Revel does not directly refute Gregory A. Fossedal, author of the previous viewpoint, his views on the staying power of communism provide a compelling counterpoint to Fossedal's vision of the future. Revel, a French political commentator, is the author of *Without Marx or Jesus, How Democracies Perish,* and other books.

As you read, consider the following questions:

1. Why does Revel believe certain communist regimes are initiating reforms?
2. Why is the author pessimistic that communism can initiate true economic reforms?
3. Why does the author believe the Third World is likely to remain totalitarian?

Jean-François Revel, "Is Communism Reversible?" Reprinted from *Commentary,* January 1989, by permission; all rights reserved.

Suddenly it seems possible to think about the reversibility of Communism. First the 1979 economic reforms in China, then the bold actions and, especially, the bold words of Mikhail Gorbachev have been pushing in the direction of a change to which some Western observers have not hesitated to apply the word revolutionary.

The many domestic plans and projects are not the only signs of transformation. Up until yesterday both doctrine and fact proclaimed that geographical entities, once added to the Communist sphere, could never be dissociated from it. Now, for the first time in its history, Communist expansionism appears to some to be holding a return ticket, as countries already conquered are being effectively partitioned, while those that have proved impossible to conquer outright are being abandoned. Does this mean that Communism may be not only reversible but destructible? . . .

It is helpful to bear in mind that to Communism, and to socialism in general, *non*reversibility has always been regarded as an organic principle. Every socialist revolution aims to abolish the existing political, economic, social, and cultural structures and to replace them, once and for all, with new ones; it even proposes to do the same for man himself. Obviously, then, a transition to socialism involves much more than a simple succession of governments, since a succession in the opposite direction is unthinkable.

Without the factor of irreversibility, socialism itself loses all meaning. This holds true even for nontotalitarian socialists, or those operating within the framework of a pluralist democracy. "We must create the conditions for an irreversible transition to socialism," said Jean Poperen, then the number-two man in the French Socialist party, at the time of that party's electoral victory in 1981. "There will be no return to the past," added Louis Mermaz, president of the National Assembly. A confidant of Pierre Mauroy, then the prime minister, writes in his memoirs: "Mauroy was a democrat, but a reversal *after* a victory of the Left was for him an intellectually vacuous idea." True, in the event none of these men could or would act in complete conformity with his convictions, but they were being ideologically consistent in uttering them.

Communists Prone to Stagnation

Although every regime, every government, every president, every official, and every official's aide everywhere seeks to remain in office as long as possible, and pursues that end by means of skill, force, cunning, and talent, day by day, in every way, it is only socialists—and how much more so Communists—who make the principle of permanence central and vital to their political purview.

A final preliminary point: it has become customary to draw a dividing line between democratic and nondemocratic societies and then, within the latter category, to distinguish further between authoritarian and totalitarian systems. But the most important political division in the world does not in fact run between the allegedly principal groupings of democrats versus nondemocrats but rather between totalitarianism and all the rest. Most of human history is the story of nontotalitarian *and* nondemocratic societies; it is from them, after all, that the democracies emerged. But can democracy emerge out of totalitarianism? That is the major question today.

Anything But Secure

In the Third World, the decline of communism's appeal will make it somewhat easier for the West to deal with inept or corrupt regimes that in the past have been able to argue that they provided the only guarantees against a communist takeover. But in many Third World countries, communism is still seen by some as a potent weapon against intolerable social conditions, and by many as a means to power. The recent advances in democracy are anything but secure.

Henry Grunwald, *The Wall Street Journal*, June 12, 1989.

It is by no means a simple question. If democracy is a system in which the electorate can turn out a government which it dislikes, and authoritarianism one in which the people cannot effect a change in government but can, over the long term, effect a change of regime, in a totalitarian system, at least up until the present, the people cannot change either the government or the regime. In comparison with the evolutions, revolutions, transformations, and downfalls suffered by all other types of political systems, totalitarianism in general and Communism in particular present us with a difference not just of degree but of substance.

Communist Systems' Internal Capacity

What is the internal capacity of Communist systems to transform themselves, through evolution or revolution?. . .

To be sure, economic failure and popular discontent in the satellite nations are themselves a source of trouble to the Soviet state, no less than the stirring of the nationalities within Soviet boundaries proper. Still, it is really only within the central systems, the autonomous mother countries—above all the Soviet Union itself and continental China—that the process of reversibility, if it exists at all, is to be observed.

The one massive fact everyone can agree on, if only because it is shouted aloud by the leaders themselves, be they Deng Xiao Ping, Gorbachev, or even Pham Van Dong, is that the socialist economy is everywhere in a state of collapse. The leaders have been *driven* to reform. To read Gorbachev's report to the party conference of June 28, 1988, with its obsessive harping on food shortages, is to be plunged back into the worried atmosphere of Western speculations in the period just after World War II. Gorbachev is hardly the first General Secretary to resort to apocalyptic language in describing the situation bequeathed to him by his predecessors. The point, however, is that the perduring penury of the Soviet Union is such as to constitute in and of itself both a definition of the crisis and a constant aggravating factor in it. Less and less can it be presented as a temporary or circumstantial condition; more and more it is recognized as conducing to the structural paralysis of the entire system. . . .

The Socialist Market

The notion of the "socialist market" is neither practical nor intellectually viable. Lenin was right: there is no "third way." The Chinese Communists gleefully rubbing their hands in anticipation of gaining control of Hong Kong imagine they will be appropriating a permanent source of wealth, when their very presence cannot but dry it up. For socialism and competition inhabit two different universes, and cannot be put into practice simultaneously. It may be amusing to try riding your bicycle out over the ocean waves, or to drive your boat up a tree; if you are a Communist country and play such games you may even be rewarded with Western subsidies, general-purpose loans, business credits, and technological aid, not to mention the enthusiastic congratulations of experts and journalists. But after you have tried organizing some rivalry among collective enterprises, after you have introduced the concept of profit (measured how?), decentralized the decision-making process, and placed management and workers on notice that they will be held responsible for their output, you will still find you do not have true competition, true competitiveness, true modernization.

And for a simple reason—competition cannot be willed. It goes against the grain, as is proved by the fact that even in a free economy rival enterprises endeavor to neutralize competition by means of tariffs and trade agreements. For competition to flourish, it must be rooted in the underlying institution of private property. Only then does it become a basic reality of life. If its powers of creative stimulation are truly to be released, the one indispensable condition, necessary if not sufficient, is private ownership of the means of production, agricultural no less than industrial. The transformation of the Soviet kolkhozes into long-term leaseholds, that is to say the transition in theory from serfdom to tenant farming, will not in itself suffice to recreate that class of competent and enterprising peasants, the kulaks, which the Soviet system set about abolishing.

True reversibility will thus entail the dispossession of Communism: not just dismantling the system of central planning but reinstituting private property, not just granting semi-autonomy to certain economic sectors, within limits determined by the party, but freeing ownership and property. In short, capitalism; everything else is froth.

Democracy and Politics

To accomplish all this in the economic realm, however, means accomplishing democracy in the political realm. And here once again socialism proves a stubborn obstacle.

In fact socialism has never been an economic system *per se.* It is a political system which in order to survive needs to destroy all economic life. One should not imagine that socialist rulers *like* presiding over economies in a condition of irremediable breakdown. Obviously, they would prefer their economies to flourish. But there is only one way to accomplish this miracle, and that is to commit political hara-kiri. Short of that, the art of managing Communist countries consists in bringing about, by means of expedients which include capitalist charity, the survival of a nonviable economic system that offers political benefits only to the rulers themselves and to the class that serves them.

The populace pays the cost of these expedients, and so does the

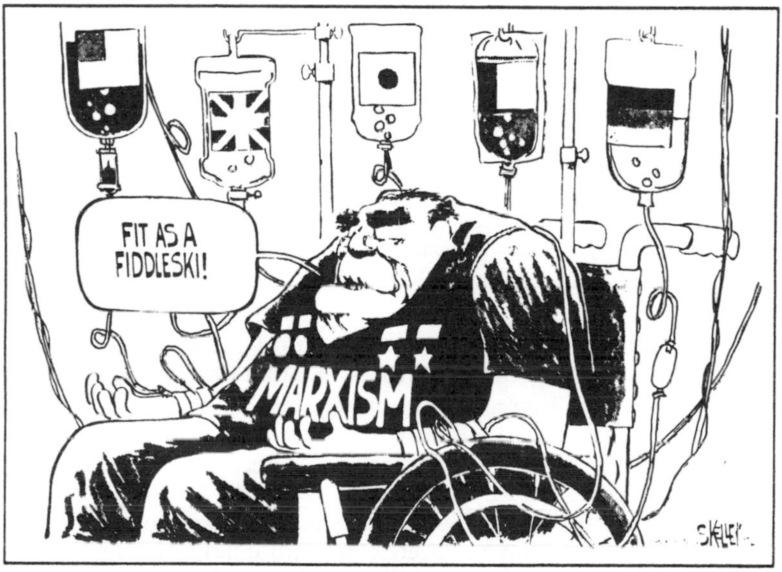

Steve Kelley. Reprinted with permission

democratic world. Capitalist patronage has for a long time functioned as a structural component of Communist economies, never more strikingly than during periods of active reform, which create currents of sympathy catalyzing new infusions of Western capital and technology. But as for setting a Communist economy on its own feet, rather than on ours, this cannot occur without democratization—that is to say, an end to the party-state, an end to the monopoly of power exercised by the Communist party. . . .

Gorbachev wants to cut down the party by building up the state, and to this end he has proposed to commingle responsibility for both within the hands of a single person: himself. Below the top, analogously, party secretaries at the regional or national level will run for election to the presidency of their corresponding regional or national soviet. The idea is that party chieftains will thus be submitting to a "democratic" vote cast by the "representatives of the people." If a party secretary fails to be elected president of the soviet, he will have to abandon his post in the party; this rule would apply to the General Secretary as well.

A Stumbling Block to Democracy

This pretty construct leaves standing an essential stumbling block to democracy, namely, the single party. In their votes the members of the soviets will be allowed to choose, at best, among various "candidates" sprung from or close to the ranks of the party. In any event, the Communists are hardly at great risk because the soviets are already in the hands of the party, which in general reserves for itself a very large majority. So before hailing, as a step toward democracy, this new requirement that party bigwigs "run" for office, we should ask how the "representatives of the people" are elected or rather appointed to the soviets in the first place.

It is not enough to have "pluralism" apply among individuals all of whom belong to the same single party. Before one can speak of democratization in the USSR it must become possible freely to create there pro-capitalist, liberal, or social-democratic parties, capable of coming to power should they receive a mandate by popular vote. Whether a particular regime is democratic is to be gauged not according to some abstract flow chart of offices and institutions but according to the essence and disposition of the forces that shape those institutions. . . .

For what is involved here? Gorbachev says: no economic reform without political reform. Westerners translate: no market economy or free enterprise without political democracy. But this is not in the least what Gorbachev means. True, he wants to revive the economy and shake up the inefficient and corrupt bureaucracy. But he wants to do this, so far as possible, within the same old administrative framework, and not by permitting real political rotation. As we have seen, the one means at his disposal (without exiting the system) is to bring the party under control of the soviets, or rather to blend the two pyramidal structures under a single apex. But this new arrangement remains internal to the system; and it has little in common with democracy as we understand it. Under the plan peremptorily announced October 1, 1988 and ratified by the Supreme Soviet on December 1, the Central Committee loses many of its prerogatives and powers, which means that the party does greatly surrender the mechanism by which it has controlled the economy, and that can only lead to greater autonomy. But the soviets are nevertheless not becoming democratic, and at the top, as Andrei Sakharov has warned, the autocracy embodied in Gorbachev is being reinforced.

If we base our assessment of Communist evolution only on what is real, and not on what we are pleased to imagine, this is qualified progress indeed. . . .

A Post-Totalitarian Society

A new political concept has been introduced by a number of Czech authors, among them Jiri Pehe, Petr Fidelius, and Vaclav Havel: this is what they call a "post-totalitarian society," a society characterized above all by the disappearance of mass terror. They are pointing to a true and palpable change that has taken place in East European Communism—though even so one should point out that Albania and especially Rumania are still practicing or have returned to the practice of terror, and in the Soviet Union itself during the 1970's, which is not exactly prehistory, Yuri Andropov made a habit of physically liquidating opponents of the regime by means of "psychiatric" treatment.

But if by and large there is considerably less fear in the USSR and its satellites since *glasnost*, mass terror and genocide have hardly disappeared from the Communist world as a whole. There may still be people who believe that Communism has been evolving spontaneously in the direction of ever greater sweetness and light; globally, however, it has seldom been so cruel as over the course of the last fifteen years. What happens in Moscow is interesting, and more interesting still is what is said there; but it is necessary to look elsewhere as well.

Elsewhere, there are the 10,000 dead in South Yemen in 1986. Elsewhere there is the pharaonic or dynastic Communism of Cuba and North Korea, countries where mass terror definitely holds sway. Elsewhere there are the mass executions in Ethiopia, the famine-by-design, the often fatal transfers of populations. Elsewhere there is Communist Madagascar, despotic and wretched. Elsewhere there is the physical and cultural genocide of the Tibetan people by the Chinese Communists. Elsewhere there are the thousands of political prisoners in Sandinista Nicaragua, lightly though they weigh on the conscience of

Amnesty International. Elsewhere there are the million massacred civilians of Afghanistan.

This little recital suggests the enduring popularity of the Stalinist model in the Third World. Despite variations, the basic pattern remains the same. In Vietnam, after the successful invasion of the South by the North, the well-worn process began anew: the forced collectivization of the land, reeducation camps, mass terror. In 1976 the Vietnamese Communist party created "new economic zones" to which several million persons were forcibly transferred to labor under military supervision. A half-million workers were sent against their will to the Soviet Union, free manual labor for the Siberian pipeline providing gas to the West. As before in the USSR or in China, drastic plans meant to build up the economy have created nothing but a shambles. Summary executions in Vietnam are estimated at 80,000 from 1975 to 1985, another 15,000 since 1985. An additional 300,000 Vietnamese have died as a result of maltreatment in the camps, and around 600,000 boat people have perished at sea.

Post-totalitarian society, in other words, is a singularly relative phenomenon.

Not a Single Communist Country Is Democratic

What is happening today in the Soviet Union, in China, and in other Communist countries is something we must consider in a detached spirit, careful not to confuse words with deeds, and mindful that up to the present moment not a single fully Communist country has been restored or has come on its own to democracy. Despite what so many in the West appear to regard as an extremely easy process, we cannot name a single *completed* instance of Communist reversibility. With hindsight we may have learned, more or less, how a country may avoid entering into that pit; we are still far from being able to say: this is how you get out.

But if we are truly aiming to induce the great Communist systems to democratize, the one thing we must not do is help them surmount their crises while remaining Communist. For unless the sickness is allowed to run its course, they will never fundamentally change. Only if we have the courage to let them evolve on their own do we stand a chance of realizing the prophetic mid-19th-century vision of Alexander Herzen:

> Socialism will go on developing through all its phases until it achieves its extremes and its absurdities. Then there will escape anew from the great bosom of the rebellious minority a cry of refusal, and the struggle to the death will begin anew, as socialism, assuming the place of present-day conservatism, is vanquished in its turn by the revolution to come, which as yet we cannot descry.

a critical thinking activity

Recognizing Deceptive Arguments

People who feel strongly about an issue use many techniques to persuade others to agree with them. Some of these techniques appeal to the intellect, some to the emotions. Many of them distract the reader or listener from the real issues.

A few common examples of argumentation tactics are listed below. Most of them can be used either to advance an argument in an honest, reasonable way or to deceive or distract from the real issues. It is important for a critical reader to recognize these tactics in order to rationally evaluate an author's ideas.

a. *scare tactics*—the threat that if you don't do or don't believe this, something terrible will happen

b. *patriotic appeal*—using national pride to sway the reader into favoring a position which flatters one's own culture

c. *personal attack*—criticizing an opponent *personally* instead of rationally debating his or her ideas

d. *strawperson*—distorting or exaggerating an opponent's ideas to make one's own seem stronger

e. *bandwagon*—the idea that "everybody" does this or believes this

f. *testimonial*—quoting or paraphrasing an authority or celebrity to support one's own viewpoint

g. *deductive reasoning*—the idea that since *a* and *b* are true, *c* is also true, although there may be no connection between *a* and *c*

The following activity can help you sharpen your skills in recognizing deceptive reasoning. Most of the statements below are derived from the viewpoints in this chapter. *Beside each one, mark the letter of the type of deceptive appeal being used. More than one type of tactic may be applicable. If you believe the statement is not any of the listed appeals, write N.*

1. An optimistic belief in America's future has been shared by millions of people who immigrated to this country in search of a better life.
2. If America's world population share continues to decline, this country may face a situation where our birthright, our legacy, and our prosperity are diluted and diluted until we become insignificant in the world.
3. Apocalyptic predictions about U.S. population decline are similar to French predictions in the 1870s of "race suicide" and the end of France. The doomsayers were wrong then, and they are wrong now.
4. Harvard's Dr. Nathan Keyfitz, one of the grand old men of American demography, states that "beyond a quarter century or so we simply do not know what the population will be." Thus worries about population declines and/or explosions are off-base.
5. Immigrants are a source of renewal for the United States because their hard work and family togetherness epitomize the values that made America great.
6. The United States is losing control of its borders and is confronted with the prospect of millions of impoverished refugees it cannot absorb.
7. America should spread freedom and democracy throughout the world because that is her destiny.
8. People who talk about American "limits" and say that the U.S. cannot be "the world's policeman," use these arguments as pretexts for inaction. Our timid leaders are afraid, and cover up their failures by talking about what cannot be done instead of what we still may accomplish.
9. Everyone knows, including the leaders of Communist countries, that socialist economies everywhere are in a state of collapse.
10. The eminent French demographer Alfred Sauvy warned a century ago against a society of old people ruminating about old ideas.
11. Some Americans like to believe that their country is exceptional and has none of the social problems that other countries face. But the facts show otherwise.
12. One of the things that makes America unique is its assumption that race should not matter. This is a noble belief: It makes America better than most other societies.

Periodical Bibliography

The following articles have been selected to supplement the diverse views presented in this chapter.

Richard J. Barnet	"The Challenge of Change," *Sojourners*, June 1989.
Daniel Bell	"The World and the United States in 2013," *Daedalus*, Summer 1987.
John Carey	"The Changing Face of a Restless Nation," *Business Week*, September 25, 1989.
Ossie Davis	"Challenge for the Year 2000," *The Nation*, July 24-31, 1989.
Francis Fukuyama	"The End of History?" *The National Interest*, Summer 1989.
Anthony Harrigan	"National Character Is Decisive," *Vital Speeches of the Day*, June 1, 1989.
R.J. Herrnstein	"IQ and Falling Birth Rates," *The Atlantic Monthly*, May 1989.
Neil Howe	"America in the Year 2007," *The American Spectator*, December 1987.
Ryzsard Kapuscinski	"America as a Collage," *New Perspectives Quarterly*, Summer 1988.
Tony Kaye	"The Birth Dearth: Conservatives Conceive a Population Crisis," *Utne Reader*, May/June 1988.
Edward N. Luttwak	"Do We Need a New Grand Strategy?" *The National Interest*, Spring 1989.
The New Republic	"It's a Small World After All," September 18-25, 1989.
Gary Orfield	"Well Along Toward Separate and Unequal Societies," *Los Angeles Times*, August 22, 1988.
Jonathan Rauch	"Kids as Capital," *The Atlantic Monthly*, August 1989.
Tom Sine	"Shifting into the Future Tense," *Christianity Today*, November 17, 1989.
Steven Steinberg	"How We Went Wrong," *The Nation*, June 26, 1989.

Organizations to Contact

The editors have compiled the following list of organizations that are concerned with the issues debated in this book. All of them have information or publications available for interested readers. The descriptions are derived from materials provided by the organizations. This list was compiled upon the date of publication. Names and phone numbers of organizations are subject to change.

The American Assembly
412 Altschul Hall
Barnard College
Columbia University
New York, NY 10027
(212) 854-3456

The Assembly was established by Dwight D. Eisenhower in 1950 as a nonpartisan think tank on public policy. It publishes books on policy issues, including *The Future of American Political Parties* and *Regrowing the American Economy*. It also publishes the pamphlets *Improving American Innovation, U.S. Interests in the 1990s: Seize the Moment*, and *U.S. Global Interests in the 1990s: A New Approach*.

Americans for Democratic Action (ADA)
1511 K St. NW, Suite 941
Washington, DC 20005
(202) 638-6447

ADA works to formulate and promote liberal domestic and foreign policies. It publishes *ADA World* bimonthly, *ADA Voting Record* annually, and *Legislative Alerts* and *Membership Alerts* periodically.

Citizens for a Debt Free America
2550 S. Sunny Slope Rd.
New Berlin, WI 53151
(414) 782-1305

The Citizens are intent on eliminating the national debt through massive private contributions to the U.S. Department of the Treasury. By doing so, they hope to ensure hope and opportunity in America. Their newsletter, *Silver Linings*, is published four times a year.

Citizens for a Sound Economy (CSE)
470 L'Enfant Plaza SW, Suite 7112
Washington, DC 20024
(202) 488-8200

CSE is an advocacy group dedicated to reducing government intervention in the economy. It supports tax reform and reduction, free trade, and deregulation. It distributes studies on economic issues and publishes *CSE Reports* quarterly.

Committee for Economic Development
477 Madison Ave.
New York, NY 10022
(212) 688-2063

The Committee is a research organization of economists. It encourages businesses to become involved in improving American education. Through its studies and reports, it seeks to eradicate the budget deficit and so improve America's competitiveness. It publishes *Newsletter* and *Statements on National Policy* periodically.

Democracy Project
215 Park Ave. S., Room 1814
New York, NY 10003
(212) 674-8989

The Project is a progressive public policy institute that was founded in 1981. It promotes strong democracy, liberal economic policies, peace between the superpowers, and respect for the law. It publishes the book *America's Transition: Blueprints for the 1990s.*

Economic Policy Institute (EPI)
1730 Rhode Island Ave. NW, Suite 812
Washington, DC 20036
(202) 775-8810

EPI is a liberal think tank that conducts research on economics. The Institute studies poverty, economic growth, unemployment, inflation, international competitiveness, and other issues. It advocates government spending on public works in order to create jobs and stimulate private businesses. It publishes *Briefing Papers* and *Directory of Economic Policy Experts* periodically.

Educators for Social Responsibility
23 Garden St.
Cambridge, MA 02138
(617) 492-1764

The Educators teach students how to think critically about global interdependence, security in the nuclear age, and U.S.-Soviet relations. They seek to help students develop a vision of a peaceful future. They publish *Forum* quarterly. They also distribute the books *Perspectives: A Teaching Guide to Concepts of Peace* and *Listening to Children: Soviet and American Voices.*

Federation for American Immigration Reform (FAIR)
1424 16th St. NW, Suite 701
Washington, DC 20036
(202) 328-7004

FAIR works to stop illegal immigration and to limit legal immigration. It believes that the increasing influx of immigrants causes higher unemployment and taxes America's social services. FAIR has published many reports, including *To Import a Poverty Class: Data on the Characteristics of Recent Illegal Alien Amnesty Applicants, Rethinking Immigration Policy,* and *Illegal Immigration: The Problem, The Solutions.*

Foundation for Economic Education (FEE)
30 S. Broadway
Irvington, NY 10533
(914) 591-7230

FEE focuses its research efforts on free-market theory. It opposes government interference in the economy. FEE also maintains a speakers bureau and library with related materials. It publishes *The Freeman* monthly.

Foundation for Rational Economics and Education (FREE)
PO Box 1776
Lake Jackson, TX 77566
(409) 265-3034

FREE consists of individuals who wish to study the Constitution. It opposes government intervention in the economy and promotes personal liberty. It conducts seminars for high school and college students and publishes the monthly *Freedom Report.* It also distributes the booklet *God, Peace, and Prosperity.*

The Heritage Foundation
214 Massachusetts Ave. NW
Washington, DC 20002
(202) 546-4400

The Foundation is a conservative think tank that conducts research on public policy. It advocates free enterprise and limiting government involvement in the economy. Its publications include the periodic *Backgrounder, Issues Bulletin,* the *Heritage Lectures* series, and the monthly *Policy Review.*

Institute for Contemporary Studies (ICS)
243 Kearny St.
San Francisco, CA 94108
(415) 981-5353

ICS is a public-policy group that studies issues which have a direct bearing on the free-market system. Its publications include *The Letter* three times a year, as well as the reports *Winning the Brain Race: A Bold Plan to Make Our Schools Competitive* and *Reagan and the Economy: The Successes, the Failures, and the Unfinished Agenda.*

Libertarian Futurist Society (LFS)
89 Gebhardt Rd.
Penfield, NY 14526
(716) 248-3112

LFS consists of futurists and science fiction fans who support individual freedom. It believes the innovations presented in science fiction are a means toward a freer society. Its quarterly newsletter, *Prometheus,* has dealt with America's future role in space and with immigration.

National Academy of Sciences
Office of Public Affairs
2101 Constitution Ave. NW
Washington, DC 20418
(202) 334-2000

The Academy is dedicated to furthering science and engineering for the public welfare. It operates three other organizations under its charter: the National Research Council, the National Academy of Engineering, and the Institute of Medicine. It publishes *News Report, The Bridge,* and *IOM Newsletter.*

National Center on Education and the Economy
39 State St.
Rochester, NY 14614
(716) 546-7620

The Center believes it is necessary to improve education so that students will have the skills to strengthen America's economy once they get jobs. It promotes increased science and math education and advocates reforming the educational system. It publishes *A Nation Prepared: Teachers for the 21st Century, Redesigning America's Schools: The Public Speaks,* and *Training America: Strategies for the Nation.*

National Council for Better Education
1001 Prince St., Suite 204
Alexandria, VA 22314
(703) 739-2660

The Council believes that the radical left is attempting to gain control of the American public education system. It conducts research on parents' rights and secular humanism in the classroom. It advocates teaching traditional values in American schools. The Council publishes *NEA: Propaganda Front of the Radical Left, 31 Flavors Rebuttal,* and *A Parent's Survival Guide to the Public Schools.*

National Education Association (NEA)
1201 16th St. NW
Washington, DC 20036-3290
(202) 822-7000

Founded in 1857, NEA is the largest teachers' organization in the U.S. It provides teaching materials and pamphlets on science education, ethnic groups in the U.S., and many other topics. NEA's publications include *Teaching Thinking Skills: Science Education in the 80s, Multiethnic Education,* and *Economics in the School Curriculum, K-12.*

National Immigration Project of the National Lawyers Guild
14 Beacon St., Suite 506
Boston, MA 02108
(617) 227-9727

This organization is a group of lawyers, law students, and legal workers that educates and organizes for progressive immigration laws. The organization maintains a speakers bureau. It publishes the *National Immigration Project Newsletter* bimonthly and the *Central American Refugee Defense Fund* quarterly.

National Science Foundation (NSF)
1800 G St. NW
Washington, DC 20024
(202) 357-7748

NSF is an independent agency in the executive branch of the federal government that supports basic and applied research and education in the sciences. It publishes the bimonthlies *Antarctic Journal of the US* and *Mosaic.*

Pacific Studies Center
222B View St.
Mountain View, CA 94041
(415) 969-1545

The Center is a public interest group specializing in analyzing and critiquing the negative impact of technology on society, the military, and the environment. Its monthly magazines are *Global Electronics* and *California Military Monitor.*

Reason Foundation
2716 Ocean Park Blvd., Suite 1062
Santa Monica, CA 90405
(213) 392-0443

The Foundation's purpose is to provide a better understanding of the intellectual basis of a free society. It promotes individual freedoms and free-market principles. Its publications include *Fiscal Watchdog* and *Reason Magazine.*

Rockford Institute
934 N. Main St.
Rockford, IL 61103
(815) 964-5053

The Institute is a conservative research center that studies capitalism and liberty. It publishes three periodicals, *Chronicles, The Rockford Papers,* and *Persuasion at Work.*

Science for the People (SFTP)
897 Main St.
Cambridge, MA 02139
(617) 547-0370

SFTP works to create a society based on human needs rather than profit and to support science that serves all people. It publishes the bimonthly *Science for the People* magazine.

World Future Society
4916 St. Elmo Ave.
Bethesda, MD 20814
(301) 656-8274

The Society's goal is to "contribute to a reasoned awareness of the future . . . without advocating particular ideologies or engaging in political activities." It publishes *Future Survey* monthly and *The Futurist* bimonthly.

World Without War Council
1730 Martin Luther King Jr. Way
Berkeley, CA 94709
(415) 845-1992

The Council seeks to build support for alternatives to war. It analyzes international conflicts and promotes nonviolent resolutions. It makes recommendations to the U.S. State Department and to other organizations. It publishes the newsletters *Steady Work* and *American Purpose* periodically.

Bibliography of Books

Annelise Anderson and Dennis L. Bark — *Thinking About America: The United States in the 1990s.* Stanford, CA: Hoover Institution Press, 1988.

Sven W. Arndt and Lawrence Bouton — *Competitiveness: The United States in World Trade.* Washington, DC: American Enterprise Institute, 1987.

Robert E. Baldwin — *Trade Policy in a Changing World Economy.* New York: Harvester Wheatsheaf, 1988.

C. Fred Bergsten — *America in the World Economy: A Strategy for the 1990s.* Washington, DC: Institute for International Economics, 1988.

Allan Bloom — *The Closing of the American Mind.* New York: Simon & Schuster, 1987.

Don Bonker — *America's Trade Crisis.* Boston: Houghton Mifflin Co., 1988.

David H. Brandin and Michael A. Harrison — *The Technology War: A Case for Competitiveness.* New York: John Wiley & Sons, 1987.

Daniel Burstein — *YEN!: Japan's New Financial Empire and Its Threat to America.* New York: Simon & Schuster, 1988.

Daniel F. Burton, Victor Gotbaum, and Felix G. Rohatyn, eds. — *Vision for the 1990s: U.S. Strategy and the Global Economy.* Cambridge, MA: Ballinger Publishing Co., 1989.

Marvin J. Cetron — *Schools of the Future.* New York: McGraw-Hill, 1985.

Marvin J. Cetron and Owen Davies — *American Renaissance: Our Life at the Turn of the 21st Century.* New York: St. Martin's Press, 1989.

Pat Choate and J.K. Linger — *The High-Flex Society: Shaping America's Economic Future.* New York: Alfred A. Knopf, 1986.

William K. Cummings et al., eds. — *Educational Policies in Crisis: Japanese and American Perspectives.* New York: Praeger, 1986.

The Cuomo Commission on Trade and Competitiveness — *The Cuomo Commission Report.* New York: Simon & Schuster, 1988.

Michael L. Dertouzos, Richard K. Lester, Robert M. Solow, and the MIT Commission on Industrial Productivity — *Made in America: Regaining the Productive Edge.* Cambridge, MA: The MIT Press, 1989.

Peter F. Drucker — *The New Realities.* New York: Harper & Row, 1989.

Benjamin Duke — *The Japanese School: Lessons for Industrial America.* New York: Praeger, 1986.

Ken Dychtwald and Joe Flower — *Age Wave: The Challenge and Opportunities of An Aging America.* Los Angeles: Jeremy P. Tarcher Inc., 1989.

James Fallows — *More Like Us: Making America Great Again.* Boston: Houghton Mifflin Co., 1989.

Gregory A. Fossedal	*The Democratic Imperative: Exporting the American Revolution.* New York: Basic Books, 1989.
James K. Galbraith	*Balancing Acts: Technology, Finance, and the American Future.* New York: Basic Books, 1989.
George Gilder	*Microcosm: The Quantum Revolution in Economics and Technology.* New York: Simon & Schuster, 1989.
Norman J. Glickman and Douglass P. Woodward	*The New Competitors: How Foreign Investors Are Changing the U.S. Economy.* New York: Basic Books, 1989.
Andrew J. Goodpaster, Walter J. Stoessal Jr., and Robert Kennedy, eds.	*U.S. Policy Toward the Soviet Union: A Long-Term Western Perspective, 1987-2000.* Lanham, MD: University Press of America, 1988.
P. Edward Haley, David M. Keithly, and Jack Merrit, eds.	*Nuclear Strategy, Arms Control, and the Future.* Boulder, CO: Westview Press, 1985
Edward K. Hamilton, ed.	*America's Global Interests: A New Agenda.* New York: W.W. Norton & Co., 1989.
Robert Heilbroner and Peter Bernstein	*The Debt and the Deficit: False Alarms/Real Possibilities.* New York: W.W. Norton & Co., 1989.
Peter Jay and Michael Stewart	*Apocalypse 2000.* London: Sidgwick & Jackson, 1987.
Pearl M. Kamer	*The U.S. Economy in Crisis.* New York: Praeger, 1988.
Paul Kennedy	*The Rise and Fall of the Great Powers.* New York: Random House, 1987.
Rushworth M. Kidder	*An Agenda for the 21st Century.* Cambridge, MA: The MIT Press, 1987.
Joel Kotkin and Yoriko Kishimoto	*The Third Century: America's Resurgence in the Asian Era.* New York: Crown Publishers, 1988.
Joel Kurtzman	*The Decline and Crash of the American Economy.* New York: W.W. Norton & Co., 1988.
Richard D. Lamm	*Megatraumas: America at the Year 2000.* Boston: Houghton Mifflin Co., 1985.
Richard D. Lamm, Richard A. Caldwell, and Ira H. Mehlman	*Hard Choices: A Book on America's Future.* Denver, CO: The Center for Public Policy and Contemporary Issues, 1989.
James Laxer	*Decline of the Superpowers.* New York: Paragon House, 1989.
Stanley Lieberson and Mary C. Waters	*From Many Strands: Ethnic and Racial Groups in Contemporary America.* New York: Russell Sage Foundation, 1988.
Robert E. Litan, Robert Z. Lawrence, and Charles L. Schultze, eds.	*American Living Standards.* Washington, DC: The Brookings Institution, 1988.
Robert S. McNamara	*Out of the Cold.* New York: Simon & Schuster, 1989.
Alfred L. Malabre Jr.	*Beyond Our Means.* New York: Random House, 1987.
Walter Russell Mead	*Mortal Splendor: The American Empire in Transition.* Boston: Houghton Mifflin Co., 1987.

Richard Nixon	*1999: Victory Without War.* New York: Simon & Schuster, 1988.
Oxford Analytica	*America in Perspective.* Boston: Houghton Mifflin Co., 1986.
Tom Peters	*Thriving on Chaos.* New York: Alfred A. Knopf, 1987.
William Pfaff	*Barbarian Sentiments: How the American Century Ends.* New York: Hill & Wang, 1989.
Jim Powell	*The Gnomes of Tokyo: Japanese Financial Power and Its Impact on Our Future.* New York: Dodd, Mead & Co., 1988.
Clyde V. Prestowitz Jr.	*Trading Places: How We Allowed Japan to Take the Lead.* New York: Basic Books, 1988.
Simon Ramo	*The Business of Science.* New York: Hill & Wang, 1988.
Marcus Raskin and Chester Hartman, eds.	*Winning America: Ideas and Leadership for the 1990s.* Boston: South End Press, 1988.
Robert B. Reich	*Tales of a New America.* New York: Times Books, 1987.
Carlton Rochell	*Dreams Betrayed: Working in the Technological Age.* Lexington, MA: Lexington Books, 1987.
Isabel V. Sawhill, ed.	*Challenge to Leadership: Economic and Social Issues for the Next Decade.* Washington, DC: The Urban Institute Press, 1988.
Craig Schindler and Gary Lapid	*The Great Turning.* Santa Fe, NM: Bear & Co., 1989.
James Schlesinger	*America at Century's End.* New York: Columbia University Press, 1989.
Brent Scowcroft, R. James Woolsey, and Thomas H. Etzold, eds.	*Defending Peace and Freedom: Toward Strategic Stability in the Year 2000.* Lanham, MD: University Press of America, 1988.
John Silber	*Straight Shooting: What's Wrong with America and How to Fix It.* New York: Harper & Row, 1989.
John D. Steinbrunner, ed.	*Restructuring American Foreign Policy.* Washington DC: The Brookings Institution, 1989.
Hugh B. Stewart	*Recollecting the Future.* Homewood, IL: Dow Jones-Irwin, 1989.
Studs Terkel	*The Great Divide: Second Thoughts on the American Dream.* New York: Pantheon Books, 1988.
Martin Tolchin and Susan Tolchin	*Buying Into America.* New York: Times Books, 1988.
Ben J. Wattenberg	*The Birth Dearth.* New York: Pharos Books, 1987.
Murray Weidenbaum	*Rendezvous with Reality.* New York: Basic Books, 1988.
Marcia Lynn Whicker and Raymond A. Moore	*Making America Competitive.* New York: Praeger, 1988.
Merry White	*The Japanese Educational Challenge.* New York: The Free Press, 1987.

Index